Soccer Analytics

IAN FRANKS & MIKE HUGHES

SOCCER ANALYTICS

SUCCESSFUL COACHING THROUGH MATCH ANALYSIS

Meyer & Meyer Sport

British Library Cataloguing in Publication Data
A catalogue record for this book is available from the British Library

Soccer Analytics
Maidenhead: Meyer & Meyer Sport (UK) Ltd., 2016
ISBN 978-1-78255-081-5

© 2016 by Meyer & Meyer Sport (UK) Ltd.
Aachen, Auckland, Beirut, Cairo, Cape Town, Dubai, Hägendorf, Hong Kong,
Indianapolis, Manila, New Delhi, Singapore, Sydney, Tehran, Vienna

 Member of the World Sport Publishers' Association (WSPA)

Manufacturing: Print Consult GmbH, München
E-Mail: info@m-m-sports.com
www.m-m-sports.com

TABLE OF CONTENTS

ACKNOWLEDGEMENTS

First we would like to acknowledge the outstanding work of illustrator Rachel Apted whose coloured figures brought the practices in this book to life. Also we acknowledge George Marjanovic whose work was an inspiration for some of these illustrations. Second, we recognize the contribution and expertise of Chris Franks (trainer and physiotherapist at the Vancouver Whitecaps F.C. and Fortius Sport and Health Clinic, Vancouver) to the chapter in the book that focuses on the warm up activities that players engage in at the beginning of a coaching practice. Third, the research into soccer match analysis would not have been possible without the creative genius of Paul Nagelkerke (systems analyst) who developed the computer programmes and video interface that were used in the data collection process. We also acknowledge the hard work of the graduate students who aided in the collection of match data at both UBC and Cardiff Metropolitan University. Finally we are indebted to Social Science and Humanities Research Council of Canada and Sport Canada for funding the research into soccer match analysis and coaching analysis.

DEDICATION

This book is dedicated to Emilly, Brynn, Hayden, Kieran, Siena and Sebastian who are all well on their way to completing 10,000 hours of active yet enjoyable deliberate play and practice.

ABOUT THE BOOK

This book explores the analysis of soccer and uses the results of this analysis to develop realistic and progressive practices that will improve the performance of both the player and the team. An historical perspective of past research is maintained when describing the logical and systematic methods used to notate the game. Analysis of the coaching practice itself is also considered whereby the behaviours of the coach are scrutinized and evaluated. Research from human decision making and motor skill acquisition is directly applied to the coaching process and therefore technical and tactical practices are designed to accommodate these findings. It is expected that this book will provide the reader with an understanding of how to develop their own coaching practice and improve their coaching style with the aid of match analysis. A comprehensive bibliography is provided for students of the game who wish to delve further into the science of soccer analysis and soccer skill acquisition.

This book is intended to be informative for all levels of coaches, from the recreational novice who has the responsibility to develop young players to the experienced coach of senior players. Part 1 provides a window into the notional analysis of soccer. It logically explains how one might develop a system of analysis and then gives a brief summary of the results from analysis. Special attention is paid to the studies that have provided information on set pieces and crosses. Part 2 illustrates how decision making is a critical process in soccer and provides a unique method of using this to advantage when coaching. For example, defending is broken down into a series of decisions all players on the team should be involved in no matter what their position. In part 3 we emphasize the need to have progressive realistic practices that maximize transfer of training from the practice field to the match. Several examples of functional training are given along with progressive practices that move from an isolated technique in a specific area of the pitch to a full phase of match play. In addition, combined attacking techniques are coached in realistic situation-specific practices and then they are progressed back into small-sided games. Part 4 provides the coach of developing young players with a brief summary of research findings and recommendations into the acquisition of motor skills as they pertain to teaching and coaching soccer skills. Then practices that adhere to these recommendations are described for several techniques. In part 5 we briefly introduce some guidelines for warming up players before training and games. Several practices are then described that could be used to begin the coaching session with an emphasis on game-related activity. This section also describes several fun conditioning games that can be used to end the coaching session. Part 6 defines the entire coaching process and illustrates how match analysis fits into the overall scheme of this process. Furthermore this section gives the coach some guidelines as to the preparation, organization and execution of a successful practice session. Within this framework of the coaching practice we emphasize the need for coaches to engage in self-reflective practice. Coaches must gather feedback on their own coaching behaviours in order to improve the delivery of information they provide players. In order to maintain an easy reading experience for the coach we have chosen not to follow the regular convention of citing references within the body of the text. However, in part 7, we do provide an extended bibliography of classic studies and recent research that directly relate to research used in writing this text. This section will aid the student of soccer to begin a more rigorous and detailed investigation into various aspects of soccer analysis and soccer skill acquisition.

ABOUT THE AUTHORS

Ian Franks, PhD, gained his full English Football Association Coaching Award in 1975. He was intricately involved in developing the Canadian Soccer Association's Coaching Program in the early 1980s and was head coach at the Olympic Soccer Training Centre at the University of British Columbia from 1980 until 1983. Professor Franks then took a position as director of the Centre for Sport Analysis at the University of British Columbia and conducted research into the computer analysis of international soccer matches. Since joining the faculty of the School of Kinesiology at UBC, he has published over 150 research articles, 22 book chapters and 5 books in the areas of sport analysis, skill acquisition and movement control. Professor Franks is also a Fellow of Canadian Society for Psychomotor Learning and Sport Psychology as well as the National Academy of Kinesiology.

Mike Hughes, PhD, is an emeritus professor of sport and exercise science at the Cardiff Metropolitan University and has conducted research into match analysis for over 30 years. He has worked with National Sports Great Britain teams as a notational analyst in squash, hockey, soccer and badminton. He has published over 160 research articles, written and contributed to 24 books and organized 18 international conferences on sport analysis. His areas of expertise include modeling, sport system perturbations, tactical and technical game analyses as well as individual movement analysis. Recent research includes work on performance indicators in soccer, racket sports, basketball, cricket, women's squash and statistical techniques in the analysis of soccer. Professor Hughes is the founder and current president of the International Society of Analysis of Sport (ISPAS) as well as being the founding editor of the International Journal of Performance Analysis of Sport. Professor Hughes is a BASES (British Association of Sport and Exercise Sciences) accredited sport and exercise scientist and a Fellow of the Royal Statistical Society.

PART 1
MATCH ANALYSIS

CHAPTER 1
INTRODUCTION

Spectators of a soccer game want to be entertained while observers search for critical information. Needless to say, we all would like to be entertained, but for the coach, watching a soccer game is hard work. Observing playing behaviour is one of the most important tasks a coach has to accomplish, and early research into the process of behavioural observation revealed some interesting findings in the field of social psychology that are relevant when examining the observational skills of soccer coaches. Darren Newtson found that adult observers used breakpoints in action sequences to organize behavioural units of ongoing events for later recall. These units then became units of comprehension and memory. For example, breakpoints in soccer game action for the observer coach could be something as simple as a change in ball possession and each component of memory could be one possession. Unfortunately, due to the length of the game and the myriad of other factors that affect memory recall, most of what the soccer coach observes and remembers about the game is not accurate. This is not surprising since a lot of events (e.g. breakpoints, changes in possession and critical incidents) take place in a 90-minute game. Research findings from our own lab at UBC have shown that at most levels of coaching, from novice to international, observations by coaches are in error by more than 50% when trying to recall such things as how goals were scored and how shooting opportunities were created.

How then can coaches improve their ability to remember key events during a game? We know that skilled observers develop a specialized set of predictive features and adopt certain monitoring priorities. Therefore the soccer coach must understand key factors in expected performance and have a clear vision of what that expected performance should look like. In order to provide an accurate recall of all game events it would obviously require a considerable amount of practice in observing playing behaviours. However an alternate method of maintaining an accurate account of a 90-minute soccer match is to use a memory aid. This could be as simple as a pencil and paper checklist or as complex as an interactive computer-video analysis system. The level of sophistication of the system is not important; the key elements of any system of analysis are accuracy, relevance and usefulness of information that is collected by the system. For instance, a video recorder can collect and store most of the information from a game, but the game still needs to be analyzed in a manner that can assist the coach in making decisions. The statistical accumulation of such things as number of possessions and number of passes is not informative if the coach requires the information to assess team or individual performance and make preparation for the next game. By way of example let us examine a simple forward pass. Diagram 1 illustrates a pass that is identical in all aspects except the position of one defending player (diagram 1a) or in its location on the field (diagram 1b). In diagram 1a the pass in case 2 is more penetrative and offers more of an attacking threat than does the pass in case 1. Also if we move the position of the pass from the middle of the field to the top of the penalty area as shown in diagram 1b, it is obvious that the pass in case 2 would be considered much more difficult to execute than the pass in case 1 and should eventually lead to a shot on goal.

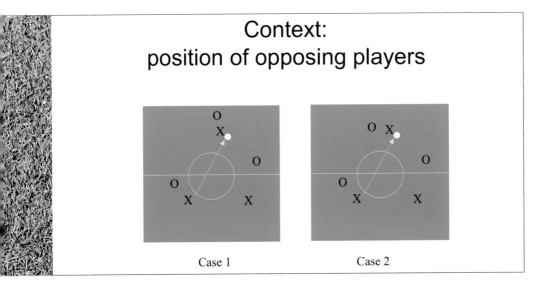

Diagram 1a

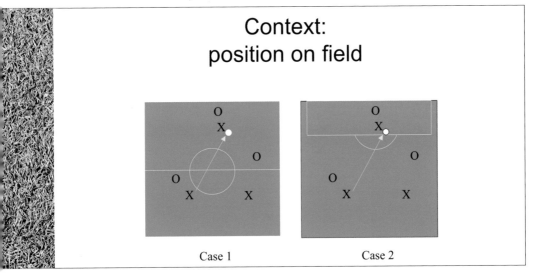

Diagram 1b

Collecting only the number of completed passes without taking into consideration the context in which they were made reduces the richness and informative nature of the data. Therefore, it is important to understand what opportunities these passes and possessions create. Hence the sequential nature (i.e. what leads to what) of data capture then becomes a critical feature in any analysis system. However if this were to be achieved by simply video recording the game without any systematic analysis system to guide the viewing then many of the problems encountered on an initial live viewing of the event may still exist.

How then can a team's performance be analyzed in a systematic and progressive manner? During an average soccer game each team has possession of the ball approximately 200 times, and since the objective of the game is to score goals, these 200 possessions could possibly translate into 200 goals. Not a very likely occurrence given that league champions usually average only 2 or 3 goals per game. The remarkable fact is that about 99% of all team possessions end up being lost to the opposing team without a goal being scored. Analyzing a soccer game is therefore a process of recording how, where and why the team lost and regained possession. A detailed analysis of these lost possessions should provide the coach with an overall view of the key factors that were responsible for both good and bad team performance.

Let us take a brief look at these lost possessions. Each possession is lost in a particular area of the field and each loss can be attributed to a particular action. It is obvious that goals can only be scored from certain areas of the field, let's say within 40 meters of the goal (we realize that there have been exceptions but these account for a very small percentage of all shots). Therefore, the task for the attacking team is to move the ball into an area of the field from which shots on goal can be taken. Team possessions that are lost in these areas would satisfy a large part of the final objective, which is to produce a shot on target that results in a goal, whereas a sub-objective would be to create the shooting opportunity. If possession of the ball is continuously lost in these shooting areas and shooting opportunities do not arise, the problem for the coach is less formidable than if ball possession is lost in areas other than the shooting area. Using this simple logic we can now identify priorities for possession loss as: first, lose possession in scoring a goal (usually 1% per game for winning teams); second, lose possession in taking a shot at goal (10% per game for winning teams); third, lose possession after creating a shooting opportunity (20% per game); and fourth, lose possession in and around the shooting area (40% per game). As you can see, we are now developing a method for systematically observing the game.

Collecting and categorizing information about how the team lost and gained possession can cover all the attacking and defending events the game has to offer. If we just recorded numbers and totals of discrete events this would provide interesting statistics for spectators and TV viewers, but the observing coach wants to know more. For example, what events led to the shot that missed the target, the lost possession in the defending third of the field or the free kick outside the penalty area? This type of information can only be gathered if a sequential history or story of the game is recorded that allows us to ask "What led to what?" Over the past 30 years notational analysis researchers have developed computer analysis systems that record the sequence of game events; these are then time locked to the video recording. Some systems automate the process such that the camera recognizes the image of all players, the ball and the officials every second of the game. Because of these systems some coaches can now view the statistics (as either numbers or graphs) after the game (or at half time) and then recall video excerpts of key events in the game. This then becomes a very powerful and useful coaching tool and provides important visual feedback for players. In addition to being an excellent coaching tool these notation systems have allowed researchers to collect data from many major soccer competitions to form a large database of information that may provide answers to several questions such as:

⚽ How are goals scored, and what leads to the creation of shooting opportunities?
⚽ What type of defensive tactic yields most regained possessions?
⚽ What are the technical demands of performance?

Let us look in a little more detail at some of the tentative answers to these questions that have been gleaned from soccer match analysis research over more than 60 years.

HOW ARE GOALS SCORED?

It appears that after reviewing a considerable amount of data from past games, the approach play that led to goals was not significantly different than the approach play that led to shots that did not result in goals. Goals were thought to occur randomly from a population of all shots. These facts were uncovered in one of the earliest examples of comprehensive match analysis undertaken by Charles Reep using a sophisticated hand notation system. In 1968 he published samples of his extensive data collection in what is now the classic paper by Reep and Benjamin. They reported on the collection of match data from 3,213 top level soccer games between 1953 and 1969. The results of the analysis were later supported by several subsequent studies from such coaches as Egel Olsen (former Norwegian national coach), Dick Bate (English FA staff coach), Charles Hughes (director of coaching for the English FA) and from researchers in laboratories throughout the world (see bibliography). For an excellent recent discussion on what has since been termed *the winning formulae* see an article written by Joao Medeiros, science editor for Wired.co.uk (also cited in the bibliography).

The predominant finding that has surfaced from nearly all analyses is that approximately 80% of goals are scored from team play that involves no more than four consecutive passes, indicating that goals are scored from team play that is direct (we have offered an alternate interpretation to these results, see Hughes and Franks article in *JSS* 2005, cited in the bibliography). The finding—that goals are not scored from many intricate passing moves—has been the centre of much controversy in England and has led certain teams to adopt a very direct style of play that has been relatively successful in terms of overall results. However, many misinterpretations exist, both of the findings from analysis and of the reasons why these teams, with the direct style of play, are successful. In order to dispel some of this misunderstanding it is important to know first what the results of past analysis are, and second what implication these results have in terms of preferred playing styles.

So let us begin with the question "What leads to the scoring of goals?" First and foremost, it does appear at first glance that direct play (i.e. few consecutive passes leading to a shot) leads to goals being scored. This is not a new finding. Experienced coaches will remember that in the early 1960s, a major principle of team play proposed by the then-director of coaching for the English FA, Allen Wade (definitely *not* a proponent of the long ball game) was termed *penetration* and defined as bypassing as many defensive players with the ball as possible. It was, and still is, extremely important that passes made, runs with the ball made and shots taken went behind and between defenders. Penetrative play often involves a long forward pass and it has been found that long, *accurate* forward passes that are made into space behind defenders are a major contributor to goals being scored. The important factor here seems to be that not only long passes be made behind defenders but that cooperating team members are in positions to either ideally receive the ball or to challenge for the ball that is played into space. Having several players who are specifically deployed in attacking positions and having the ball played into the opponents third of the field would require that the rear-most players (the ones who are making these long passes) move forward and keep the team compact from front to back. That is, keep the ten outfield players playing in an area that spans, at most, one half of the length of the field. Data from analysis has shown that if opposing teams win possession of the ball in their own defending third of the field and if these players are pressured defensively by a number of players who are in the immediate vicinity of the ball, then there is a higher probability of them losing that possession in their own half of the field. In addition, compact team play, once possession is won, leads to good supporting play and an improved percentage of completed passes. When a team emphasizes playing penetrative passes behind the opposing team's defenders and all team members strive to keep play compact, then the game will be played at a fairly fast pace. This requires a high level of physical and mental fitness from all team members. Teams that choose to play this direct style of soccer, and are fit, tend to score a large proportion of their goals in the final 20 minutes of play or just prior to half time.

This particular style of direct play dictates certain other qualities required of the team apart from fitness. For example, all members of the team have to be able to defend as an individual and as a team unit (see the chapter on defending). Moreover, all team members are required to involve themselves in physical challenges for the ball. Full backs and midfield players have to be technically proficient at playing accurate passes in excess of 30 meters behind and between opponents, and midfield players also have to be skilled at predicting where the second ball (or knock-down pass) will be played after such a long pass. These midfield players are required to make sure this secondary possession is won in the middle or attacking third of the field and also to be skillful enough to maintain possession and begin the next attack. It is this middle third area that attracts more action than any other part of the field. Therefore, players working in this area should be extremely fit, both physically and mentally. Front players should be fast and able to create space and arrive in that space at the correct time, for it is these players that should strive to fully utilize the penetrating passes.

As can be seen, the simple statement of direct play brings with it many other essential features, the above being only one small example. Therefore, for a coach to read into the descriptive statements of analysis concerning how goals are scored, the fact that long, high balls should be kicked into the opponent's goal area and chased by one or two players is incorrect. This will produce an unsuccessful performance and also give a false impression of the benefits of direct play. A complete understanding of all the ramifications of this style of play, including the selection of players, must be thought through carefully and with the facts of analysis available to guide the coach's thinking process. For example, one recommendation that could be useful given the data on how goals are scored is to lose as many possessions in the attacking third of the field as possible (preferably with a shot on target—don't forget scoring a goal is losing possession). Winning teams have been recorded as losing over 60% of all possessions in their attacking third of the field.

WHAT TYPE OF DEFENSIVE TACTIC YIELDS THE MOST REGAINED POSSESSIONS?

The results of soccer match analysis that are concerned with regaining possession provide possibly the most conclusive evidence in favor of using tight defensive pressure in critical areas of the field. If possession of the ball is regained in the opponent's third of the field, the chances of a shot at goal is approximately 65%. If possession is regained in the middle third of the field, then the chances of that subsequent team possession resulting in a shot on goal is reduced to 25%. If, however, possession is regained in your own team's third of the field, the chances of scoring have been reduced to only 10%. More importantly, when possession is won in the opponent's third of the field in free play (i.e. not from a set play), the chances of scoring goals will increase dramatically. Two implications would seem to be obvious from these data. First, do not increase the probability of losing possession in your own half of the field. Making short intricate passing plays in and around your own team's penalty area when pressured by defenders increases the probability of a loss in possession. Secondly, the team's first defensive priority should be to regain possession in at least the opponent's half of the field.

A further recommendation from a defensive viewpoint would be to reduce—to zero if possible—the number of possessions lost in free play in one's own defending third of the field and win back the ball in the opponent's half of the field. Teams should win possession of the ball early and organize the defensive structure of the team, such that possession is regained in predictable areas of the field. Therefore, players not involved in challenging for the ball can move quickly into the attack from defense (sometimes referred to as transitional play). When possession is won, players should attack directly and quickly (i.e. transition quickly from defense to attack) in an attempt to produce a strike at goal. More information about the results of analysis and defending will be covered in the chapter on defending later in the book.

WHAT ARE THE TECHNICAL DEMANDS OF SOCCER PERFORMANCE?

The first and most important technique is that of receiving the ball. Players should be able to bring the ball under control from all possible positions, especially balls that arrive at head or chest height. Allied to this, players must understand under what conditions they should bring the ball under control with their first touch, and under what conditions they should play the ball away with their first touch (usually called one-touch play). These building blocks of technical expertise for all players are also a priority for developing young players. Practice sessions should be designed that allow players the opportunity to experience many and varied receptions of the ball in many and varied realistic playing environments. The practice should enable the player to provide him- or herself with time, and this time should be spent in deciding upon the opportunities available for the upcoming attacking option. For the player this is about selecting the next appropriate technique (e.g. shot, dribble or pass).

The second important technique, especially for developing young players, is that of dribbling and running with the ball. Although dribbling should probably be limited to areas of safety (i.e. the attacking half of the field), it is important that all players have the ability to take on opposing players in 1-vs-1 situations. With more experienced players it should be stressed that there are certain areas in which dribbling yields the best results. Also running forward with the ball through areas of no opposing pressure is a critical technical component of any team that wishes to advance ball possession into the attacking third of the field. Along with these techniques the coach should stress to the players an understanding of when to run with ball, when to dribble past opponents and when to shoot or pass.

A third priority is that of passing. Over the past 50 years, short passing (i.e. less than 20 meters) has received more attention than any other technique in coaching practices. While this technique is important for players (especially young players) in order to understand the principles of good supporting play, its importance has tended to overshadow that of long passing (i.e. greater than 30 meters). Teaching players how, when and where to play accurate long passes is as important as teaching them to make short passes. It is interesting to note that when teams are running out of time (e.g. 5 or 10 minutes remaining in the game) and need to score goals in a closely contested game, the number of long forward passes increases dramatically. The technique of long passing should be stressed with all players, including the goalkeeper clearance. Goals that arise as a result of long goalkeeper kicks are increasing in number. Goalkeepers can now, with practice, deliver the ball into the attacking third of field and with the correct arrangement of team members; this ball possession can ultimately result in a shooting opportunity. One caution to coaches of players younger than 11 years of age: the necessary muscle strength to deliver a 30-meter pass in the air is not fully developed in younger players and, therefore, reduced objectives should be given to these players and more priority given to the other techniques.

Fourth, since shooting and crossing are considered to be the primary sources of goals, they should also be given high priority in every coaching practice. The usual methods used in teaching these two techniques have not taken into account the need for players to transfer learning from the practice session to the game. This is because events unfold in time and certain events precede others in a game, and this feature of sequential dependency is not clearly understood by many coaches. Having players realize that there is an opportunity is essential. From a player's perspective, the game is a series of opportunities to produce a given technique. There are opportunities to play the ball forward, opportunities to cross the ball, opportunities to shoot and opportunities to tackle, and these opportunities can either be taken or not. The first objective is to create the opportunity and, having done so, the players must recognize the opportunity and then take it. If the opportunity is not taken then nothing can be said about the technique. Only when the opportunity to produce the technique is taken can the coach assess the quality of that technique. If players are made aware of how the coach sees the game in terms of opportunities, then the players can fulfill the objectives given by the coach.

Finally, the technique that has received the least amount of attention in coaching practices is that of individual defending. All members of the team should practice individual defending as they would any other attacking skill. Without the correct defensive skills, players will always be a liability to the team for that portion of play that their team does not have possession of the ball. Only after individuals know and can execute the technique of defending is it possible for the coach to address the components intrinsic to defending as a team unit.

THE PHYSIOLOGICAL DEMANDS OF SOCCER

Although it is beyond the scope of this book to detail the many advances made in the area of physiological analysis of soccer performance, it is worth noting the historical context of movement analysis during the game. As early as 1974, John Brooke and colleagues conducted a study into the description of methods and procedures for the recording and subsequent analysis of field movement behaviour in soccer, and then established the reliability of that method. Shorthand symbols were used to represent variables and parameters to be measured. However, the definitive study that used time and motion analysis in soccer was completed in 1976 by Tom Reilly and Vaughn Thomas. They used hand notation to record and analyse the intensity and extent of discrete activities during an entire match. Hand-notated data was synchronised with the use of an audiotape recorder to analyse in detail the movements of English First Division soccer players. The study was able to specify work rates of the players in different positions, distances covered in a game and the percentage time of each position spent in each of the different ambulatory classifications. For example, they were able to specify work rates and distances covered by each player, as well as the percentage of time walking, jogging, sprinting and so on. This led to the calculation of physiological demands for each player that was followed up by bringing each of them into the lab in order to replicate movements performed on the field. In the lab, measurements such as lactate and VO_2 consumption were taken. Tom Reilly continually added to this database enabling him to define clearly the specific physiological demands in soccer, as well as all the football codes. Following on from the work of Tom Reilly, a very detailed analysis of the movement patterns of the outfield positions of Australian professional soccer players was completed by Withers and colleagues. Their players were classified into four categories: full backs, central defenders, midfielders and forwards, and then videotaped whilst playing. At the end of the match they were informed that they were required to calibrate the different classifications of motion by reproducing the various actions of walking, running and sprinting and so on. The data produced by Withers et al. agreed to a great extent with that of Reilly and Thomas. Withers then went on to link their very detailed data analysis with training methods specific to the game and the player's position in the team. Although these research studies now seem to be dated in their design and methodology—especially with the advent of automatic digitization of each player offered by systems such as Prozone and the real-time assessment of physiological measures using remote devices—the work by Brooke, Reilly, Thomas and Withers has become a standard against which other similar research projects can compare their results and procedures. The importance of these studies is that they set up a template of analysis of movement that has enabled position specific training demands for today's players (see the bibliography for a sample of recent research using modern techniques and methodologies).

SUMMARY

This introductory chapter has provided only a brief summary of results gained from analysis but it can be the foundation for new performance criteria. It is also worth noting that several exceptions to the above findings can be found in specific games when coaches have adapted their strategy to meet the challenges of particular teams or environments. However these instances account for only a small percentage of game data.

Coaching by analysis is relatively easy in concept for the players to understand but requires a great deal of logical thinking from the coach. Understanding what analysis to conduct directs the observations of the coach and allows for the development of priorities in performance and practice. If the coach can relate these priorities to the players then the expectations of both coach and player are known. The player has realistic, objective goals of performance and can use the facts gained from analysis for comparison. The feedback process for coach and player is now a tangible item that can be viewed (video recording) and quantified (analysis). However, the player should not be inundated with the many aspects of statistical game data that is now available. It is the task of the coach to filter out and reduce this information into simple key factors that will be useful in changing player and team behaviour for the better.

Analysis guides coaching and the facts of performance should be available before the coach undertakes any drastic changes in technical or tactical thinking. Therefore in order to provide the coach with some relevant facts about soccer techniques and tactics, the coaching practices in this book are based upon the research findings from years of study in the area of soccer analysis as well as research findings into the acquisition of motor skills. Most chapters deal with a technical aspect of play while progressing through realistic coaching practices that offer maximum transfer of training and outline the key factors that are responsible for successful performance in each technique. In doing this we recognize that highly skilled players are the key to successful teams. If emphasis is placed upon coaching and practicing techniques, players will be able to adapt to any system of play that coaches wish to impose upon the team. The organization for each practice and its progression toward realistic game situations is outlined clearly along with diagrams of the practice. In addition, several brief coaching points are provided for each practice.

CHAPTER 2
ANALYSIS OF SET PLAYS

Set plays have always been an excellent source of goals in soccer. Research suggests that approximately 40% of all goals scored at every level of the game are scored in set-play situations. This has profound ramifications for the organization of players in attacking and defending roles during set plays. A stoppage in play usually allows a team time to arrange its players in field positions that are not dictated by any system of tactical play. For example, tall centre back defenders are brought into the attacking penalty area for corner kicks and free kicks, and players who have the capability of throwing the ball long distances can be used on either side of the field. This should make it clear to the coach that the system of play that teams adopt is not as important as once thought when considering the specific way in which all goals are scored. What is important to the coach is the time spent in practice dealing with set-play situations. If such a large percentage of goals are scored from set plays then it would seem logical that coaches should spend larger proportions of their practice time on set plays. In our analysis of set-play situations we sought to answer two fundamental questions: What events led to set plays that were located in and around the penalty area, and what are the key factors of scoring goals from these set-play situations? In this chapter we will address these questions with reference to goals scored from free kicks that are awarded in central and wide areas in addition to goals scored from throw-ins, corners and penalty kicks.

FREE KICKS

Directness appears to be the common factor that underlies the majority of successful free kicks, both in the attacking play leading to the free kick being awarded and in taking the free kick itself. Attacking players that run the ball at and past defenders and attacking players that play penetrating passes to the back of defenders create 1-vs-1 situations close to the penalty area. These situations are a major source of free kicks. Defensive players—especially at the international level—who foresee danger in regions just outside their own penalty area are more likely to concede a free kick in an attempt to stop the attacking player entering the penalty area. Interestingly, once attackers enter the penalty area with the ball under control, defenders tend to allow them more space and time than if the attacker was 20 meters from goal. This is obviously an understandable reaction to the growing number of penalty kicks being awarded in international competition—and not all of them resulting from any infringement of the laws. Television cameras that are now positioned at several locations around the ground can provide information that would verify a referee's decision. Although this places undue pressure upon the referee, it does allow an analysis of a disturbing trend in modern football, that being players who simulate being fouled (i.e. dive) and are falsely awarded a free kick. The TV-viewing public is made aware of this problem during nearly every televised game. Hopefully the governing bodies of soccer initiate a process of analysis that can be used post game to stop this unwanted behaviour.

Once a free kick is awarded, the attacking player who is on the ball, should be alert as to potential early opportunities to advance the ball forward and score. During the stoppage in play defenders are susceptible to lapses in attention. At this instant in the game the defending players are most vulnerable. However, if there is no opportunity to take an early advantage then several key factors should be considered when organizing attacking players at free-kick situations in and around the penalty area.

FREE KICKS WIDE OF THE PENALTY AREA

Essentially, these are crossing opportunities and the key factors for successful crosses apply (see a later chapter dealing specifically with crosses). However, the placement of players in critical positions is much easier than during free play when it is a dynamic crossing opportunity. However, defenders also have time to choose appropriate marking positions. Briefly, the key factors are:

- play the ball behind defenders;
- do not play the ball too close to the goalkeeper (but entice the goalkeeper off the goal line);
- attacking players should attempt to be first to any ball played into the penalty area; and
- three areas should be covered: near goal post to mid goal, far goal post and outside this post, and top of the penalty area (area that is called the D).

Two advantages exist at free kicks that are not possible during free-play crosses. Specific players who have special talents can be chosen for particular roles and the cross can be both an out-swinging cross (played away from the goal), or an in-swinging cross (played toward goal). The in-swing cross is played with speed and directed to the mid- and far-post areas, and has been very successful at producing shots and goals since its successful introduction on the international scene by Paul Gasgoine in the 1990 World Cup (e.g. Mark Wright's goal for England against Egypt).

FREE KICKS LOCATED CENTRALLY WITHIN THE SHOOTING ANGLE

The key factors arising from analysis into these free kicks are given below.

- The player taking the free kick should be direct and maximize the shooting opportunity. Free kicks from this position that do not produce a strike on goal can be considered a missed opportunity to shoot on target.
- Arrange attacking players such that they will expect rebounds and they can challenge for any knock downs from defenders or goalkeepers.
- Players who can impart swerve and spin on the stationary ball should be encouraged to strike directly on goal, with emphasis being placed on hitting the target.

A final and most important aspect of all set plays is the delivery of the ball. It matters little how good the organization of players are in the penalty area. Unless the player taking the free kick can deliver the shot, pass or cross accurately, both in space and time, the free-kick success rate will be at chance levels. Therefore, players must practice taking free kicks and delivering the ball into designated areas within the penalty area, assuring at least a 75% probability of producing an accurate free kick. This means that the player can deliver the ball to a precise place on the field 7 or 8 times out of 10 attempts. This is not an easy task and is one that requires considerable practice.

THROW-INS

The throw-in has received little attention as a potential source of goals, but analysis has revealed that defenders become extremely poor markers and trackers when the ball goes out of play for a throw-in. Successful throw-ins that produce shots and goals are mostly direct. Either the throw itself is played directly behind defenders or the player who receives the throw quickly runs or plays the ball into shooting positions. In recent years several teams have used the long throw with some success. These throws are usually delivered to the near post and headed back into the goal area. If sufficient numbers of attacking players are placed in and around the goal area this tactic will produce strikes on goals and also goals. The benefit of this play is that no attacking player can be offside from this direct throw. It would appear that there would be great rewards for teams that encourage all players to practice long throws from all positions along the touch line, since this is also an opportunity to move the ball, without defensive pressure, into potential shooting areas in the attacking third of the field.

CORNERS

Corners are an excellent source of goals, and teams that have wide attacking players that dribble on the outside of defending full backs increase their chances of gaining corners and, therefore, improve their chances of scoring goals from corners. In-swinging corners that are played to the front half of the goal—and that clear the defenders at the near post—appear to be the most profitable for producing shots on goal. These corners are usually hit with force and are not played high with a long hang time. However, teams should place attacking players in three key areas of the goal in anticipation of the corner. At least two players should cover the area in the front half of the goal, one player should be positioned just outside the far goal post and at least one player should be moving into an area near the penalty spot. In addition two players should position themselves in anticipation of the ball being cleared by the defenders or goalkeeper to the edge of the penalty area, just outside of the D. It is important to choose players who have special talents for these particular roles. For example, aggressive players who will attack the ball should be stationed at the near goal post, and players who are accurate at shooting first time, on-the-volley should be placed just outside the penalty area. As with free kicks, the one key element in all corner kicks is the quality of the kick itself. Players who are designated to take the kick should practice regularly (e.g. at every coaching session) and achieve over a 75% success rate. However not every kick will go where it is intended and the positioning of cooperating players will accommodate for errors in performance or when secondary chances from defensive mistakes occur.

One important aspect of defending at corner kicks is the need to have players in the area positioned next to the goal posts. A large number of goals are scored because goalkeepers do not deploy players on both near and far posts. This is a mistake. The responsibility of these post players is to block any ball going into an area about a meter wide and inside to the post. The goalkeeper can then be responsible for only approximately a 6-meter wide area in the center of the goal, positioned just forward of the goal line. It is also important that these post players remain on their post until the danger from the corner has been cleared.

PENALTY KICKS

The penalty kick is becoming an important factor in the results of major international soccer tournaments. This is due to the requirement of penalty shootouts as a method to decide the winner of a game after the provision of extra time could not produce a winner. In addition it appears that more penalty-kick decisions are given during regular time. Clearly the importance of practicing penalty kicks should become an essential component of each practice. Research conducted at UBC into the penalty kick with researchers Todd Hanvey and Dr. Tim McGarry appears to be both timely and relevant. The question asked in this particular research was "Can we provide the goalkeeper with information that will enable him or her to predict where the penalty kick will go?"

It was suggested in earlier research that it was possible to distinguish between novice and expert goalkeepers on the basis of the anticipatory cues they used during the penalty kick. However, it was evident in our own research that expert goalkeepers were not always successful at predicting the direction of the penalty kick. This analysis revealed that goalkeepers correctly predicted shot direction on only 41% of all shots (no better than chance). Furthermore, only 14.5% of these shots were saved by the goalkeeper. Clearly, expert (i.e. international) goalkeepers were not using effective strategies in trying to predict the direction of the shot and consequently save the penalty. Therefore, our first step was to identify reliable response cues that could be used effectively by goalkeepers.

The penalty shot can vary in both speed and direction as can the goalkeeper's movement. From the studies we conducted it appears the average ball time (time from the ball being kicked to when it crosses the goal line) was approximately 500 milliseconds (half a second), and goalkeeper movement time (time from the goalkeeper's first observable movement to when the body intersects the plane of the ball flight) was 600 milliseconds. Assuming that the goalkeeper detects an appropriate stimulus or response cue given by the kicker before moving, they then have to decide on movement direction. Therefore we must factor in reaction time (time from the stimulus onset [foot contact on the ball] to the first observable movement of the goalkeeper) as an added time delay. In laboratory based studies, reaction time for correctly anticipated events can be as short as 100 milliseconds while reaction times for choice decisions are usually in excess of 250 milliseconds. Based upon these predicted times it would appear that if the goalkeeper waited until the ball was kicked before diving they would be too late to stop the shot. The rule change (brought in after 1996) allowed goalkeepers to move before the kick. At first glance, this would appear to be a reasonable attempt at improving the goalkeeper's chance of saving the shot. However, results from our analysis led us to believe that the strategy of moving too early does not help the goalkeeper. If they move too early they will not benefit from late anticipatory response cues provided by the penalty taker, and if the goalkeeper is moving in the wrong direction the time taken to readjust and then move in the correct direction can exceed a full second in some instances. Moving too early also provides the kicker with information prior to the kick, which they will use to their own advantage.

The problem then is to find response cues that are reliable and presented early enough to allow the goalkeeper the opportunity to move in time to stop the shot. We identified the following possible response cues in chronological order:

- The penalty taker's starting position
- Angle of approach to the ball
- Forward or backward lean of the trunk
- Placement of the non-kicking foot just prior to contact
- Point of contact on the ball of the kicking foot

We reasoned that on the occasions when prediction from an early cue was incongruent with a later one, the time taken to disconfirm the first cue would inflate the reaction time causing the goalkeeper to move too late. The only response cue that was both reliable and time efficient was the placement of the non-kicking foot. This allowed the goalkeeper between 150 and 200 milliseconds to react after detection. The position of this foot placement dictates the direction of the shot on over 80% of penalty kicks we analyzed. If the non-kicking foot points to the left the ball will be placed to the left; if placed to the right the shot will go to the right. A further test of the response cue's reliability was completed on the penalties from various competitions (e.g. English Premier League, European Championships, World Cup, etc.) and the accuracy of predicting shot direction using this cue was in excess of 85%.

From the results of our research it is clear that goalkeepers can improve the detection of the direction of the penalty kick by using reliable late response cues. The coach should therefore spend time with the goalkeepers helping them to identify the best response cue for them. Once selected the goalkeeper should practice this technique of detection and movement at every coaching practice. The aim for the goalkeeper would be to first detect the correct direction more than 80% of the time and then to be confident enough in the choice of direction to initiate a forceful dive in that direction. Missing a penalty shot that is struck powerfully into the corners of the net is not a failure. Some penalty shots are unstoppable, but the goalkeeper should not try to predict direction based upon past performance of known penalty takers. This will again give only a 50% probability of making the correct decision regarding direction of the kick.

An interesting development occurred when the rule changed to allow goalkeepers to move along their line. On average, penalty takers slowed down their approach run to the ball in order to wait and see if the goalkeeper was moving early, which usually occurred. The kicker would then place a slower moving shot into the side of the goal opposite to that of the goalkeeper's movement or in some cases into the middle of the goal where the goalkeeper was last standing. This type of strategy by penalty takers would be extremely useful for goalkeepers who wait until the non-kicking foot has been placed because it improves their ability to save the slower moving shot.

The antithesis to the goalkeeper's strategy therefore is for the kicker to shoot the ball into the corners of the goal with a shot as powerful as possible without losing accuracy. The player taking the shot should first go for accuracy, then develop a powerful shot. The corner of the goal that has been chosen for the shot should be selected early and not changed. Once again it should not be forgotten that some penalties are unstoppable and penalty takers must try to achieve this level of skill. Practice is the only way to improve the penalty kick. Penalty shot competitions are always a good way to end a practice. Furthermore this is an ideal time for the coach to analyze the kick using a video recording of the goalkeeper and the penalty taker. The coach can then determine who in their squad of players is the most successful penalty taker and rank order them according to percentage of successful attempts. This rank order will change throughout the season but it will be invaluable when deciding the ordering of players in a penalty shootout situation.

CONCLUSION

One key point for coaches to take away from all the analysis into set plays is that each player must understand his or her role at every set play situation in every area of the pitch. They must also understand what the expected (i.e. probable) outcome of the set play will be. This understanding can only come from practice and good organization on the part of the coach. In order to achieve this understanding all set plays must be practiced in realistic settings.

CHAPTER 3
ANALYSIS AND PRACTICE
OF SUCCESSFUL CROSSES

In many team games when a ball is passed into the scoring area from the perimeter of the playing area, defenders have a great deal of difficulty in preventing a strike on goal. Crosses are as much of a problem for defending players in field hockey and ice hockey as they are to soccer players. Why? The answer is relatively simple. In order to defend the goal correctly in any invasive team game, the defensive player tries to keep the goal behind them while maintaining a view of the ball and their opposing attacking player in front of them. When the ball is played to a wide position and the opposing player pulls wide (on the opposite side) of the defender, it is very difficult to maintain a good covering (marking) position while maintaining a view of the ball, unless the defender moves back into the goal and beyond the net (certainly not recommended).

It would seem reasonable, therefore, that attacking teams should maximize this potential defensive weakness, and it appears that most soccer teams in the past have done just that. More than 30% of all goals scored at all levels of play arise because the ball crossed into the penalty area. However, although teams score many goals from crosses, can we say that the tactic of increasing the number of crosses would be an efficient strategy? A cursory examination of the World and European Cup data would lead you to believe that crosses were a very *inefficient* method of scoring goals. For example if we were to average the data from several tournaments, approximately 30% of goals were scored from crosses but the ratio of goals to overall crosses played into the penalty area was only 1 in 40. This is certainly *not* an efficient means of scoring goals. Therefore, the fundamental questions of interest may be "What makes some crosses more successful than others? and "What are the key factors of these successful crosses?"

David Partridge, a researcher at The Centre for Sport Analysis at the University of British Columbia, produced one of the most comprehensive analyses of crosses in soccer ever undertaken. He produced a detailed examination of all the crossing opportunities that were presented to players during a single World Cup competition. A total of 1,867 crossing opportunities were analyzed and over 40 items of information were recorded for each opportunity, such as

- ⚽ position from where the ball was played;
- ⚽ the technique of the cross;
- ⚽ the position that cross was first contacted in the penalty area;
- ⚽ the position of the cooperating and opposing players at the time of the cross and their movements after the cross;
- ⚽ the results of the cross after contact was made, and much more.

From this study we identified several key factors of successful crosses and also suggested the most appropriate coaching practice that would highlight these factors for players. Since the time of the original research we have verified our finding at UBC and at Cardiff Metropolitan University with information from many international soccer tournaments. What follows is a summary of the key factors of crosses gained from this analysis.

KEY FACTORS

- ⚽ *The player on the ball should take the opportunity to cross if a) the target attacking player can contact the cross and b) the player taking the cross has the chance to play the ball behind defenders and eliminate the goalkeeper (i.e. play the ball to a position such that the goalkeeper will not come and collect it).*

  A common fault of many players is their failure to recognize situations in which they could have made a crossing attempt. Players should be coached to recognize the opportunity to cross; this can occur if realistic coaching practices are organized.

- ⚽ *The cross should be played behind defenders, past the near goal post and the ball should not be played high with a long hang time.*

  More than 60% of goals that are scored from crosses are the result of early crosses swept in behind defenders. In Partridge's analysis of the World Cup data, 37 of the 38 goals that were scored from crosses were delivered into the space behind the back line of defenders but in front of the goalkeeper. These crosses do not have to be delivered in the air. High lofted crosses tend not to produce goals or strikes on target. Also, early crosses usually cause defenders to run back toward their own goal and many own goals are scored by defenders trying to clear a cross only to find it goes past their own goalkeeper into the net. Many notable examples in top level competitions illustrate this scenario.

⚽ *Target players should be in a position to contact the cross by a) individual moves that get them goal side of the marking defender, b) being as direct as possible in their runs, c) not running too far past the near goal post to contact the ball and d) always making an attempt to contact the ball.*

In our analysis, if the cross was first contacted (not necessarily a shot) in the penalty area by a target player then the cross-to-goal ratio was reduced to 9:1 from 40:1 for all crosses. These data alone should provide enough impetus for target players to become aggressive and courageous in the penalty area in an effort to be "first to the ball" (response cue) that is crossed into the penalty area. In contrast, another interesting statistic was that one particular team, which failed to qualify from their group stage, delivered more crosses into the penalty area than any other team in the first round of the competition, but their ability to have target players contact these crosses was one of the poorest of all the teams. The majority of this team's crosses either passed through the penalty area without being contacted, were contacted by a defender or were collected by the goalkeeper.

⚽ *Supporting players should position themselves to seal off the space at the top of the penalty area and the area around the far (back) goal post.*

In other words, do not let the ball get out of the penalty area once it is in there. Secondary chances (knock-downs) are a great source of goals and players should be positioned such that they will benefit from either a cross played over the crowded goal area or an unintended defensive knock-down that was not cleared out of the penalty area.

⚽ *Certain techniques for crossing the ball are more successful than others from different areas of the field.*

First, if the ball is approximately 20 meters from the end line on the side of the field and the opportunity to cross arises, the ball should be swept-in or bent around the back of the defenders with some speed (see diagram 1).

Diagram 1

Second, if the ball is by the side of and next to the penalty area, it is best to pass the ball square across the penalty area into the path of the attacking target player (see diagram 2).

Diagram 2

Finally, if the ball is along the by-line (end line) then the player should try to chip the ball (coaches could use the response cue "digging the ball out") over what will be a congested near post and front goal area to supporting attacking players moving into the far goal post area. This would also lift the ball over the goalkeeper causing the goalkeeper to readjust position and potentially be moving when the player at the far post shoots or the attacker heads the ball down for a cooperating player to shoot (see diagram 3).

Diagram 3

These key factors were derived from performance analysis of past international games. What lessons can the coach learn from this information? It is essential that coaching practice arise from real performance and not from an imagined performance. When designing drills the coach should ask "Is this situation likely to occur during the game?" If the answer is "Not very often," then the coach must question the usefulness of the practice and not be surprised that little or no transfer of training occurs. The following practices were designed to teach players how to maximize the results of successful crosses.

PRACTICE A

Diagram 4

The practice that we suggested after reviewing the analysis of crosses is shown in diagram 4 and described below. It begins close to goal.

⚽ As illustrated in diagram 4 the crosser (X9) begins the practice by playing the ball into the coach who returns a first time ball to various places down the side of the penalty area or in front and to the side of the penalty area. The purpose of the varied service is to allow the coach a chance to suggest to X9 the best type of cross from certain areas.

⚽ As the coach plays the ball, one attacking player (X4) moves to seal off the space at the far post while X7 moves into the target areas along the goal area line (see target areas in diagram 5 below) and X6 moves to seal space at the top of the penalty area.

⚽ Between two and four defenders can be brought in as the crosser and the target attackers achieve success.

Target Areas

- Far post area for the chipped cross or to seal off space
- Target area for crossing
- Top of the penalty area to seal off space and keep the ball in the area

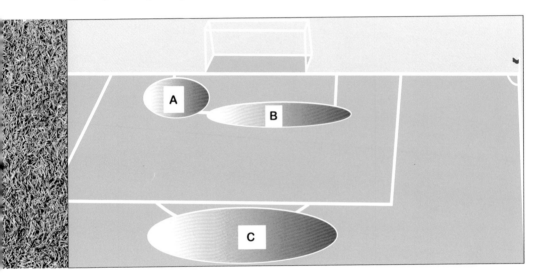

Diagram 5

Coaching Points

- First contact of X9 should be either a cross or to play the ball down toward the end line.
- X9 should be making a decision as to which type of cross they will make from which area.
- The cross should be delivered with enough speed to allow the target players to just redirect the ball toward goal.
- X4, X6 and X7 should learn to anticipate a certain type of cross based upon the position of X9. They should therefore readjust their runs into space based upon this expectation. Their runs should be "late and fast" (response cue). It may also require individual moves to lose their defensive markers. If they wait in a particular area, the defender will likely be able to prevent their contact with the ball.
- X9 should cross as early as is possible.
- X7 must attempt to get a contact on the ball.

Although most coaches realize the importance of crosses to successful game performance the practice does not always produce a maximum transfer of training. This is mainly due to the fact that the coaching practice is not realistic. Realism can be achieved if coaches analyze match performance and plan practices based upon this analysis. Review video of your team's performances and then videotape the practice sessions. Ask the questions "Is there any relationship between the two?" and "Do the players understand the key factors of successful performance that have emanated from analysis?"

PART 2
DECISION MAKING

One assumption we make in the following section of the book is that humans take time to process information, albeit in some instances very short amounts of time. One of the earliest researchers who provided evidence to support this assumption was Frans C. Donders. He published a classic paper in 1868 that is still cited by many researchers today. Donders believed it possible to measure the time course of human information processes. In his study he found that reaction time (i.e. time from observing a change in the environment that required a response to the initiation of that response) is longer when people have to make more than one choice. Hence he concluded that the extra mental processing in dealing with more than one stimulus–response alternative was responsible for this increase in reaction time. It was thought that if we know exactly what to do before seeing the stimulus to react, we can prepare our actions ahead of time. This allows people to anticipate future events and have the actions prepared and ready to go, thus saving the time to process information.

The hypothesis that human information processing slows down when people are faced with many possible actions was later supported by Julius Merkel in 1885, and then by Ray Hyman and William Hick in the 1950s who showed that there was a lawful relationship between the number of uncertain elements present in the environment and the speed it takes to respond to one of them. For example the reaction time to process information increases linearly as the number of stimulus–response alternatives double. There are, however, several factors that can affect this relationship; importantly, learning is one of these factors. Individuals can learn the predictability of certain environmental changes and therefore anticipate. This anticipation reduces the processing lag time considerably.

Given that this is a very robust phenomenon found in the laboratory and the real world, we felt it worthwhile to apply these findings to the soccer game and try to assist players in reducing the number of alternatives they face during the game. This then would aid in reducing mental processing time and eventually result in speeded actions. The question of interest for the coach is "Can we reduce the number of possible actions the player has to deal with and therefore speed up their information processing of the chosen event?"

CHAPTER 4
A MODEL OF DECISION
MAKING FOR SOCCER

Individuals who play soccer are involved in three basic processes. They perceive a changing environment, they make decisions relating to their perceptions and they select and execute an appropriate response. The speed with which a player can make a correct decision has a profound effect upon the performance of individuals within a game setting. The purpose of this chapter is to give the coach a basic framework whereby the

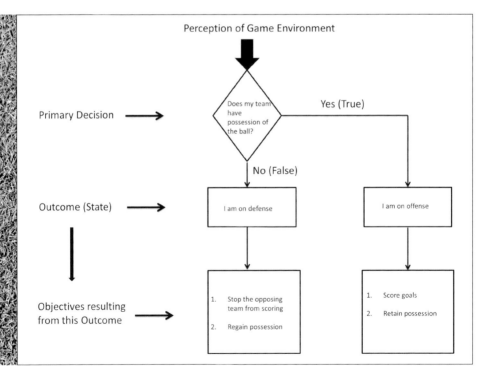

Diagram 1

process of decision making can be made simpler. This chapter is intended to develop a logical model of decision making as it applies to the game of soccer.

The development of tactical thinking has mainly revolved around the principles of possession as discussed in chapter 1. That is to say, possession of the ball is required before goals can be scored therefore the principles of maintaining and retaining possession should govern most decisions that are made in soccer. Since ball possession is at the apex of tactical reasoning, the first decision each team member should make is with relation to who has possession of the ball: "Does the team I am playing for have possession of the ball?"

By answering this question the player can arrive at certain states (see diagram 1). If the answer is "Yes," then that player's team is in possession and that player is on the attack. Two key objectives result from this state of offence and these relate to the fundamental aim of the game itself. Firstly, the main aim of the game is to score goals. If this is not possible then the tactical objective of ball possession could be considered. Conversely, if the answer to the initial question relating to the ball is "No, my team does not have ball possession," then the objective must first be to stop the opposition from scoring and secondly try to regain possession of the ball. From this basic framework, players within a team can now work together with a basic understanding of what is required from them.

Obviously achievement of these objectives involves further decision making in order to specify exactly what action the player should take. The information load placed on the performer by these decisions can be reduced to a minimum by presenting the player with one decision requiring a "yes" or "no" answer at any point in time. The subsequent actions can be viewed as the results of the player successfully traversing what could be termed a binary decision tree of the game. The binary decision tree displayed in diagram 2 illustrates the decisions that each player has to make during any one game, the apex of the tree being the initial ball possession question asked in diagram 1.

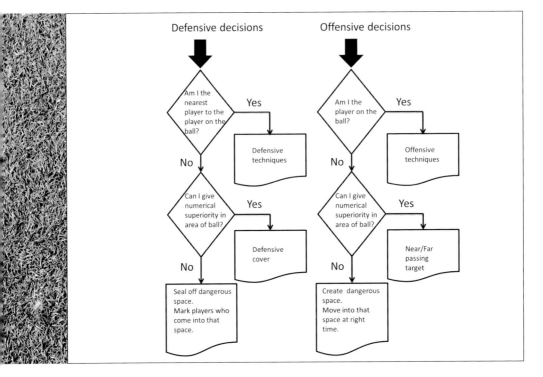

Diagram 2

THE ANSWER TO INITIAL QUESTION IS
"YES, OUR TEAM DOES HAVE BALL POSSESSION."

This affirmative response leads directly to team attacking play and if the answer to the next question (see diagram 2) is "Yes, I am the player in possession of the ball" then the attacking player will be involved in producing technical actions. These on-the-ball activities are the focus of the coaching practices described later in this book. Improvement of the techniques involved consumes the attention of most coaches, whereas the decision-making skills used to arrive at these actions within a game setting are sometimes neglected. Moreover, during any one game only a very small proportion of the time is actually spent performing these techniques. Reports from several top-level soccer games show that on average during a 90-minute game, individual players come into contact with the ball for only approximately 90 seconds. It is therefore important that all players within a team understand all the alternatives involved in off-the-ball attacking behaviour (i.e. answering "No" to the question posed in diagram 2).

If an individual player is not in possession of the ball and his or her team is on the attack then the player's next decision relates to whether he or she can be directly involved in play; that is, can the player become an immediate target for a pass in the area of the ball? It is interesting to note that younger players (8 years and under) seldom traverse the decision tree beyond this branch. One of the reasons why young players assemble around the ball and move around the playing area in swarms is due to their inability to see beyond direct involvement in play (i.e. they have possession or they are the immediate target for a pass). This is largely a developmental problem and resolves itself when players become aware of indirect involvement in team play. It would be unnecessary and unproductive to try to explain the problem of the situation with the young player. However, the number of players in each team should be reduced such that the players do have the potential to be directly involved in all play. Small-sided games offer an excellent platform for explaining age-appropriate decision making and techniques.

If the players who are on the attack are not in possession of the ball, and are not required to be a direct passing target they should now ask questions related to the attacking space. This leads players to become indirectly involved with attacking play. Questions now asked could be "Can I create attacking space?" or "Can I move into potential attacking space?"

THE ANSWER TO THE INITIAL QUESTION IS "NO, OUR TEAM DOES NOT HAVE BALL POSSESSION."

The principles of team play outlined here have equal and opposite components in both attacking and defending aspects of play. Diagram 2 illustrates similar questioning for both offensive and defensive decision making. Since the first option for attacking players is to perform individual techniques while in possession of the ball, the counter behaviour displayed by a defender would be to prevent the attacking player who is in possession of the ball from performing the required techniques. The performance of a skill is influenced by two important factors: time and space. Decreasing the time in which the skill may be executed and decreasing the playing space available will place more demands on the attacking player and possibly cause a decrease in skilled performance. The defensive challenging player therefore should strive to reduce both the time and space available to the attacking player. The defending challenger at this level in the decision tree is involved in individual defensive techniques such as pressurizing opponents and tackling.

A defensive player who is not involved directly challenging for the ball must consider the next problem, that being one of numerical superiority. By offering oneself as a passing target, the offensive player is trying to gain numerical superiority in the area of the ball. Therefore defending players must counteract this influx of attacking players by adding extra defenders. These defenders, who are not involved in challenging for the ball, should put themselves into good covering positions (see diagram 2). Further defensive questioning relates to space and how defenders overcome problems of marking space or marking players. This problem is the basis of much tactical defensive reasoning related to zone or man-to-man defensive tactics. These tactical considerations are at the centre of most defensive coaching and yet the individual decision making that precedes this problem is again often neglected.

FACTORS AFFECTING THE DECISION PROCESS

(1) Learning: It is possible for this model to account for learning. The more often the player meets certain environmental changes that cause him or her to traverse the decision tree, the more likely the player will be able to predict certain outcomes. That is of course, presuming the player is guided and coached through the process of making decisions. Too frequently players within a team are left to their own devices in regard to individual decision making. Hence, the player's only concern becomes decision making in and around the area of the ball, and those players who are not directly involved with play do not consider themselves an intricate part of team play.

Guiding players through the decision tree is important in the learning process and allows players to predict certain occurrences during the game with respect to this questioning framework.

Anticipation, therefore, plays a major role in the optimization of a team's performance. For example, a skilled player who, during the course of the game, has traversed the decision tree down to indirect involvement in offensive play can predict whether there is a danger of his or her team losing possession. This prediction may lead the player to prime their defensive behaviour so that the time it takes to switch from offensive thinking to defensive thinking can be minimized.

(2) Area of Play: Certain priorities relating to where the ball is in relation to the goals affect the importance given to feedback and response priming. If a player is in an offensive state and is on the ball then this player will be more ready to prime scoring responses (e.g. shooting) than passing responses when he or she is close to goal. Conversely, a challenging player will prioritize defending techniques (e.g. pressurizing, tackling and shot blocking) the more imminent the possibility of conceding a goal. It would follow, therefore, that in addition to understanding the basic principles of offensive and defensive team play, a player also needs to know when to use these principles in relation to the proximity of the goal.

(3) System of Play: The basic principles of team play that are illustrated via the decision tree apply to each individual. Whereas all individuals will be asking themselves similar questions in order to fulfill common objectives (i.e. offensive, scoring and retaining possession), each player will have to make decisions relating to all aspects of play. Systems and formations are inherently restrictive. They are needed to organize and align players to certain responsibilities during any one game. The amount of organization of individual players depends upon the game that is being played. *The more restrictive the system of play is on any team, the more limited the individual player is in making personal decisions.* Therefore, the binary decision tree can be aborted at any branch depending upon the limitations placed upon the individual. Hence, the initial question relating to ball possession with its eventual outcomes applies to a limited number of players in a limited area of play.

IMPLICATIONS FOR THE COACH

The decision-making model that is described here is one of total individual involvement within a team game. Players are asked to think and make decisions continually during the game. The model makes assumptions relating to the fundamental aims and objectives of the team game. These objectives may not span all of the game, but it is essential that all members of the team attempt to fulfill the same objectives during a game. Therefore several assumptions are made relating to individual decision making within a team sport; what then are the problems facing the coach? First, the coach should realize that the player is involved in three processes during a game: perception of a changing environment, decision making relating to all aspects of play and selection and execution of the correct action. Second, the coach must be aware that the practice time is best spent when maximal transfer of training is achieved. That is, performance in situation A (practice session) is directly related to performance in situation B (game). *It is important, therefore, for the coach to create a practice environment in which the player has to perceive, decide and act.* In the majority of unopposed drills used in various team sports, the decision stage is usually omitted. Fast, efficient drills very rarely involve the player in making decisions as to what response to select. The selection problem is taken away by the coach who will usually demand a specific technique in a specific drill.

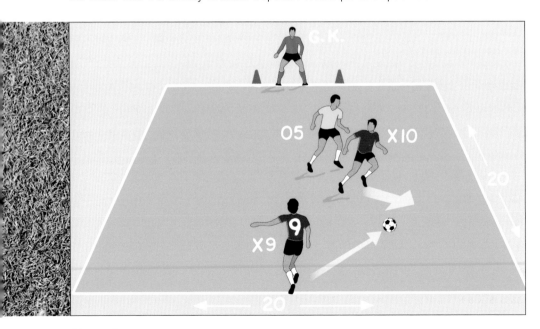

Diagram 3

The following practice is an example of a situation that attempts to involve the player in making individual decisions. These decisions can only be brought out by using the correct realistic environment; it is therefore essential that the coach plan and set up the correct learning environment (see diagram 3).

The practice situation illustrated in diagram 3 has been set up to stress several coaching points to player X10. This player is receiving a pass and has their back to goal. What decisions must X10 make, and how can a coach ease the burden of decision making?

Diagram 4 is a flow chart of the decisions and actions that are possible for X10. In this particular scenario several techniques are important for the attacking player, notably:

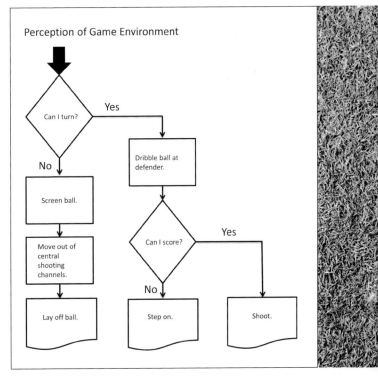

Diagram 4

- receiving the ball with their back to goal;
- screening the ball away from opposing players;
- being able to lay off (pass back) a pass to oncoming cooperating players;
- dribbling;
- shooting; and
- combined play with another cooperating player called, in this case, a step-on (covered later in the book).

The initial question the player should be asking themselves as they move to receive the pass is "Can I turn?" The answer to this will determine subsequent actions. If the receiver can turn, they should try to dribble at the defender and attempt to score by finding a channel to goal. The next question relates to scoring opportunities. If the player cannot find a channel to goal then a combined play with another player could open up a channel to goal, hence a shooting opportunity.

Diagram 5a illustrates one possible combined play termed a step-on (see chapter on Combined Attacking Play). This combined play opens up a shooting channel for X9 to score, whereas in diagram 5b the player under consideration, X10, used the technique of deception to open their own shooting channel.

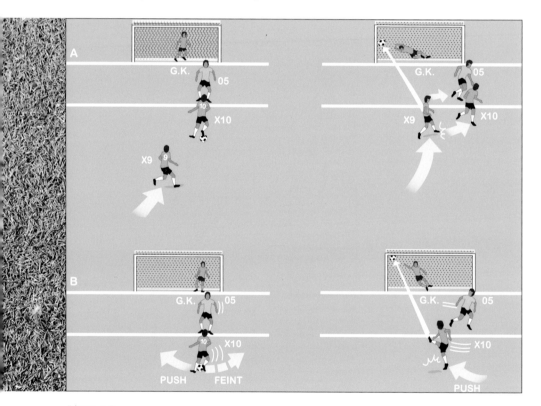

Diagram 5

Returning to the flow chart of diagram 4 and considering the situation in which X10 cannot turn because the player is too closely marked by O5, other alternatives are open. First, X10 must not give the ball away and second, X10 should create space or shooting channels for other players—in this case, X9. By screening the ball and moving out of central areas, X10 can accomplish both of these tasks. The problem facing X10 is now when and where to lay off (see chapter on Combined Attacking Play) the ball so X9 can have a good opportunity to score. Diagram 6 illustrates how X10 moves out of central areas and collects the pass for an immediate lay-off pass back to X9 who has a shooting opportunity.

Diagram 6

CONCLUSIONS

Individuals within a team continually make decisions during a game. The decision-making process can be structured to align all players to similar game objectives. If all players within a team are trying to fulfill similar objectives by different actions, the team performance should improve. Also, if all players understand the reasons behind each other's actions then cohesive team play is inevitable. The binary decision tree has been used to illustrate how the players within a team game can be guided in their thinking process. The implications for both coach and player are far reaching. More importantly *the coaching practices should include the process of decision making.* The player's understanding of direct and indirect involvement in team play has to be tested by intelligent use of the practice environment. Also, the restrictive nature of the system of play that is used has to be weighed against the potential of each individual contributing totally to the team effort. Individual technical excellence is still considered to be of paramount importance. However, the model that is proposed in this chapter highlights the events that occur prior to the execution of these techniques. Consideration should be given to the fact that the performer processes information, and that the perceptual and decision processes cannot be overlooked when considering the player within a game.

CHAPTER 5
DECISION MAKING
AND DEFENDING

Coaches often neglect defensive aspects of the game and spend most of their time concentrating on the more creative techniques of attacking play, perhaps because players would rather attack with the ball than defend and try to regain possession. During a game we can conclude that on average, half of the time a team does not have possession of the ball, though this sometimes depends on the tactics employed by the coach. It is therefore important that every member of the team be aware of their defensive responsibilities at any time during the game.

Upon analysis it appears that a few general factors are responsible for an attacking team giving up possession of the ball. For example:

⚽ With very little defensive pressure, the attacking players lose control of the ball, play inaccurate passes or take inaccurate shots on goal due to poor technique.

⚽ Due to defensive pressure, the attacking team is *forced* to lose control of the ball, play inaccurate passes or take inaccurate shots.

The position outlined in (a) is evident at all levels of the game but especially at lower levels of recreational league play. No defensive consideration is needed in this case. All we can ask of our players is to be alert and ready to capitalize on these mistakes by attacking players (i.e. get speedy and composed control of the ball early when the opposition give up possession).

The coach's major concern lies with (b). How can we force attacking players to give up possession of the ball? Several further questions stem from this general one. What are the priorities involved? How does the coach most profitably spend their time in practice? And what does a player need to know when defending?

The major problem for the coach in dealing with defensive aspects of the game is organization and understanding. Players should have very simple decisions to make while defending. The simplicity of the decision speeds up the entire information process. The environment is continually changing and requires respective changes in action from the defending players. Having players understand their specific responsibilities whilst defending is a realistic goal for coaches at all levels.

Teaching the technique of tackling is often given a higher priority than is necessary. During any game, the techniques of passing, heading and shooting are evident, and mistakes can be attributed to a possible breakdown of the skill. Moreover it is not often during any one game that the block tackle or the slide tackle can be seen executed as laid down in many textbooks (and recently most sliding tackles draw some type of punishment from the referee). The reason for this is that due to the rate at which the environment changes, execution of all the points related to the block tackle takes too long and on some occasions it becomes anatomically impossible.

Before introducing players to the tackling technique they should be first be made aware of where and when to tackle. Once they understand these important prerequisites, the efficiency of how to tackle can be coached. Since a player cannot effectively defend unless they are in the correct position, it seems illogical to spend most of the coaching time on the technique of tackling. For many young teams just being goal side of the ball is sufficient for opposing players to give up the ball.

Reassessment of the present teaching methods relating to defending is needed. A prioritized list of the objectives is given below. It should be kept in mind that these objectives are related to specific areas of the field and not necessarily the whole field; for example, it would be impractical to ask a front striker to get goal side of a lofted clearance played into their own penalty area.

OBJECTIVES

Players should understand:

- Where the dangerous defensive space is in relation to the ball, their own goal and their own position on the field
- How to get goal side
- How to pressure and challenge for the ball
- How to give cover to a teammate who is applying pressure to the ball
- When to tackle
- How to tackle
- How to track down an opposing player
- How to seal off dangerous space

The first two objectives could be dealt with in a small-sided game situation (4 vs 4 or 5 vs 5). A method of stopping or freezing play should be used to illustrate these objectives. Examples are given on the following pages.

"Where is the dangerous defensive space?"

First it is important for players to realize that dangerous space is continually moving.

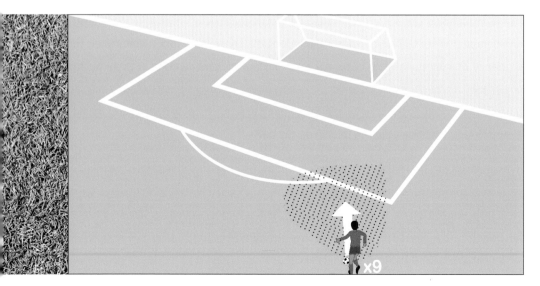

Diagram 1

⚽ In diagram l, X9 is an attacking player in possession of the ball. In this example the dangerous defending space is between the near post of the goal and the attacker and is shaded in diagram 1. For defenders every effort must be made to stop X9 moving the ball forward into this space.

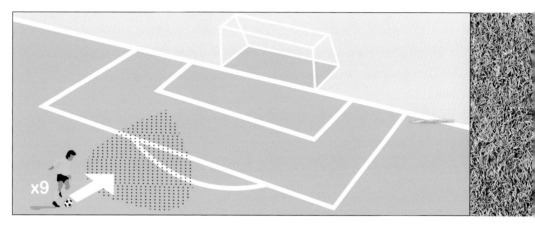

Diagram 2

⚽ In diagrams 2 and 3 the dangerous space has moved with respect to the movement of the ball and the near goal post that is being attacked by X9.

Diagram 3

A defender must judge the potential danger of space by considering the following:

⚽ The position of the ball

⚽ The position of the goal being defended

⚽ Their own position on the field with respect to opposing and cooperating players

A series of questions should be used to direct the small-sided game. Stop play intermittently and ask the defensive team where their dangerous defensive space is. Each player on the team just having lost possession must first ask themselves a similar question.

"Am I goal side?"

Is the defensive player positioned between the ball and their own goal? If the answer is *"No,"* then the player should move towards the back of the dangerous space as quickly as possible. Once the defender has passed the line of the ball they should look up and reassess their position while moving (see flowchart A-D).

At this point in the practice, players should have an understanding of the first two objectives and are now either positioned goal side or are moving goal side of the ball.

FLOWCHART A-D

If the answer to the question in flowchart box C is *"Yes, I am goal side of the ball,"* then the next question, in box D, is *"Am I the nearest person to the ball?"* If the answer is *"Yes,"* then this player becomes the challenging and pressuring player. The coaching objective then is to coach the player how to pressure and how to challenge for the ball.

"How do I pressure and challenge for the ball?"

Key Factors

⚽ The stance and movement of a challenging player who is applying pressure should:

⚽ Keep the body weight forward and low

⚽ Position one foot forward and one back, with knees bent and weight resting on the balls of the feet not the heels

⚽ Maintain the ability to move backwards quickly while staying well-balanced and ready to turn and sprint

⚽ Allow defending players to be looking at the ball not the opposing player

⚽ Be likened to a boxer's stance

It is important that players work hard at mastering this type of pressuring movement as well as moving backwards and turning and sprinting from this stance since the essence of dribbling is to counter all of the points made above.

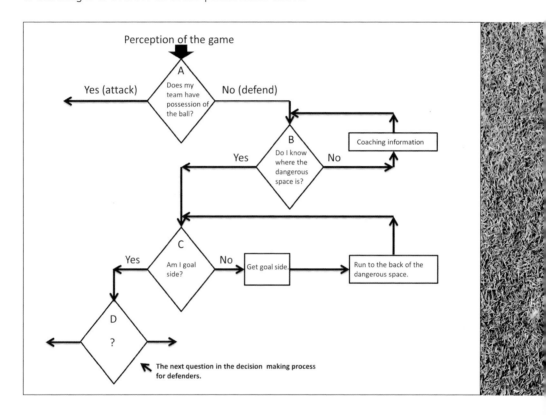

PRACTICE A

Diagram 4

- ⚽ One ball between two players.
- ⚽ Area of work (see diagram 4).
- ⚽ The X team are attackers and attempt to dribble the ball, under control, onto the target line.
- ⚽ The O team are defenders and must try to keep the distance between themselves and the ball a constant 1 or 2 meters.
- ⚽ The O player must reach the line target line before the X player scores.
- ⚽ After either team has reached 5 goals, reverse roles with Os becoming attackers and Xs becoming defenders.
- ⚽ Attackers are encouraged to change pace and direction frequently.
- ⚽ No tackling by the O team.

PRACTICE B

- One ball per two players.
- Area as in diagram 5 (10-by-10-meter grid).
- The practice begins with the defender O5 serving the ball into X9 and following in the service.

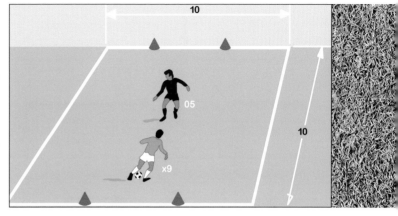

Diagram 5

- X9 has a time limit of 20 seconds in which to score.
- O5 should move in to pressure and contain X9 while remaining goal side for the 20-second time period.
- If the ball is won by the defender O5, then O5 becomes an attacker and attempts to score.
- O5 should not move in to tackle but can entice X9 into giving up the ball (early shots etc.) by feinting to tackle.

Coaching Points

- Pressure is applied to X9 by O5 with a speedy but controlled approach to a position approximately 2 meters away from the ball. Slowing down quickly as the challenging player approaches the attacker is an important skill to master.
- The angle of the defender's run is dependent upon where the cooperating defending players are positioned (introduced later in practice) and the closeness of the out-of-bounds lines.

Before progressing to the technique of tackling, the problem of the covering a defender should be dealt with. It would be instructive therefore to return to the unfinished flowchart.

FLOWCHART D-H

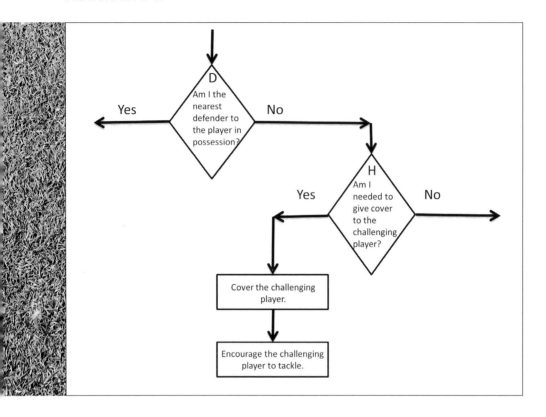

If the answer to the question in question box D is *"No"*, then the next question is related to giving cover to the challenging player.

"How do I cover the challenging player?"

The aim of the covering player is to try and gain numerical superiority for their team in the area of the ball. In diagram 6, X6 is the covering defender. The position of X6 is important.

Key Factors

- ⚽ The position of the covering player X6 (given in diagram 6).

  - ⚽ When the opponent is being forced down the touch line, the position is just backward of straight as in diagram 6a.

  - ⚽ When the opponent is being forced across field into cooperating defenders, the position is just backward of square as in diagram 6b.

  - ⚽ If in doubt (maybe due to the fact that X5 is not pressuring closely enough) then the defender X6 selects a position approximately 45 degrees as in diagram 6c.

  - ⚽ X6 should be positioned such that a tackle for the ball can be made if O4 dribbles past X5 or immediate pressure can be applied to O4 to contain the forward movement into dangerous areas after dribbling past X5.

  - ⚽ X6 must be close enough to X5 so that O4 is faced with a 1-vs-2 situation. If X6 is too far away from X5, O4 is faced with two 1-vs-1 situations and is therefore more likely to dribble past both players.

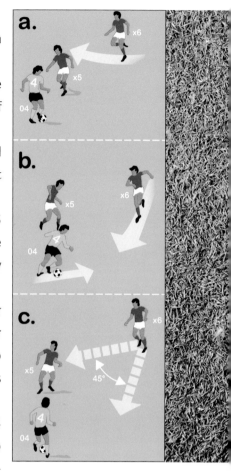

Diagram 6

- ⚽ It is important that X5 is continually alerted to readjusting this covering position.

  - ⚽ Communication between the two defenders.

  - ⚽ The covering player must make the cooperating players aware of changes to his or her position.

  - ⚽ The covering player should encourage and inform the challenging player of when the cover is in place and where their defensive strengths lie (e.g. "Push the opposing attacker inside or outside!").

  - ⚽ Although the covering player does not decide when the challenging player tackles, the covering player must encourage them to challenge for the ball when it is safe to do so.

PRACTICE C

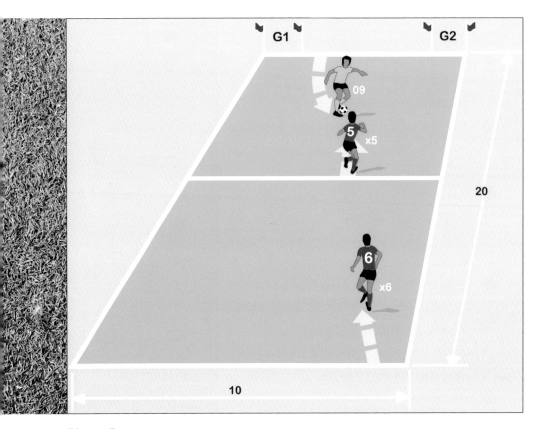

Diagram 7

- ⚽ One ball per 3 players.
- ⚽ Two defenders versus one attacker.
- ⚽ Area of 20-by-l0-meter grids (see diagram 7).
- ⚽ X6, X5 and O9 all begin each practice from their respective lines.
- ⚽ O9 must place the ball in control on the target line vacated by X6.
- ⚽ X5 and X6 attempt to win the ball and score through either G1 or G2 goals.
- ⚽ X5 should be encouraged to tackle when cover is correctly in place.
- ⚽ The practice begins with X5 serving the ball to O9 and then moving in to challenge for the ball.

ALTERNATIVE PRACTICES
FOR BOTH CHALLENGING AND COVERING PLAYERS

This series of practices could be used for front strikers and midfield players who would like to improve their ability to seal off play in concentrated areas in the front third of the field and regain possession back early.

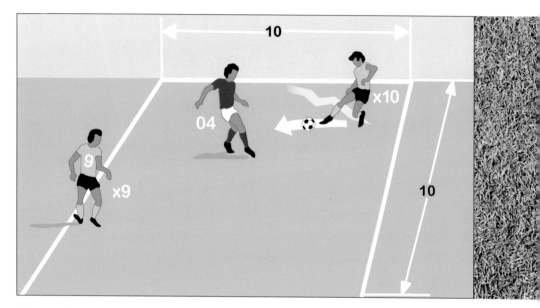

Diagram 8

⚽ Diagram 8 illustrates a 2-vs-l practice in a 10-meter grid.

⚽ X9 and X10 attempt to score by making 5 consecutive passes.

⚽ O4 scores a goal by touching the ball.

Coaching Points

⚽ O4 should try to isolate one attacker with the ball by cutting off the passing angles.

⚽ O4 should use the boundary lines to their advantage by forcing play into the corners.

⚽ O4 must be ready to challenge for the ball when X10 is most likely to pass and look down at the ball.

Diagram 9

⚽ Diagram 9 illustrates a 3 vs 1 in a 10-meter grid.

⚽ X9, XI0 and X11 attempt to score a goal by making seven passes.

⚽ 04 scores a goal by touching the ball or by forcing the X players to play the ball out of bounds.

Coaching Points

⚽ 04's movement toward the player in possession of the ball should allow only one passing possibility.

⚽ While this predicted pass is moving, 04 should close down the receiver at speed and tackle as the player receives the ball or cut out the return pass from the attacker.

⚽ Speed of movement and predicting play is of utmost importance.

Diagram 10

⚽ Diagram 10 illustrates a 4-vs-2 game in a 15-meter grid.

⚽ X7, X8, X9 and X10 attempt to score by making five consecutive passes.

⚽ O4 and O6 score by touching the ball or by making the X team play the ball out of the area.

Coaching Points

⚽ O4's movement toward the player in possession has to indicate early where the cover is needed. Make the opposition's play predictable (response cue).

⚽ O9 is the covering player and must predict from O4's challenge where the subsequent pass is most probably going to be played.

⚽ O6 must act with speed and pressure or tackle the receiver of the pass early.

The challenging player is now in a position (with cover) to ask the question posed earlier in the flowchart.

FLOWCHART D-G

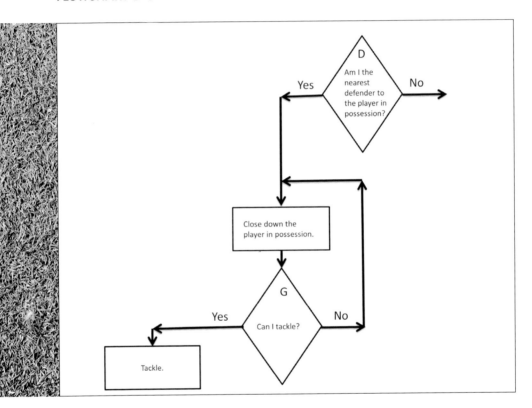

"When do I tackle?"

Key Factors

- ⚽ The challenging player should have encouraging and vocal cover.
- ⚽ The challenging player should allow the distance between the ball and themselves to reduce. This is done by jockeying backwards at a slower rate.
- ⚽ At this time the challenging player must be alert to a highly probable attacking move from the player in possession.

- The challenging player can tackle when the attacking player in possession of the ball has momentarily lost control. When does an attacker momentarily lose control? As soon as the attacking player has made contact with the ball. At this point the distance between the attacker and the ball is increasing and the player requires another step before they can touch the ball again.

- The challenging player can tackle when they can reach the ball in one step. Unless a defender can touch the ball with one step they are not then in a position to execute the tackle.

"How do I tackle?"

Key Factors

- The tackling player should be well balanced.
- The tackling player should try to remain on their feet during and after the tackle.
- The tackle should be executed with speed and determination.
- The tackling player should be committed (response cue) to the tackle.
- The tackling player should move their body forward and through the ball.
- The tackling player should keep their eyes on the ball.
- Very few tackles are won cleanly after the first contact. Therefore the tackling player should be ready to try and regain possession, whatever the outcome of the first contact.

PRACTICE D

Diagram 11

- The organization of this practice is designed to allow lots of tackling.
- The practice should be strictly controlled by the coach to discourage reckless challenges for the ball.
- As in diagram 11 the area is only a 10-by-10-meter grid.
- The goals for the teams are cones placed in the two opposite corners.
- It is a 4-vs-4 game.

Coaching Points

- Players should not commit to a tackle if they are not balanced and are not within one step of the ball.
- Players should concentrate and keep their eyes on the ball.
- Players should stay on their feet.
- If the player can steal the ball with the front foot then they should do so, but then move toward it quickly.
- If tackling with the back foot, the player should bring all their weight into and through the ball.

We now return to the flowchart. If the answer to the question about cover is *"No"*, then the next action for the defender may be to track down opposing attacking players.

FLOWCHART H-I

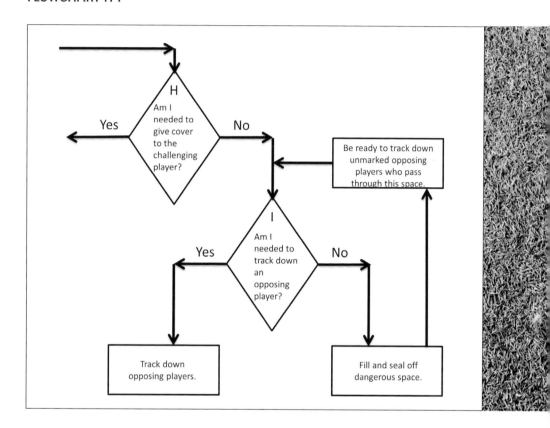

"How do I track down opposing players?"

Key Factors

⚽ Peripheral awareness:

　⚽ The defender should not allow themselves to have their vision or stance narrowed down (i.e. do not watch only the ball and do not watch only the player [response cue]).

　⚽ The defender should be aware of the changing positions of opposing players, ball, covering players, pressuring players, own goal and area of the field.

,Interception judgment: consider the defender who is marking an opposing player and then the ball is passed to this opposing player. The defender should:

- Pressure the attacker such that the defender has their back to their own goal and the ball and the attacker can be moved away from dangerous space (mark inside to out [response cue]).
- Try to be first to the ball (intercept); if this is not possible then try to tackle as the attacker receives the ball. If this is not possible then close down the opponent and be balanced on arrival, ready to move back as fast as the opposing player moves forward.
- Force the opposing player to the side of defensive strength and away from the opposing player's attacking support (i.e. isolate the attacking player if possible).
- These priorities can be achieved if the defender moves in to intercept, tackle, or pressure when the ball has just been passed to the opposing player.
- Caution should be taken that the defender is not drawn into the interception run too early. Go fast but late (response cue).

PRACTICE E

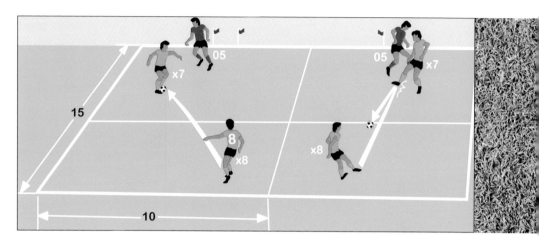

Diagram 12

- ⚽ One ball between three players.
- ⚽ As in diagram 12 there is an area of 15 by 10 meters.
- ⚽ X8 is the feeder who cannot move into the grid but who can be passed to.
- ⚽ X7 must try to score and is also encouraged to play back to X8 and try to get behind O5 for a return pass.
- ⚽ O5 must stay goal side of X7 and stop X7 from scoring.

Coaching Points

- ⚽ O5 should move in with low body position.
- ⚽ If possible O5 should try to intercept the pass.
- ⚽ If O5 cannot intercept the pass then they should try to tackle X7 as they receive the ball.
- ⚽ If O5 cannot tackle then they should prevent X7 from turning. With the low body position the defender should be able to see the ball and not be so close that the attacker can turn (role) the defender.
- ⚽ Be patient (response cue) and don't tackle from the back of the attacker.
- ⚽ The task for O5 now is to force X7 away from goal (and preferably back towards the attacker's goal) while keeping their body goal side of the player and the ball.
- ⚽ Do not go to ground to tackle for the ball and do not foul the attacker.

PRACTICE F

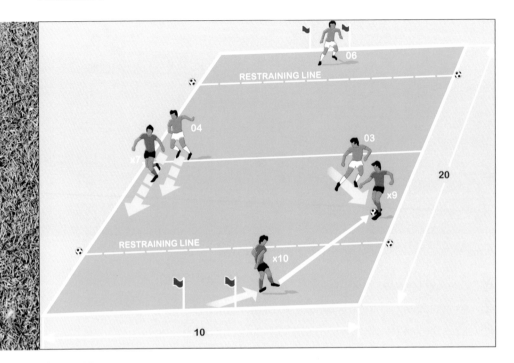

Diagram 13

- ⚽ One ball between 6 players (two teams of 3).
- ⚽ Area is 20-by-l0-meter grid as in diagram 13.
- ⚽ Two goals, 4 meters apart.
- ⚽ The aim of game is to score goals.
- ⚽ Cones mark off two restraining lines marked on diagram.
- ⚽ Feeder, goalkeeper, X10 and O6 can move laterally with ball.
- ⚽ Defenders have a responsibility of marking an individual attacker (O4 covers X7 and O3 covers X9).
- ⚽ Feeder (X10) is asked to vary the quality of service to the attackers (long, short, forceful, high passes, etc.). Because the attackers will now have some problems in controlling the pass, the defenders should have a chance to choose between intercepting the ball or tackling or jockeying their attacker.
- ⚽ While team X is attacking, O6 acts as goalkeeper.

We now return to the final coaching question of the flow chart (see flowchart H-I).

"How do I seal off dangerous space?"

The following are key factors in understanding dangerous space.

Key Factors

⚽ Players should be ready to offer themselves as a covering defender.

⚽ Players should be ready to intercept balls played into and through dangerous space.

⚽ Players should continually adjust their position with regard to the changing dangerous space.

⚽ Players should take in and organize larger amounts of information from the playing environment (i.e. be aware of sealing off attacking play into one area of the field but also recognize any runs from attackers around the back of defenders).

⚽ Players should make cooperating players aware of changes in their own positional situation.

PRACTICE G

This practice emphasizes when defenders should mark attackers very closely (when they are threatening dangerous space) and when to cover (seal off) dangerous space, or when to split responsibilities between marking attacking players and sealing off space. Man-to-man marking requires a special type of discipline and players who understand how to mark players can adapt more easily to zonal responsibilities.

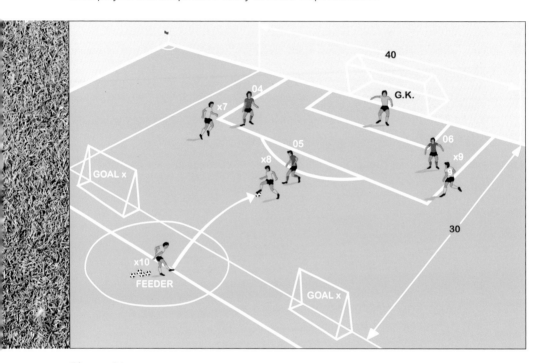

Diagram 14

- ⚽ The area is 40 by 30 meters as in diagram 14.
- ⚽ One goalkeeper, one feeder and three goals as in diagram 14.
- ⚽ The practice is 3 vs 3 and each defender is given a specific attacker to cover (mark).
- ⚽ One feeder (X10) for attackers.
- ⚽ Players keep strict man-to-man marking responsibility.
- ⚽ X10 cannot enter field of play but can be passed back to by the attacking players.
- ⚽ Offside rule should be enforced by the coach.
- ⚽ X team try to move behind O defenders with the ball, then shoot on goal.
- ⚽ If O team wins the ball it should be played into the goals on the sides of Xl0.

Coaching Points

⚽ In diagram 15, if X9 is not directly threatening the dangerous space, O6 can afford to move slightly back from the attacker and offer cover to this space. This means the defender is now covering dangerous space.

⚽ O5 should try to split defensive responsibilities between offering cover to O4 as well as being ready to intercept or challenge for a ball played to X8 or pressure if that is not possible.

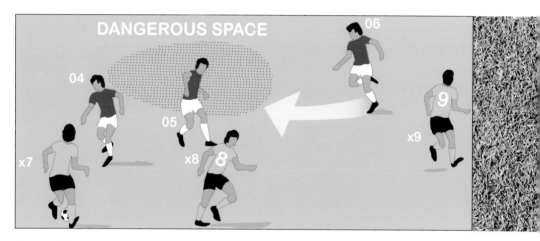

Diagram 15

PRACTICE H

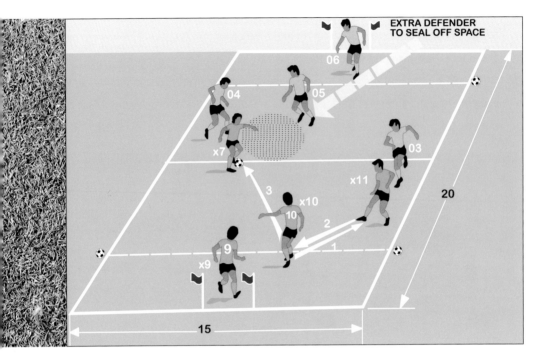

Diagram 16

- ⚽ This practice can be a progression from practice F with the addition of two more players to each side.
- ⚽ The area is 15 by 20 meters as shown in diagram 16.
- ⚽ O5 becomes the defender with whom the coach should be concerned.
- ⚽ X11 and X10 can both start the practice or can pass between themselves to unbalance the defense.
- ⚽ When the Os have possession X10 becomes the defender of concern.

PRACTICE I

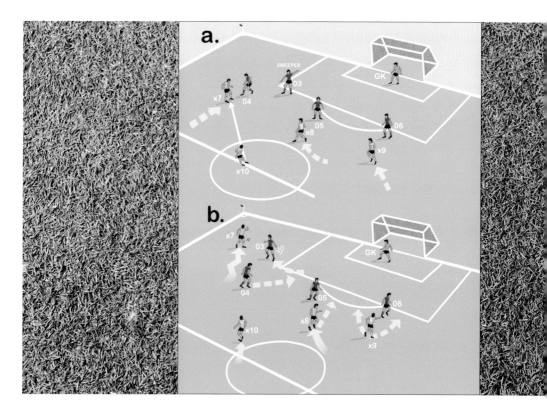

Diagram 17

⚽ Introducing a sweeper (O3) into the practice should ease space responsibilities for the markers, and O3 will now apply cover to challenging players (see diagram 17).

⚽ Attackers should be encouraged to be as mobile as possible to test the defenders.

Coaching Points

⚽ O3 should offer cover to the challenging player.

⚽ If the marking defenders are beaten then O3 should either move in to tackle and win the ball or delay the attacking player until the beaten marker (in diagram 17, this is O4) takes over the role of sweeper.

⚽ When the ball is passed into the marked attackers the sweeper should not be involved in challenging for the ball.

⚽ O3's primary responsibility is covering space and not marking attacking players.

⚽ Organizational information and control of co-defenders should come from the sweeper.

SUMMARY OF DEFENDING

The defending player makes several decisions as to what their role is when their team does not have possession of the ball. The questions that have been used in this chapter via the decision tree flow chart enable the coach to illustrate the principles of defending to the players. The main concern is not what system of defending a team is using (e.g. man to man or zone), but that the players operate within the principles of organized defending.

- ⚽ Here we re-emphasize some of these defending principles outlined in this chapter.
- ⚽ Defenders are the team who are not in possession of the ball. This means the whole team is defending.
- ⚽ Defenders should understand what *goal side* means and also understand how to get there.
- ⚽ Defenders should realize where the dangerous defending space is and how to get there.
- ⚽ Defenders nearest to the player in possession of the ball must pressure that player in a direction that makes the attacking play predictable.
- ⚽ Covering players should move into positions behind challenging defenders with knowledge of direction, distance and opposing players.
- ⚽ Dangerous defending space should be filled and sealed off by defending players.
- ⚽ Attacking players who enter this dangerous space should be tracked down and marked closely.
- ⚽ Defending players should know when and how to tackle.

The important limiting factor that was placed upon the decisions emanating from the flow chart was with respect to the area of the field in which play was occurring. However, the major emphasis in this chapter has been on individual and team understanding of defending and the application of decision making. All players become better players if they understand what is expected of them and if they utilize their own thought process throughout the changing game. This thought process can only be engaged if the player is continually asking themselves relevant (yet simple) questions.

COMPLETE DECISION TREE FLOWCHART FOR DEFENDING

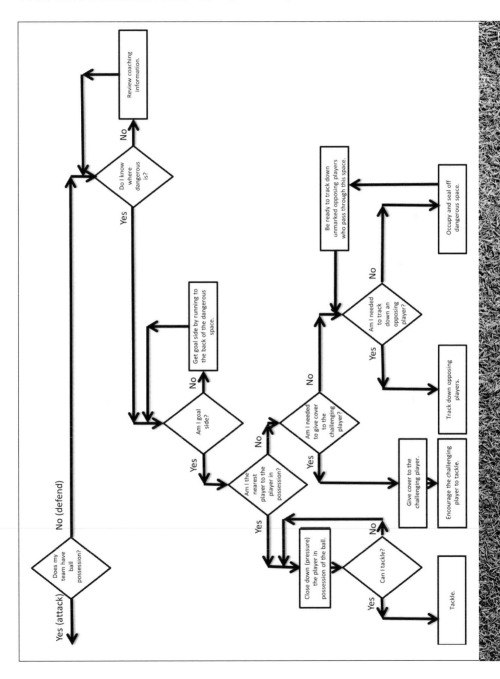

PART 3
TEAM PLAY

In the next section and throughout the rest of the book we will stress the need for the coach to recreate the game setting in practice, albeit in some modified way to accommodate the needs of the team they are coaching. Before doing this, the coach should be encouraged to analyze play and use this analysis as a basis upon which they can create the area of interest for what may be some corrective or developmental practices. The coach is hoping for maximum transfer of training. A concept called the Specificity of Learning Hypothesis was first put forward by psychologist Edward Thorndike in 1906; applied to the learning of motor skills by Franklin Henry in the 1950s; and then highlighted in the work of Denis Holding in the 1960s. Its application in soccer is best illustrated by the question "To what extent will the skills practiced in situation A (the practice session) transfer to situation B (the game)?" One way to ensure such an efficient learning process is to make the environment of the practice as close to the game as possible. Why not then practice within the framework of a full 11-vs-11 game for the entire practice? The reasons are many:

⚽ A full 11-a-side game is far too complex a situation in which to isolate and improve individual technique.

⚽ Information overload, whereby players are faced with too many game-related items to process, occurs.

⚽ Coaches cannot manipulate the session to guarantee success at a technique for each player.

⚽ There is limited involvement for each individual.

⚽ The time the player is in contact with the ball is considerably reduced.

How can we then fulfill the requirements of transfer of training and develop skillful players while avoiding these pitfalls? In order to accomplish this, the coaching practice must have several characteristics.

In terms of using practice specificity principles in a coaching context, the coach can return to game analysis (perhaps even a video of the game) and attempt to ensure the context in which the player is going to be working has some relevance to the actual game. Planning and preparation of the coaching session then becomes of paramount importance. Functional practice and combined attacking play, as described in this section, are excellent vehicles whereby situation-specific techniques can be practiced and learned. Functional practices can then be progressed back to the full game situation as skills improve. In this type of practice the relevance of the information provided by the coach becomes much more meaningful to the players involved and maximum transfer of training is ensured.

CHAPTER 6
FUNCTIONAL PRACTICE

Before any functional practice can be effectively implemented, areas of poor individual technique or organized team play should be identified and isolated by the coach from available analysis. These weaknesses or developmental concerns can then be prioritized: first, an assessment by the coach; then, joint assessment by players and coach. The coach should strive to build up within the team an enthusiasm for critical self-analysis, a willingness to be criticized and to criticize in a constructive manner. From such a relationship the goal of what is to be achieved (i.e. successful performance) for both players and coach will become attainable.

In a functional practice a coach will be concerned with the performance of an individual player or small group of players. The coach will analyze the player's function by examining the techniques which the players may be required to use in a particular situation and also by examining the need to develop an understanding with other players in circumstances relevant to the game. The coach will be involved with part of the team for the specific benefit of one or more members of that team.

The emphasis is on decision making in specific situations. Players are required to apply the individual techniques with respect to the position of opposing players and cooperating teammates. The requirements placed upon the player should be focused upon making the correct decisions after reading the changing environment. It is therefore important that the coach structure a practice to allow relevant instruction to take place in a realistic situation that the player will face in the full game. The situation begins in its simplest form with limited decision making required. This will allow the coach to bring out the key factors of individual technical performance. It builds up to a complex realistic game situation although the emphasis would still be on the particular aspect of play under consideration.

The playing environment should allow the coach to work on the problem technique or tactic that will be under review. Organization of this practice is of primary importance and the following should guide the organization of any functional practice.

⚽ The area of the field where the action takes place within the game should be demarcated and the players that are initially involved in action should be decided upon. A good analogy to keep in mind is one of a movie camera. The coach should imagine a zoom lens attached to a camera that makes it possible to isolate the problem area in detail and answer the following questions:

⚽ Where does the action take place?

⚽ When does the action take place?

⚽ Who is involved in the action?

⚽ The specifics of the setup can be taken from analysis of the game. A video recording of the problem and its area of play can be extremely useful here.

⚽ The practice must have a clear objective for the attacking and defending players. For example:

⚽ Attackers must try to score a goal.

⚽ Defenders regain possession and find target players or goals.

⚽ Boundaries must be realistic with relation to space and players involved in that space.

⚽ Functional practice is not designed to improve physical fitness, but is aimed at decision making and applying some cognitive pressure to the players involved. Fatigue will interfere with the decision-making process, therefore the coach should not make intense physical demands of the players during the practice.

⚽ Functional practice can be related to a jigsaw puzzle. The players involved are made aware of the whole picture and are encouraged to continually refer back to it. Pieces of the puzzle are added until the whole picture is once again recreated.

⚽ It is not always advisable to weight the odds too much in favor of the coached players. Sometimes this produces an atmosphere of not hurrying because numerical superiority is assured (e.g. 5 attackers [coached players] vs 3 defenders). By equalizing the odds one can get closer to the real match-like situation and the type of responses needed. However the coach should progress only when success is obtained in the practice (i.e. don't make the situation too difficult too soon). This becomes a difficult balance for the coach to achieve.

- ⚽ The player should contribute as much as the coach. Discussion with the player must be undertaken in order to find out the player's ideas in certain situations. Understanding at this point is as important as technical excellence.

- ⚽ The functional practice should progress toward a phase of play (more players and larger area of the field).

- ⚽ Finally the players should be allowed to implement their skills once again in the full game. In order to facilitate frequent practice of the function under review, the coach may condition or modify the rules slightly in order to concentrate on the situation under review.

The organization of any practice session is very important in ensuring that the relevant coaching points can be brought to the player's attention. An integral part of the functional practice therefore is knowledgeable planning. The playing environment should be such that it allows positive instruction to be given to players. To give this positive instruction the coach should be knowledgeable of all phases of play, specifically the analysis of the technique and its application in any given game situation.

Beginning a Functional Practice

This session is conducted practically. A full game (11 vs 11) is the vehicle by which the objectives of the session can be met.

- Begin with two teams in clearly distinguishable colors. Team positions should be as they are in competition.
- Allow play to continue for approximately 10 minutes while the coach acts as referee.
- After this preliminary time of play the coach should then try to observe instances where it is possible to freeze play for all 22 players (a whistle is the best method to freeze all players in this situation).
- The instances when play should be frozen will be in relation to the functions the coach wishes to illustrate (having gained this information from match analysis). For example, if the coach wants to illustrate where a functional practice on two front strikers will originate, they may stop play when a midfield player has the ball entering the opponent's half and is looking for target players (front strikers) to pass to. The coach should then ask all players not directly involved in play to sit down on the outskirts of the field and observe and listen while the coach makes the coaching points to the players involved. The progression and development of play can then be illustrated by asking selected players in certain areas to stand up and participate in the practice. This development continues until all players are once again playing and involved in play.

What follows are several examples of various functional practices.

FUNCTIONAL PRACTICE ON A FULL BACK
IN THEIR OWN DEFENDING THIRD OF THE FIELD

PRACTICE A

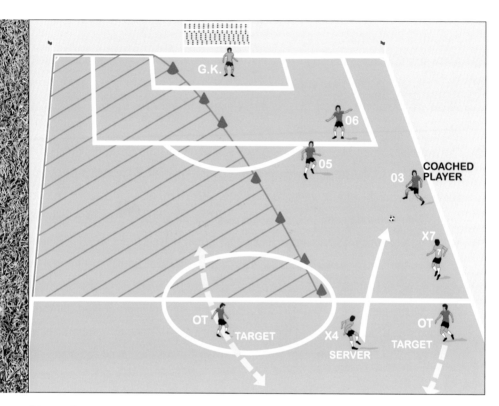

Diagram 1

⚽ The area of the field is marked with cones as shown in diagram 1.

⚽ The player being coached is O3.

⚽ The objective of attackers (X7 and X4) is to try and score goals.

⚽ The objective of the defenders is to make an accurate pass to two target players (OT) or in emergency situations to clear the ball out of the marked area.

⚽ Before the ball is played into the area of O3 and X7, the position of O3 should be inside and goal side of the opposing player X7.

⚽ O3 should be at the correct distance allowing O3 to move in close to X7 if ball is played to X7's feet.

⚽ Early services of the ball by the coach may be aimed directly toward O3, allowing the coach to make the point that no chances should be taken in this area of the field and that the first requirement will be to select techniques which produce the least possibility of advantage falling to the attacking side.

Coaching Points

⚽ When in doubt O3 should take the ball early, heading, volleying or driving the ball for distance and playing the ball away from central areas towards the sides of the field.

⚽ Where O3 does have time to keep the ball (because X7 is not close) then it will be important to select a controlling technique which will allow the player to take the ball away from the direction of the challenge; it may even be possible for O3 to allow the ball to run on occasionally while looking up and around to make a selection of a forward pass.

⚽ The angle through which the forward passes are to be made will be important, since any ball played into a central area from this deep defensive position will almost certainly mean the full back will play themselves out of the game should that central pass be intercepted by opposition.

⚽ The need for a quality pass to the target players cannot be overstated since this will initiate a new attack for the team.

⚽ The composure of the full back at this time is most important and the controlling technique should be well learned as this will provide the player with confidence to retain possession of the ball. Quick implementation of the controlling technique will give O3 the time to make a good pass forward.

⚽ The cooperation and communication between the defenders will be important to the full back's performance, since the goalkeeper, O5 and O6 can all assist the full back in making correct decisions.

⚽ A back pass to the goalkeeper may be a useful outlet if there is the possibility of an intercepted pass forward.

⚽ Indecision is the greatest problem here and if the full back lingers on the ball before releasing it then clearly this will give opposing attackers time to anticipate such a pass and intercept it.

PROGRESSION 1

The service can now be varied to allow the ball to be played directly to X7. This will prompt the coach to outline other priorities for the full back to consider.

Coaching Points

⚽ Now the defenders marking position before the ball is served into X7 should enable an interception if a less-than-perfect service is made.

⚽ Where interception is impossible it will be vital for O3 to move quickly toward X7 while the ball is travelling to X7 in order to get close to the attacker and stop them from turning and moving toward the goal. O3 will now have to apply defensive pressure to X7 until the ball is released. If O3 stands off X7 and allows the attacker to turn, it will make the opposition's play less predictable. It should be emphasized that the job of the pressuring defender is to make the opponent's play predictable for all the cooperating defenders.

⚽ If X7 does turn, then the full back needs to move more cautiously in order to avoid over-committing themselves and being beaten by X7.

⚽ O3 should then try to contain X7. This containing position will require attention, and the defensive support which O3 receives from the O5 and O6 will determine whether X7 is forced infield or towards the touch line. Whichever way X7 is to be directed, the player will have to be challenged closely from a distance of two or three meters in order to prevent playing the ball forward easily.

It must be stressed that it may not be necessary and certainly will not be desirable to make all the points mentioned above in one functional practice situation. As always, it will be the job of the coach to recognize the needs of the players and to structure practices to meet those needs. Technical inadequacies may best be dealt with in individual practice situations, always bearing in mind that the performance of the technique is only relevant in the proper context, which means in the game environment.

PROGRESSION 2

The functional practice outlined above can be further developed by:

- ⚽ A variation of service by X4 (e.g. the ball can be played directly to X7 or past O3).
- ⚽ X4 moves into play as soon as the pass is made.
- ⚽ An increase in the number of players in this sector of the field.
- ⚽ An increase in the area of the field used with the removal of some field markers (cones).

FUNCTIONAL PRACTICE ON TWO CENTRE BACKS

PRACTICE B

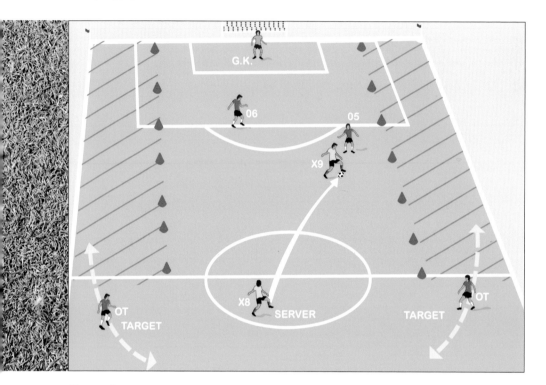

Diagram 2

- ⚽ The area of the field is marked with cones as shown in diagram 2.
- ⚽ The players being coached are O5 and O6.
- ⚽ The objective of the attackers is to try and score goals.
- ⚽ The objective of the defenders is to make an accurate pass to two target players (OT) or, in emergency situations, to clear the ball out of the marked area.

Coaching Points

Made to the challenging player O5:

- ⚽ As the ball is served in to X9, the closest defender to X9 becomes the challenging defender (in diagram 2 this is O5) and O6 becomes the covering defender.
- ⚽ If the attacker receives the ball with their back to goal, O5 should prevent them from turning and attempt to force them back towards their own goal by moving in close and low enough to see the ball through the opponent's legs. Standing upright and

too close to attacking players will allow the attacker to roll (turn) the defender or cause the attacker to fall and claim a free kick.

⚽ It is important, especially in this position on the field, that the defender does not concede a free kick by fouling the attacker.

⚽ If the attacker does turn, it is important to stay close and make sure the attacker is concentrating on the ball and not looking up.

⚽ The defender should force the attacker away from dangerous central areas.

⚽ If the attacker is running with the ball toward the goal, the defender should use a body position that will force them (show them) to one side. This will make play more predictable and allow the covering defenders and the goalkeeper to react appropriately. The challenging player is moving the attacker into a concentrated areas of defending players or into poor shooting angles (wide of the goal).

⚽ If the attackers do dribble around the challenging defender and move goal side with the ball, then the challenging defender should quickly recover to a good covering position as soon as possible. The covering defender (O6 in this instance) then moves in to become the challenging defender.

⚽ If the attacker does shoot on goal, then both the challenging and covering players should be prepared to block the shot. This may require them to go to ground and offer a large surface area for the block.

Made to the covering player O6:

⚽ This covering player should provide loud vocal information to the challenging player (e.g. "Challenge!" "Hold them!" "Get tighter!" etc.).

⚽ The covering player should move into a good covering position (i.e. close enough to challenge the attacker if the challenging defender is beaten).

⚽ If another attacker (X10) is brought in to become another front striker, the practice becomes essentially a 2 vs 2. The covering player then takes into account a further problem of being able to challenge the supporting attacker should they receive the ball. The angle of cover and the speed with which the covering players engage the supporting attacker are of importance.

PROGRESSION 1

Progression of this practice would be to add another striker X10 and X8 as a supporting midfield player with the inclusion of O4 as a recovering midfield defensive player.

FUNCTIONAL PRACTICE ON TWO FRONT STRIKERS

PRACTICE C

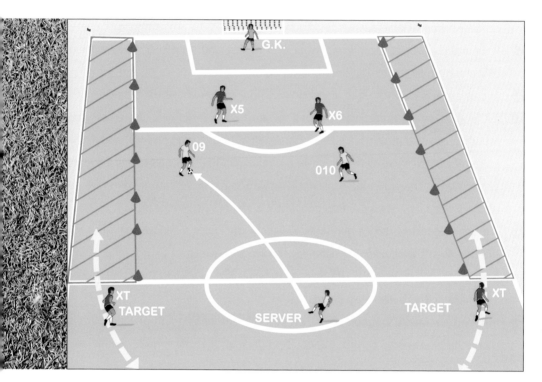

Diagram 3

- ⚽ The area of the field is marked with cones as shown in diagram 3.
- ⚽ The players being coached are O9 and O10.
- ⚽ The objective of the attackers is to try and score goals.
- ⚽ The objective of the defenders is to make an accurate pass to two target players (OT) or, in emergency situations, to clear the ball out of the marked area.

Coaching Points

- ⚽ Before the ball is played in by the server, O9 and O10 must be aware that their combined runs can stretch or contract the space between the defenders. This can be done from side to side or up and down the field.

⚽ When the ball is played in, different coaching points can be made to either the player receiving the pass or the player not in possession. These points can be best illustrated once again by a simple decision tree flow chart (similar to that used in chapter 4) outlining several decisions and options for the player receiving the pass.

Made to the striker receiving pass (using the decision tree):

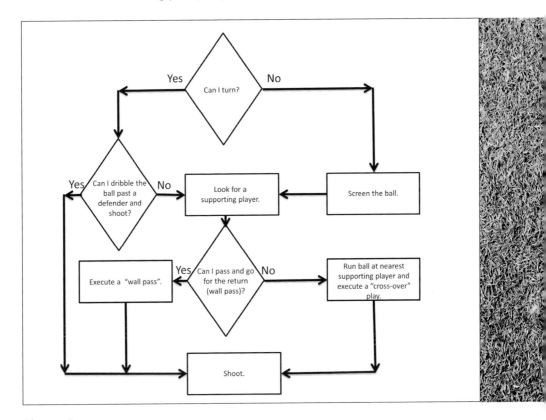

Diagram 4

Made to the striker who is not in possession of the ball:

⚽ "Show" (response cue) they are available for the pass as a supporting attacking player. OR

⚽ Make a run that will attempt to breakdown defensive cover and create space for the player on the ball to run the ball at the defenders, and create a shooting opportunity.

FUNCTIONAL PRACTICE ON A WINGER

PRACTICE D

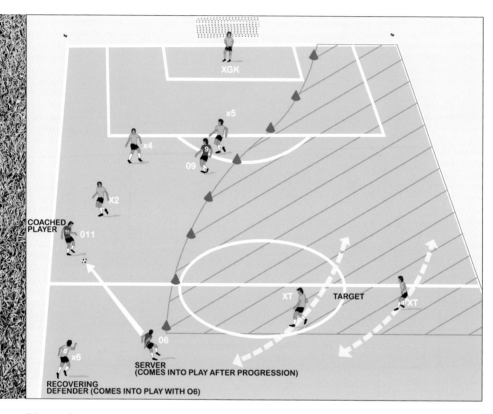

Diagram 5

- ⚽ The area of the field is marked with cones as shown in diagram 5.
- ⚽ The player being coached is O11.
- ⚽ The objective of the attackers is to try and score goals.
- ⚽ The objective of the defenders is to make an accurate pass to two target players (OT) or, in emergency situations, to clear the ball out of the marked area.

Coaching Points

- Before a pass is made to O11, the coached player must try to make space to receive the ball. This can be achieved by making an attempt to run behind the challenging full back (X2 in diagram 5).
- If X2 does not go with O11's first run, then the ball can be passed into the space behind X2 for O11 to run onto and cross the ball for O9 to take a shot.
- If X2 does move backwards towards their own goal, space will be created for O11 to receive the pass. This move back for the pass should be done at an angle out to the touch line in order to offer a good target for the pass and allow O11 to partially turn and face X2.
- When O11 is receiving the pass the question being asked should be "Can I turn?"
- If the answer is "Yes" then O11 has 2 alternatives.
    - Dribble the ball at X2 and attempt to move past the defender with the ball if there is space behind X2.
    - If there is no space to attack behind X2, then look to use O9 as a supporting player for a combined attacking play.
- If the answer is "No" then O11 has three alternatives.
    - Hold on to the ball and screen it.
    - Look for supporting players to the side or back.
    - After giving the pass to supporting players, attack the space behind X2 with a penetrating run.

The important point to stress, both before and during this practice, is that these moves are designed to create enough space for the winger to cross the ball into dangerous areas in the penalty area.

FUNCTIONAL PRACTICE FOR AN ATTACKING THROW-IN

PRACTICE E

This example illustrates how a set piece can be organized and coached in a functional practice framework.

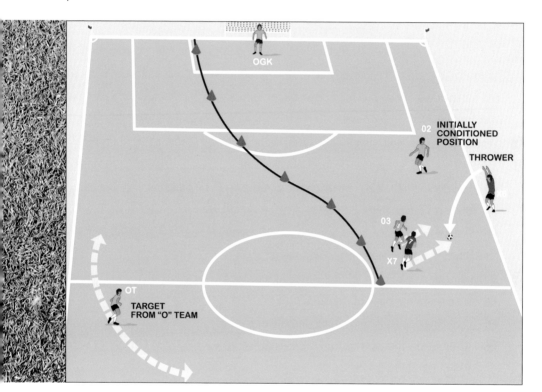

Diagram 6

- ⚽ The area of the field is marked with cones as shown in diagram 6.
- ⚽ The players being coached are X6 and X7.
- ⚽ The objective of the attackers is to try and score goals.
- ⚽ The objective of the defenders is to make an accurate pass to the target player (OT) or, in emergency situations, to clear the ball out of the marked area.

Coaching Points

- ⚽ The space between the attacker (X7) and the thrower (X6) is of vital importance. The thrower should be given enough room in which to control the possible return pass after the throw. This will allow X6 to come immediately back into play.

- 🌐 The thrower must have a target to throw at, either a player (X7) or space into which X7 can move.
- 🌐 The type of run which will enable this target to be shown is a crucial coaching point (e.g. accelerative, dummy runs, etc.).
- 🌐 The quality of the throw should be such that it poses no control problems for the receiver.
- 🌐 Possibilities for the attacking player receiving the ball:
    - 🌐 Control the ball and run with the ball toward goal if possible.
    - 🌐 Pass the ball back to the thrower and then run for a return pass into space.
    - 🌐 Run in close to thrower realizing the ball will not be played to them and clear a space behind them.

PROGRESSION 1

- 🌐 Introduce X8 (another attacker) and O4 (marking defender).
- 🌐 Initially begin with O2 as a defender (sweeper) to give realism when ball is in play and under control of the X attackers.

Coaching Points

Made to the supporting attacker X8:

- 🌐 Leave space for the player on the ball and make a run to take the defender away from the throwing area.
- 🌐 If support is needed for a pass, give it early after the throw.
- 🌐 If support is not needed after the throw, clear space for the receiver (X7) to make a run on the goal.

PROGRESSION 2

Later in practice give the thrower the option of throwing to either receiver (X8 or X7) and allow O2 to vary their defensive covering role, sometimes marking the thrower, sometimes covering behind defenders.

Coaching Points

- 🌐 When unmarked, X6 (thrower) must consider moving away from congested areas after the throw and becoming a target for an attacking pass.
- 🌐 Combined runs off the ball by X7 and X8 (e.g. cross-over runs) are important to create attacking space. These players should look for space that has been cleared.

ORGANIZATION OF A FUNCTIONAL PRACTICE
WITHIN A COACHING SESSION

EXAMPLE 1: Whole squad involved in different functional practices.

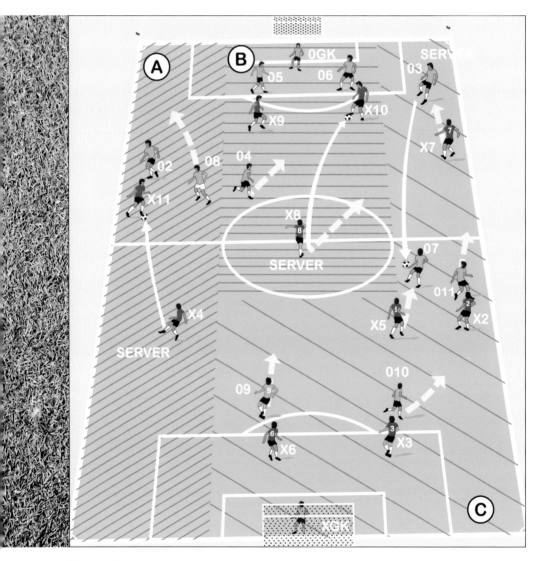

Diagram 7

Example 1 (diagram 7) illustrates how a squad of 22 players (20 outfield players and 2 goalkeepers) can be employed in three functional practices using the whole field.

AREA A

This is a functional practice on O2 being able to contain the opposing winger X11, until O8 provides defensive cover. The practice begins with server X4, who may also come into play if required.

AREA B

This is a functional practice on the defensive understanding between O5 and O6 (two centre backs). X8 is the server and may come into play. When X8 does come into play, O4 is used as the defending midfield player who is recovering to mark X8 or cover either centre back.

AREA C

This is a functional practice on the midfield player's (O7) technical ability to control a pass, turn toward goal, and initiate an attack using O9, O10 or O11. O3 is the server and can come into play if required. X7 is used as a recovering defender to mark O3.

EXAMPLE 2: Part of the squad is involved in a functional practice while other members are involved in skill practices utilizing marked grid areas. Also, the goalkeeper is working on technique practice.

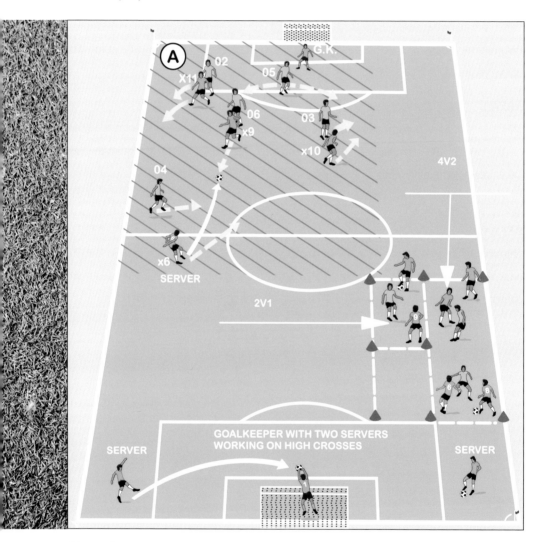

Diagram 8

AREA A

This functional practice develops into an attacking phase of play dealing with mobility between three front strikers (X9, X10 and X11), specifically concentrating on X9's function within the attacking formation.

EXAMPLE 3: Unopposed technical practice leading to functional practice.

All functional work demands a degree of technical excellence on behalf of the players involved. This close tie between the technique and its application or function within the game setting is the root of the problem of transfer from practice to the game. Therefore the method by which a coach detects the need for functional training should be equivalent to how a coach organizes unopposed technique work. The player should practice a technique while being able to refer to its function within the game. The technique practice should not be unrealistic and without relevance. A method by which players can see the relevance of practicing a technique is one of whole-part-whole practice, a game-like situation presented to a group of players. The techniques which the players use within this game are then broken down and practiced in the same physical setting. At the end of each technique practice session, the group of players are once again involved in the game-like situation and allowed to apply the technique within the game. This method of practice-test is also a good evaluation method for players and coach. One example of how this methodology can be used is given below in diagram 9.

GROUP PRACTICE

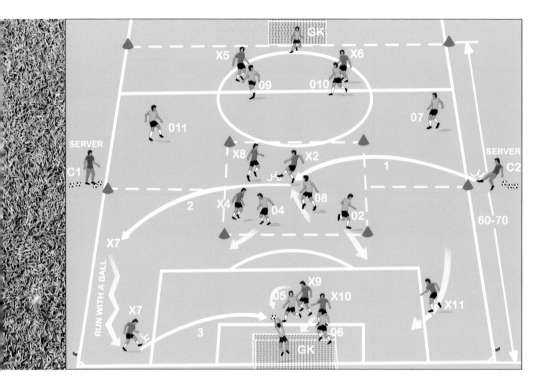

Diagram 9

- ⚽ Diagram 9 shows a reduced field size (60-70 meters long).
- ⚽ A 25-meter square is marked off with cones in the centre of the field.
- ⚽ In the center square there is a 3 vs 3 involving midfield players.
- ⚽ Coaches C1 and C2 serve balls from each side of the field into the 25-meter square alternately.
- ⚽ The three X midfield players and three O midfield players challenge to gain first possession of the ball.
- ⚽ If the Xs win first possession it becomes three X players vs one O player (with two O players dropping out of the square until the next service).
- ⚽ Any X can then play a forcefully driven pass to either wing (X7 or X11).
- ⚽ X7 or X11 then have three touches to cross the ball to either the near or far post for X9 and X10 to move onto and shoot.

⚽ X9 and X10 are opposed by O5 and O6 and OGK.

⚽ The O players try to clear the cross from the danger area and out of play, or gain possession and pass to the servers (C1 and C2). After each strike on goal or each clearance, another ball is fed into the square.

INDIVIDUAL PRACTICE

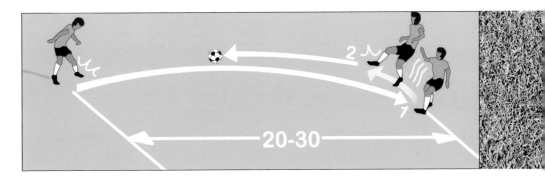

Diagram 10

⚽ Forcefully driven passes from midfield to the wings. The six midfield players from the group practice example in diagram 9 pair off and practice (two touch) driving accurate passes over distances of 20-30 meters (see diagram 10).

⚽ Near and far post crosses from wingers. The wingers X7, X11, O7 and O11 from the group practice example in diagram 9 practice using separate goals. Therefore two goals will be needed.

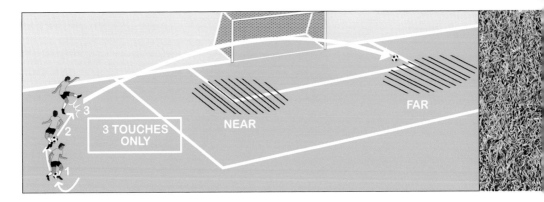

Diagram 11

⚽ Goalkeeper dealing with crosses. Each goalkeeper from the group practice shown in diagram 9 work with one of the wingers and the two centre backs (O5 and O6 in this case).

⚽ This practice can be used to help the two centre backs improve their technique of clearing crosses (see diagram 12). The centre backs work with the goalkeeper in order to reach an understanding on how to deal with crosses.

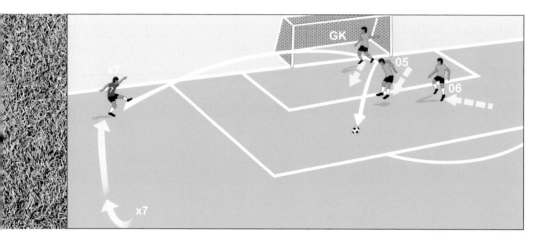

Diagram 12

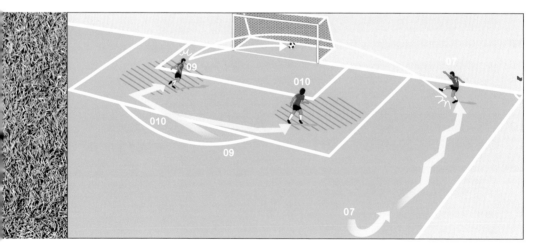

Diagram 13

Two strikers shooting for goal when receiving a cross. From the group practice two sets of strikers each work with two wingers in an open goal and practice unopposed heading and shooting (see diagram 13).

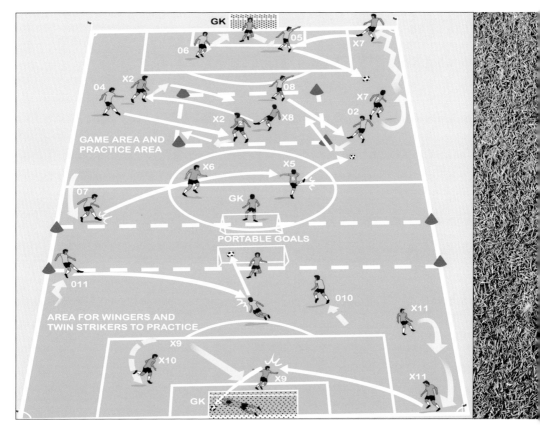

Diagram 14

Diagram 14 illustrates how these individual technical practices can be organized within one field.

The above techniques are practiced in the same physical location as the game was played. Technique errors should be identified by the coach and players should be encouraged to help each other by offering suggestions on problems they observe. Good technique should be emphasized and fatigue should be avoided. This individual practice of technique can continue for approximately 15-25 minutes. It is important to re-emphasize here that lots of practice within the correct environment and with the correct feedback will produce skillful players. After this practice the coach can then call all the players together and put them into another game-like situation (whole-part-whole practice). This would give a schedule of 10 minutes of group practice, 20 minutes of technical practice and another 20 minutes of group practice. Coaching tips can be brought out in the practice setting and mention can be made of any good or bad points during the game.

CHAPTER 7
COMBINED ATTACKING PLAY

ATTACKING PLAY AND UNDERSTANDING BETWEEN TWO PLAYERS

The combined team play of two or more players is in essence what makes soccer so engaging to the spectator. The fact that the player in possession has several options available to them makes understanding between cooperating attackers important. To be successful in gaining realism within the practice, the coach then has to provide the players with attacking options (while still being cognizant of the priorities that will make one option more predictable).

A further essential quality of soccer is the creation of shooting opportunities and the shots that these opportunities allow. There are many ways that two or more players can create a scoring opportunity, but it is imperative that all the players involved in these attacking moves understand how each can contribute to a successful strike on goal. Because of the concentrated efforts of defenders around their own goal, the understanding between attackers has to be explicit and efficient. An ill-timed run into space will certainly bring defending players into areas that should be free for attackers to move into. A shooting opportunity can only be created when the space from which to take the shot is available. The creation of attacking space behind and between defenders is then what is required. A rule of thumb (and response cues for players) for the temporal order of events should be as follows:

⚽ First, the space is created by attacking player.
⚽ Second, the ball arrives from a penetrating pass.
⚽ Third, a cooperating attacking player arrives very shortly after the ball has arrived.
⚽ Finally, the defender arrives last of all and hopefully too late to challenge for the ball.

If the order of the first three is rearranged by poor attacking play, the defenders will *not* be late.

The following series of practices will involve two or more players in attacking situations that should end with a shot on goal. The main coaching problem within this set of practices will be developing an understanding between the two attacking players being coached. The following practices will emphasize understanding between these two attacking players.

PRACTICE A

COACHING THE TAKE-OVER

⚽ As in diagram 1 the practice starts with one ball between two players.

⚽ Both players move down field in pairs.

⚽ The player without the ball mirrors the actions of the player with the ball.

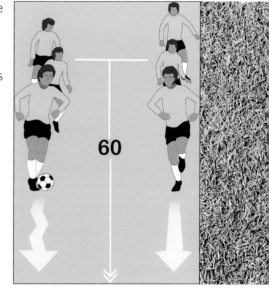

Diagram 1

⚽ When the players' movement is toward one another, the player in possession increases the speed of approach and keeps dribbling with one foot.

Diagram 2

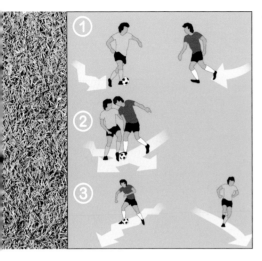

⚽ The players continue as before but now they cross over and take over the ball as shown in diagram 3.

⚽ Players dribble the ball with one foot with the ball outside of the body.

⚽ Players will then accelerate into and then away from the take-over.

⚽ The player who is now not in possession continues a run in their direction of travel away from the ball.

Diagram 3

Coaching Points

⚽ Players in possession should not pass the ball to their cooperating attacker.

⚽ The player initially in possession should leave the ball for the cooperating attacker to take over.

⚽ Play can be initiated when both these players see the opportunity and make eye contact with each other.

⚽ Space is created in the area left by defenders as seen in diagram 4.

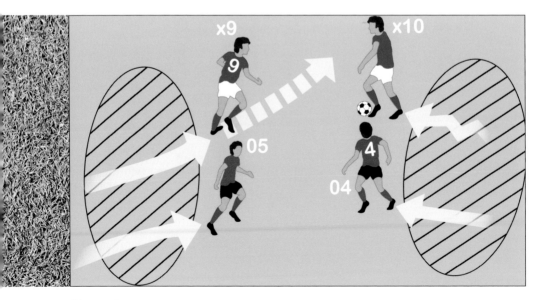

Diagram 4

⚽ After the take-over both players must accelerate away at speed.

⚽ Space is created (shaded areas in diagram 4) behind the attacking players.

Progression 1

Diagram 5

⚽ Pairs of attackers have to advance through the three 10-by-10-meter grids as in diagram 5.

⚽ In each grid there is a defender who cannot leave their grid. Their task is to win the ball and play it out of the grid.

Coaching Point

The alternative option for the attacker is to complete the crossover with the cooperating player but not complete the take-over. The player in possession will then take the ball themselves and move quickly into the next grid. One method for the player in possession to see this possibility is for the colleague to indicate by moving in a wider angle and accelerating earlier before the crossover. It is important therefore that the decision to either have the ball taken or to keep the ball rests solely with the player in possession.

Progression 2

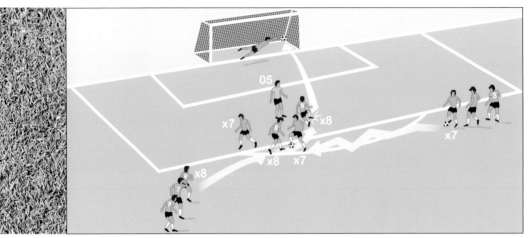

Diagram 6

- 🏈 Introduce a goal, a goalkeeper and one defender as in diagram 6.
- 🏈 The defender O5 is conditioned to only try to win possession when the ball is not screened properly.
- 🏈 X7 dribbles the ball in toward X8.
- 🏈 X7 steps on the ball.
- 🏈 X8 times the run to coincide with taking the shot just after the ball has been stopped.
- 🏈 The shot has to be a controlled shot placed into the corner of the net.

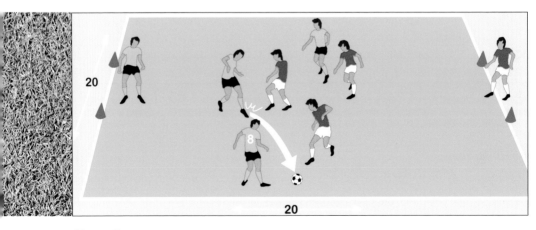

Diagram 7

Progression 3

- The practice is a 3 vs 3 in a 20-by-20-meter grid with goalkeepers as shown in diagram 7.
- One point for a goal, one point for a successful take-over and three points for a take-over ending in a goal.

Coaching Points

- Within the game, the players should be made aware of when there is a possibility to complete the take-over.
- The coach will be looking for understanding between two players.
- The third attacker should vacate any space that is required for this take-over.
- A further option open for attackers can be a stationary take-over where X10 passes to X9 who screens the ball while X10 moves in to take it off X9.
- It is important for either X10 or X9 to move directly to goal or take a shot on target immediately after the take-over. This ensures the space that is created by the move is exploited as quickly as possible before this space is filled once again by defenders (see practical example in diagram 8).

Diagram 8

COACHING THE WALL PASS

The simple explanation of a wall pass is that the attacking team uses a fast inter-passing play which utilizes one of its attacking players as a figurative rebounding surface (i.e. wall). Although the simplicity of its explanation is easily related to players, many coaches fail to practice this skill in a realistic setting. The failure to have the players fully understand the uses of the wall pass comes initially in the organization of its practice. The mistake is to have players in prearranged positions where attacking players are instructed to implement the wall pass in robot-like fashion.

The wall pass should be given to players as one of several options they could add to their attacking repertoire, and it should be practiced in realistic situations.

PRACTICE B

Diagram 9

⚽ As shown in diagram 9, there are 3 players with one ball in a 10-by-10-meter grid.

⚽ Two attackers against one defender.

- ⚽ The goal of the attackers is to make consecutive passes while the goal for the defender is to win the ball or play it out of the grid.
- ⚽ After 3 minutes the players rotate their roles.
- ⚽ Each successful wall pass is a goal.

Coaching Points

- ⚽ The player in possession dribbles at the defender to commit the defender.
- ⚽ The timing of the release of the first pass is important. If it is too early the defender will not be beaten.
- ⚽ The receiver should move to the path of the first pass and offer an open body position to the passer.
- ⚽ The first passer should accelerate around the defender after the pass to the wall.
- ⚽ The force of the first pass is critical to allow a good rebound pass from the wall player.
- ⚽ The pass from the wall player should be one touch into the space that the cooperating attacker is moving into.
- ⚽ The player in possession always has the option of dribbling past the defender if the wall pass is not available.

Progression 1

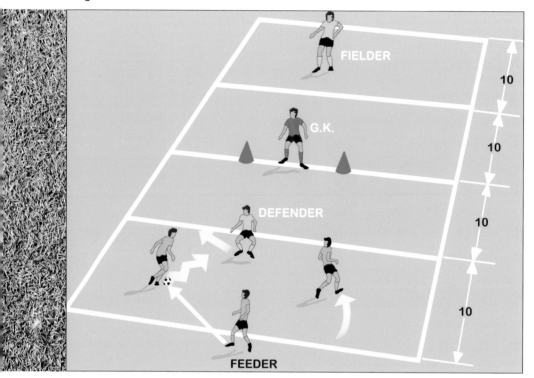

Diagram 10

- ⚽ Central goals are used in a 40-by-20-meter grid as shown in diagram 10.
- ⚽ Six players are assigned to one set of goals.
- ⚽ Defenders are one person fielding the ball that goes behind or through the goal, one goalkeeper and one active defender.
- ⚽ Attackers will be one feeder and two active attackers.
- ⚽ After a shot on goal, the positions change and the other team become attackers.

Coaching Points

Encourage the attackers to use the following options:

- ⚽ The player in possession of the ball should dribble at the defender and commit them to challenging for the ball.
- ⚽ The attacker can either pass or dribble

⚽ The player receiving the pass can either turn and shoot or initiate a wall pass to the back of the defender.

⚽ The wall pass will not be used in a completely realistic setting in this practice because it is a 2-vs-1 situation and not a 2 vs 2.

Progression 2

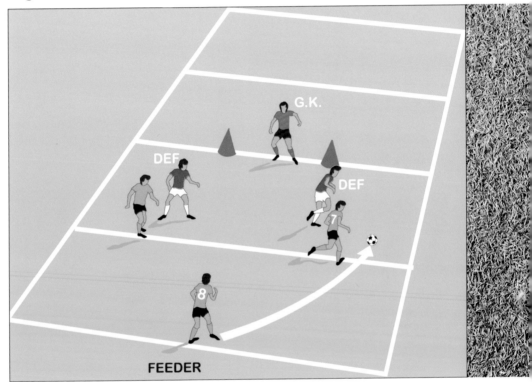

Diagram 11

The fielding defender now becomes a second active defender setting up a 2-vs-2 situation.

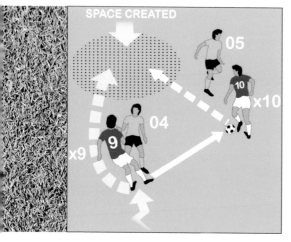

Diagram 12

Coaching Points

⚽ The timing and force of the wall pass has to be good if a good return pass is to be made (see diagram 12).

⚽ If X9 passes the ball too early to X10, then X9 can feint to run past O4 but check back and receive a pass back from X10 (see diagram 13).

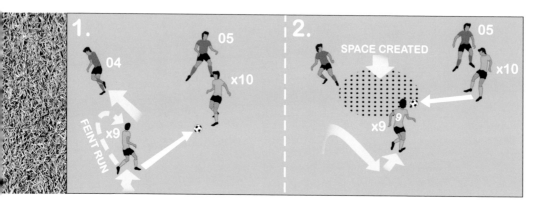

Diagram 13

⚽ This situation also gives X9 and X10 another option. X10 may be encouraged to spin around the outside of O5 with the ball if O5 is defending too closely (see diagram 14).

Diagram 14

Progression 3

Diagram 15

This practice starts with a 2 vs 2 with goalkeepers in a 20-by-10-meter area as shown in diagram 15.

Coaching Points

⚽ Coach players when a wall pass can be used.

⚽ Encourage players to also attempt the previously learned take-over play as another option.

COACHING THE LAY-OFF PASS AND THE STEP-ON PLAY

As with the wall pass, the lay-off pass should be progressively coached as another option of attacking play. The prerequisite for an effective conclusion (i.e. a shot on target) is that the front striker or target player is able to screen the ball effectively from the pressure of the defending player. Technical knowledge of screening and receiving the ball is an intricate part of these coaching practices. The introduction to the step-on that results in a shot on target is another option to the attacking colleagues if the player screening the ball can turn on their defender.

PRACTICE C

⚽ As in diagram 16 the practice starts with four players per ball in a 20-by-20-meter grid.

⚽ X10's task is to score goals or keep the ball screened for 10 seconds.

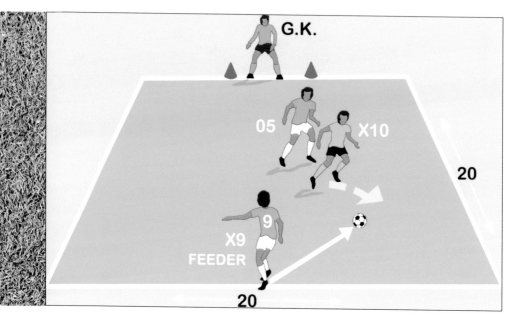

Diagram 16

Coaching Points

⚽ X10 should move away from the defender O5 at an angle in order to ensure that the ball stays close to the attacking goal. Moving straight back to X9, the feeder closes the area that X10 can work within. The intent is to draw the defender away from the central goal areas.

- X10's body position should be half turned and should offer a good target for the pass.
- X10 should receive the pass on the outside foot away from the defender if the defender is close (i.e. in good screening position).
- If the defender is not close, then X10 should be encouraged to take the ball with the inside foot and spin on the ball in order to face the goal and the defender.
- If O5 is too close and marking on the inside (back to goal) of X10, then the attacker should be encouraged to roll and turn the defender while taking the shot on the outside of the defender.

Progression 1

- The area of play has now moved to the penalty area.
- X9 can now move in to support X10 but X9 is only allowed one touch after the initial pass, that being a shot. Therefore, X10 has to work hard to get X9 free space for a shot (see the shaded free space in diagram 17).

Diagram 17

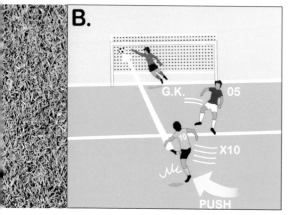

Diagram 18

Coaching Points

⚽ If X10 cannot turn on O5 then they should screen the ball.

⚽ If X10 moves O5 from central areas the player can lay off the ball into this central area where X9 can move in and take the shot.

⚽ If XIO can turn on O5, then they should try and attack the space behind the defender. Two options are then open to them:

    ⚽ Push the ball to side and shoot (see diagram 18).

       OR

    ⚽ Run the ball to the side of O5 and step on the ball, leaving it for X9 to shoot (see diagram 19).

Feinting to the right and pushing to left—the player does not have to completely round the defender—creates space in central areas on the inside of the defender.

Coaching Points

⚽ In diagram 19, X9 has passed the ball to X10 and X10 is facing O5.

⚽ As X10 attacks the space behind O5, X9 follows X10 in toward the goal.

⚽ X10 moves away from the goal.

⚽ X10 steps on the ball and accelerates away from the ball.

⚽ X9 arrives immediately afterwards to shoot on target.

Because this practice does not differentiate what attacking movements can be used, the priority for the coach is to give the players clear and simple options to use. These options require some decision making. These decisions should be simple and easy for all players to make. As we have done previously, these decisions can be simply illustrated using a decision tree.

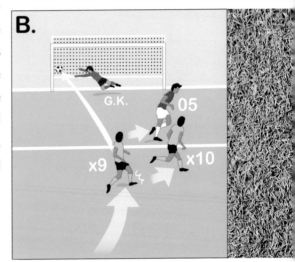

Diagram 19

QUESTIONS THE ATTACKERS CAN BE ENCOURAGED TO ASK

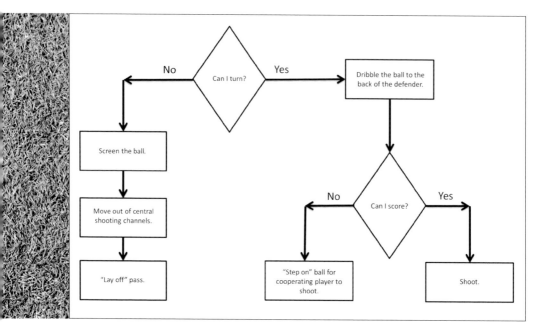

Coaching Point

The cooperating attacker (in this case X9) should delay their move into the ball until X9 is sure of the decisions that X10 has made or is likely to make space. If X9 comes in too early, the space will be filled and the shot cannot be taken.

Diagram 20

Progression 2

A recovering defender can be added to ensure that a quick strike on goal is made by X9 or X10.

PRACTICE D

To ensure the players understand these combined attacking plays that have been covered previously, a 6-vs-6 game within a 40-by-30-meter area can be used. The stop method of coaching can be used for about 10 to 20 minutes to see if, when and where these attacking moves can be used. Players not involved in these moves should realize their part in clearing areas of defenders to allow smooth execution of either:

- ⚽ the take-over,
- ⚽ the wall pass,
- ⚽ the lay-off pass or
- ⚽ the step-on play.

Coaching Points

- ⚽ Ask players who are in possession of the ball and are being closely marked to look for a colleague to execute one of the combined plays.
- ⚽ Players in near support positions should offer themselves as a cooperating player.
- ⚽ Players that are not in near support positions and not involved in the combined play should move defenders away from areas near the central goal channels.

ATTACKING PLAY AND UNDERSTANDING BETWEEN THREE PLAYERS

The previous section illustrated how two players could be involved in creating opportunities to shoot on goal. This involved the creation of space behind and between defenders. To fully utilize all aspects of combined attacking play, it is often necessary to involve more than two players in setting up shooting possibilities close to goal. Understanding the priorities of options open to attacking colleagues is the essence of the problem for the coach. When setting up play involves three players, it is important that players understand the problems of space creation, combined mobility runs while off the ball and when to play the safe option while on the ball.

Attacking play that involves three players often involves a combination of fast inter-passing moves, intelligent running off the ball and either a pass into space or a shot on goal. For this reason it is essential that technical performance in practice is of the highest quality. A well-executed run into space (that was previously cleared of defending players) is of little use if the pass does not arrive into the space at the appropriate time and with the correct amount of force. Likewise, a speedy mobile run off the inside of a player in possession is not necessary if the ultimate shot is not on target. The following practical coaching sessions are examples of combined attacking play between three players.

PRACTICE A

⚽ One ball between seven players in an area of 20 by 40 meters (as in diagram 21).

⚽ X7 begins the practice in the middle of the grids.

⚽ X7 plays the ball to any of the three X players (X5, X4 or X3).

⚽ These X players play a one-touch ball back to the side of X7.

⚽ X7 (using a one-touch pass if possible) plays another attacker into the practice (in the diagram it is X3).

⚽ X7 then moves into line of X players.

⚽ X3 then plays a first-time ball into the space where X5 has made a bent run into space as illustrated in diagram 22.

⚽ X5 then plays the other three attackers (X9, X10 and X4) into the practice by passing the ball to them and the practice repeats itself.

Coaching Points

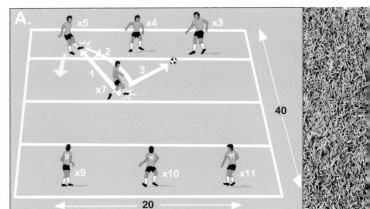

Diagram 21

- 🌑 The task for the players is to pass the ball such that it does not offer any control problems for the receiver. The timing and force of the one-touch play is stressed.

- 🌑 In this practice the body position of X7 has to be open in order to allow the ball to go first time to X3.

- 🌑 X3 has to chip pass the ball that is slowing down into the path of X5.

- 🌑 X5 should only need a maximum of two touches (one control, one pass) after the run.

- 🌑 X's run into space should be first away from play then back into the line of the ball.

- 🌑 The timing of the run has to coincide with the ball arriving into the space. The player should begin by drifting slowly away and then move into the ball and accelerate after judging the line of flight of the ball.

Progression 1

Diagram 22

The player who plays the other attackers into the practice (X7 in diagram 22) can become a defender after the transfer pass to X3. If this player wins the ball, they should begin to set up play again as an attacker would.

PRACTICE B

⚽ A small-sided game of 6 vs 6 with goalkeepers is set up on part of the full field as shown in diagram 23.

⚽ Within the game four defenders play against two attackers and are restricted to their own halves of the field until they have played the ball into one of their own front attackers (in diagram 23 this pass is made from O8 into the front attacker O10).

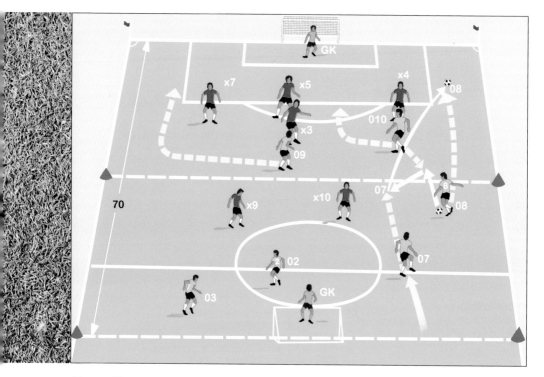

Diagram 23

Coaching Points

⚽ Controlled and composed possession between the back four players must occur before any moves forward can be initiated. This is therefore a good opportunity for the back four players to practice passing whilst being challenged from the front two opposing players.

⚽ The front two players should work hard to show themselves (e.g. going behind defenders before moving off them at angles to show for a pass from the back four players).

- A good pass into attackers must be played if the return pass is to be used as a spring board for a chip pass behind defenders.

- The player moving up to deliver the chip pass (in diagram 23 this is O7) has one of three options, either of the two front players (O9 and O10) or a back player who was originally involved in setting up this combined play (O8 in diagram 23).

- The dangerous space behind defenders has to be maintained by the front players until O7 is ready to deliver the pass.

- If any of the runs is not an option because the space is filled by defenders, the run should be checked (reversed) and the play should be set up again (response cue, "Be patient!").

PRACTICE C

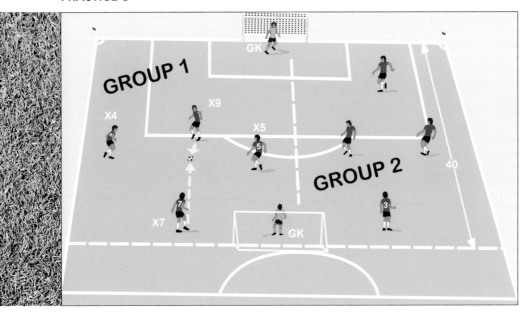

Diagram 24

- ⚽ As shown in diagram 24 this practice begins unopposed with no defenders.
- ⚽ Two groups of four players with goalkeepers and full-size goals are positioned in one half of the field.
- ⚽ Each group works in alternating directions attacking opposite goals.
- ⚽ In diagram 24 when the ball is played up to X9, the player's task is to concentrate on the techniques of turning with the ball and then moving forward and shooting.

- ⚽ When X9 has turned, X4 is encouraged to run past the inside (to the goal) shoulder of X9 as shown in diagram 25.

Diagram 25

- ⚽ X9 now has the option of passing the ball to X4 for them to shoot or X can shoot.
- ⚽ As X4 makes a run, X5 moves outside (blind side as in diagram 26) of X9.

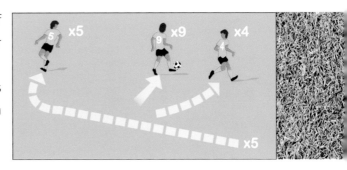

Diagram 26

- ⚽ These runs past X9 give the player on the ball three options: shoot, pass the ball inside to X4 for a possible shot or pass the ball outside to X5 for a possible cross.
- ⚽ If X9 cannot turn (because of tight marking by the defender), then X9 can play the ball back to X5 who can play (chip pass or low drive) the ball through for X9 or X4 to run onto and shoot (see example of this play in diagram 27).

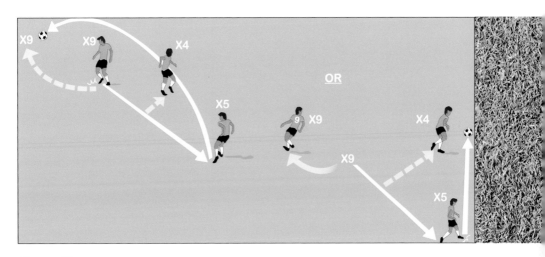

Diagram 27

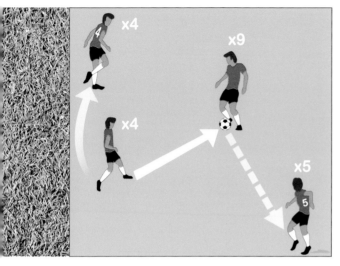

Diagram 28

Diagram 29

Alternative Play

- ⚽ X5 moves early into good supporting positions for a pass from either X4 or possibly X9 as shown in diagram 28.

- ⚽ X4 passes the ball early to X9 and then runs past possible defenders.

- ⚽ X9 then has to decide to turn and pass the ball into the space X4 is running into or play a one-touch pass back to X5.

- ⚽ X5 can then play the ball through to either X4 or X9 (see diagram 29).

Progression 1

The defenders that are shown in diagram 30 can be added one at a time starting with O3, then O2 and finally O4.

⚽ O6 can be used to start the practice by passing the ball into X7 and then moving toward X7 to challenge for the ball. This will apply pressure to X7.

⚽ Initially X7 or O6 cannot enter the practice once the ball has been passed into X9. However they can be brought in later when the combined play has been successful.

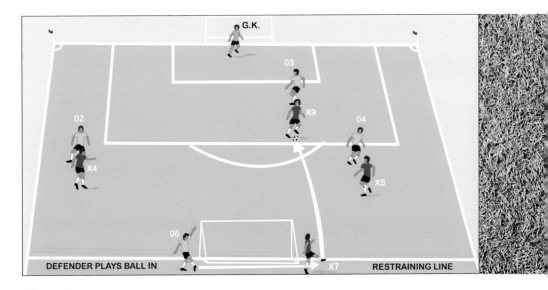

Diagram 30

COACHING THIRD-MAN RUNNING

PRACTICE D

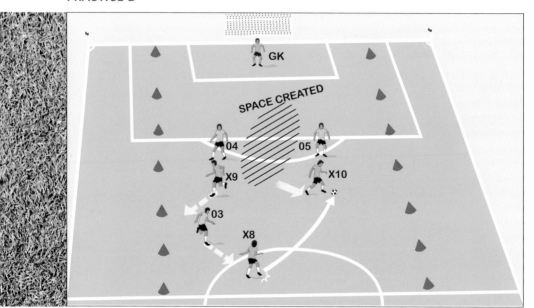

Diagram 31

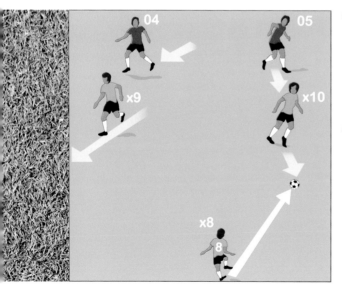

Diagram 32

⚽ The phase of play is set up as in diagram 31 with two forward attackers (strikers), X9 and X10, and one midfield player, X8.

⚽ O3 begins the practice by passing the ball into X8 then applying defensive pressure (if the practice breaks down initially, O3 can be eliminated until success is achieved).

- Both attackers move out of central areas to create space but X10 moves closer toward X8 with X9 holding the space in front of them.

- Dangerous space is now created (see diagram 33).

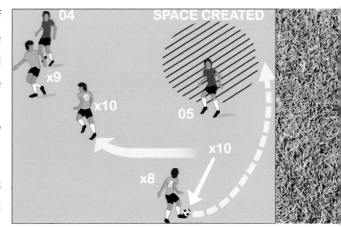

Diagram 33

- X10 passes the ball back to X8 and then turns inside toward X9.

- X9 moves out behind O4 then cuts inside to meet X8's chip pass into space.

- X10 will then be moving to space vacated by X9 (see diagram 34).

- If X9's run is too early or does not pull O4 away from the space, then X8 can pass the ball into space for X10. Note that before players can move into dangerous attacking space, defenders have to be moved out!

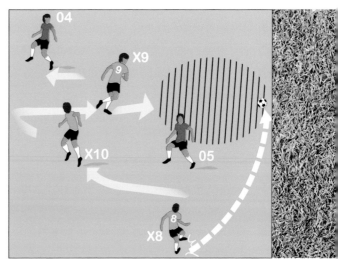

Diagram 34

PRACTICE E

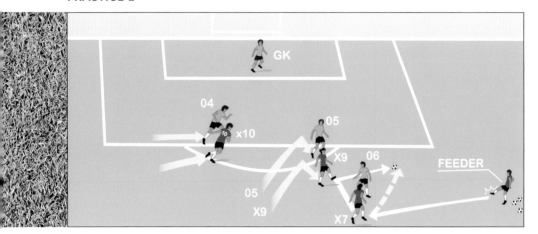

Diagram 35

- ⚽ The practice is located just outside the penalty area.
- ⚽ X7 gains possession from the feeder who begins the practice as in diagram 35.
- ⚽ X9 moves toward goal and then checks back to show as a target for the wall pass from X7.
- ⚽ X10 moves across into an area that also offers a possible target for a pass from X7.
- ⚽ The type of run X9 makes is critical to the success of this move. The final position X9 takes should not block X10 as a target.
- ⚽ Instead of playing the ball into X9, X7 also has the option of passing the ball into X10 and moving for a return pass as in diagram 36.
- ⚽ At the same time the pass goes to X10, X9 should draw O5 away from potential attacking space.

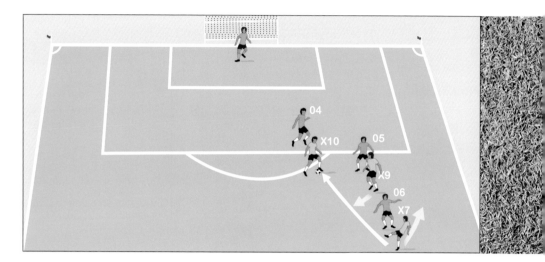

Diagram 36

⚽ As shown in diagram 37 X10 can either turn and shoot or play X7 in for a cross to X9.

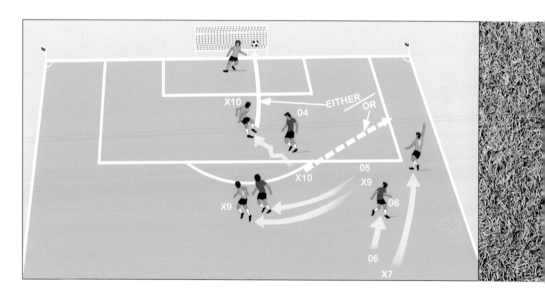

Diagram 37

INTERCHANGE OF THREE FORWARD ATTACKERS
IN THE ATTACKING THIRD OF THE FIELD

PRACTICE F

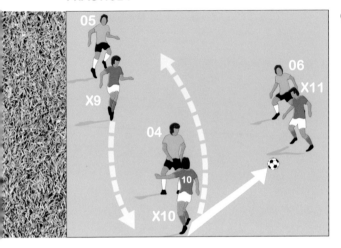

⚽ As shown in diagram 38, instead of movements laterally across the front third by the strikers, it appears from analysis that movements back and forth towards the goal could be just as profitable.

Diagram 38

⚽ The ball is initially passed into X11 and at the same time X9 comes away from the goal in the hope of bringing the marking defender O5 out of dangerous attacking space.

⚽ X10 then moves into space vacated by X9.

Coaching Points

There are three alternatives now available to X11:

⚽ Turn on the outside (away from goal) of O6 and shoot.

⚽ If O5 is moved out of attacking space, pass the ball into this space for X10.

⚽ If O5 is not moved out of this space and defends X9 closely, then X9 can receive the lay-off pass from X11. X9 then turns and dribbles the ball into the space in front of O5.

PART 4:
COACHING INDIVIDUAL TECHNIQUES

Whereas match analysis can provide a plan whereby a realistic environment for players is developed for them to learn soccer techniques, there are several factors that can also aid in the efficient acquisition of these soccer skills. Below we briefly outline some of the important factors affecting skill acquisition that coaches should be mindful of before setting up their coaching practice. In addition, we have provided further readings on these factors in the bibliography under headings associated with the term *motor skill acquisition*.

It is important for coaches to consider that during the game the players are involved in producing a series of sequential actions or techniques toward an ultimate goal. For example, when the player receives the ball there is a purpose and subsequent action attached to that reception. This could be a movement away with the ball, a pass, a shot, a clearance, etc. We know from motor learning research (see bibliography) that the most difficult aspect of learning a sequential series of actions is mastering the juncture points between the actions (e.g. receiving a ball followed [juncture point] by a pass). If the player is introduced to these techniques in isolation (individual parts of the whole) they will have trouble combining the techniques during the game. Research has also shown that when learning a sequence of actions people tend to acquire the general features of the overall task first and then deal with acquiring the finer details of the task as learning proceeds. It would therefore not be advantageous to break down the skill into artificial segments for learning purposes. This will not make the task easier to learn and will only slow the learning process and cause problems and time lags at the juncture points during the game. The goal of the practice should be (once again) to attain realism. The game is not a series of separate events but has overall continuous objectives as discussed in the section on decision making. For example in coaching the technique of receiving the ball, emphasis should be placed not only on the reception of the ball but the coach should also stress that the ball should be received and then moved (dribbled), shot, passed, etc., and the overall goal of this practice should be to end with a shot, dribble or pass (see chapter 9 for a detailed practical example of these types of practices).

During these practices coaches are not required to provide extensive detailed and corrective information about the player's previous attempts. If too much feedback is provided, many problems occur. The first of these is memory overload. Such a problem is evident in all aspects of everyday life and it is no different in learning soccer techniques. It is difficult for people to remember and understand more than about seven separate bits of information and remembering movements poses even more of a cognitive challenge. The important point for the coach is to highlight only the key elements of a specific technique that needs correcting and then only provide one or two of these key factors at any one time to the players. Understanding these key elements of performance and the sequential nature of all techniques (i.e. what leads to what) when considering the biomechanics of the techniques, and being able to detect an error in one or more key factors during performance is not an easy task. Therefore the coach will need to study and be able to detect and analyze deviations away from what they believe to be successful skill during an ongoing performance. This type of observation is a skill in itself and should be practiced by the coach.

Related to the issues of memory is the hypothesis that too much information given to a player after each attempt at a skill will produce a reliance on the feedback that is provided by the coach. This reliance on continuous feedback from the coach will negatively affect learning of the skill when it is transferred to the game setting where the coach will have less or no control over the information that they can provide. That is, the coach will not be able to give continuous feedback to the player as was the case in practice. How much information, and when to give it, becomes an important factor in helping players maximize their transfer of training to the game situation. Key points of information that are given in summary form after several trials of practice appear to be preferable to giving large amounts of information after each attempt. Coaches should give the information and then allow the player to practice without intervention. Encourage the players to detect their own errors and make the appropriate corrections. This emphasis on giving more power to the player as to how and when to receive feedback has been the focus of research that considers self-regulated learning as an extremely effective method of acquiring skill. Self-controlled feedback allows the player to select when they wish to receive feedback rather than have the coach direct when it is best to offer information. The coach can provide key points in summary to adjust the player's model of what they believe to be the perfect performance only when the player is ready to receive the feedback. However when asked, the coach should remember to give an ounce of information and a ton of practice to your players during each coaching session.

Practice is another factor affecting the learning of skill. Much has been written on the work of Anders Ericsson and his theory of deliberate practice (see bibliography). The idea that success at a skill is highly positively correlated with physically practicing that skill has been popularized by authors such as Malcolm Gladwell (author of the book *Outliers*) who used the research to suggest that 10,000 hours of practice will make you a champion. However, it is unfortunate that some of the details of Ericsson's work have been lost in this type of knowledge translation. The so called 10,000-hour rule has been hotly debated in recent literature, some of which is included in the bibliography and will not be dealt with directly here.

When one examines Ericsson's work it does appear that mental effort and attention during these many practice hours are critically important to performance improvement. The question of interest is then "What are the performers (soccer players) paying attention to?" They pay attention to feedback, both internal (e.g. proprioceptive) and external (e.g. coaching feedback, visual information, auditory information). Athletes who receive appropriate performance-related feedback and are able to make adjustments to their next practice based upon this feedback are more likely to make improvements in performance than athletes who are not provided with practical response related feedback and who do not pay attention to the results of their performance. We have emphasized the need to provide valid and reliable feedback at the right time so that athletes can pay attention to correcting errors or reinforcing their good performance. It is not the result of the player's last performance that is important but the knowledge of the last performance as it relates to the criterion performance they are trying to achieve. Players should try to make each trial as good as they can produce (as close to the model performance as possible) and then use both the internal and external feedback provided to assess their own performance. This would then make the attempt (in Ericcson's words) effortful. Hopefully the coach will not only demand the players practice but also demand this type of effortful practice during each and every attempt.

Although deliberate practice has received much attention, both in research and in the media, the concept of deliberate play has not been so prevalent, despite its importance to talent development. The term *deliberate play* was first introduced by researcher Jean Côté in 1999. Along with several others researchers, Côté makes a telling distinction between practice and play. Practice is considered to be organized skill development related to a specific sport outcome, whereas play is thought to be informal in nature and is undertaken solely for the purpose of enjoyment. However play can contribute to skill acquisition and eventual expertise. Soccer coaches should be aware that young children beginning to play soccer will lay a strong foundation for later expertise if they are involved in deliberate play, rather than only concentrating on deliberate practice in an organized setting. Côté believes that expertise in sport can still be developed by introducing young children (6-10 years of age) to a variety of sports with enjoyment being the key to participation. Specialization can follow when the child decides on one or two sports. It is at this stage in skill development that the player can become focused, and accept the concept of deliberate practice. More importantly, encouraging young children to sample a variety of sports in their early years will engage them in physical activity, which has been shown to have long-lasting health benefits. Both coaches and parents alike are encouraged to read more about the distinction between deliberate practice and deliberate play (see bibliography).

Given the importance of feedback in this process it would be prudent therefore to recognize that the type of feedback players receive would be considered a further important factor affecting the learning and performance of a soccer skill. Feedback can be thought of as being information that is used by the player. The nature of this information has been shown to be an important factor in the learning of skill. How then does the athlete acquire this vital information about their actions? First, a large part of the information comes from intrinsic feedback. This can be information from the body's own proprioceptors, such as muscle and joint movements. A second source of feedback for the player is that which augments the feedback from within the individual. This is termed extrinsic information. Although intrinsic feedback is of vital importance to the soccer player there is little that coaches can do to directly improve upon this hardwired system. However the coach is able to provide the best possible extrinsic feedback that will enable the player to accurately compare what was done with what was intended. Usually the coach observes the performance and provides verbal feedback along with a demonstration of what is expected. Demonstrations are either performed by the coach or by a designated player who the coach believes can provide this model of performance. Whereas this method has its benefits and will be used by the majority of coaches, it does have its drawbacks. The coach's observations can be in error and the information given to players can be both imprecise and inaccurate. Furthermore the model (demonstration) may not be of sufficient quality to provide a valid representation of what is expected. Players are left without a perfect performance with which to compare their previous attempts. However, modern technology can now make it possible for coaches to use video images of the performance as models and as feedback.

Using pictorial images to analyze sporting actions has its roots in the early work of French scientist E. J. Marey and English photographer Eadweard Muybridge. In 1895 Marey suggested that photographing the phases of movement may be a useful analytic tool in understanding skilled performance. This technique (termed cyclography) allowed Marey to study in detail the kinematic representation of such everyday movement skills as walking, running and descending a staircase. His subjects wore black body suits with phosphorescent markers or strips placed over the key link segments of the body. With the camera shutter open, a strobe light could project a point light movement display on a single photographic plate. Marey's techniques were subsequently adopted in the early 1900s by the Russian physiologist Nicholai Bernstein using kymocyclography. Bernstein was instrumental in bringing into joint focus the areas of biomechanics and motor skill acquisition. The detailed analysis of human skills via film recording is now commonplace in many kinesiology laboratories, and can be used as an essential element in understanding how players learn and perform soccer techniques. Although high speed film analysis is still used by some biomechanists, the introduction and development of the videotape recorder by Ampex in 1956 led to the establishment of video technology that was eventually adopted by a large number of professional sports organizations. While we recognize that well-executed real-life skill demonstrations are now an accepted tool for modeling performance, we believe there does exist the possibility that video could be used to good effect within a coaching setting.

Clearly, the use of video has the potential to provide accurate and precise information in real time and in slow motion. The benefits of using such aids are intuitively obvious as the video record not only provides instant error information but can serve as a motivator and can also reinforce behaviour when performance is correct. The act of coaching then becomes one of mediation in the process of providing video information to players. Because of their knowledge of the perfect performance the coach can structure and direct the viewing of the players toward any errors in performance. Coaches can highlight the key points of the performance for players as they observe and pay attention to the video. It is now also possible for a computer program (see the bibliography for commercially available analysis systems) to highlight the errors in performance between a perfect model and a player's recent attempt at a skill.

Good, effortful practice depends upon the player's ability to understand the actions of the model performance for any particular technique. Giving the player a clear understanding of what is expected of them will make it easier for the player to pay attention to the error feedback they receive from their own perception of the just-completed performances and the corrective information provided by the coach. Modeling allows the player to create an image or some other form of internal representation that enables them to learn the task. What then is the best way to provide a model performance to the player? Do we show a video of world-class performance to our players before they begin to practice their technique? Some caution should be exercised when considering the use of demonstrations in which the model is far superior in performance to that of the player. Those who have a less-than-positive perception of themselves may trap themselves in an ever-increasing negative spiral. Models that are less similar to the observer make a less significant impact on those trying to imitate the modeling performance than more similar models. It is also important to note that the disparity of performance abilities between the player and the model can be mediated by the explanation that the superior performance seen in the demonstration represents future behaviour, rather than present behaviour.

Given these issues with the use of a world-class model of performance, it may be worthwhile to consider using a self-model; that is, a video of the player's last performance. However the problem here is that the errors in that last performance will be viewed and inherent errors possibly reinforced without the intervention of the coach, as would be used in a feedback session. Also the player will still require an expert model of performance that can be used as a comparator. We argue here that acquisition of sport skill can sometimes be achieved by video self-modeling, in which subjects are shown images of themselves, but not as they have performed in the past (including error) but as they will perform (correctly) in the near future. This can be achieved by editing the past performance video before showing it to the player.

As early as 1976, Peter Dowrick used what he termed feed-forward self-modeling in a clinical setting to teach special population individuals to swim and navigate obstacles. His student Larry Maile then showed that athletes can also dramatically improve performance using this technique. This method entailed the compilation of video images that displayed a behaviour that the performer was expected to complete but had yet to succeed at achieving. In effect it was creating a fake video of the performance that the athlete had never completed but was capable of performing. This was done by cutting and splicing images of the past performance to assemble an attainable model performance. Athletes in Maile's study were aware this was a fake video as they had never completed these actions before. Nevertheless the athletes using feed-forward self-modeling showed a marked improvement over athletes who used more conventional methods of modeling. Because the technology available at the time of Maile's study was limited, the method was time consuming and heavily dependent on expensive video-editing equipment. However, this method of feed-forward self-modeling should be much more accessible today for coaches at all levels with the advent of computer-controlled video-editing systems and the commercially available video-editing suites.

The following chapters in this section provide technique practices that not only adhere to the principle of providing a realistic setting for practice derived from match analysis of soccer, but also to the factors affecting skill acquisition that were detailed above. Several techniques are described and progressive practices are used to enable players to improve their ability at performing these techniques in the game situation.

CHAPTER 8
DRIBBLING

Dribbling can be defined as a player moving with the ball. This definition is broad and general and many options can be added to bring this technique toward a realistic situation. If a player in possession of the ball is moving, what alternatives do they have? A player can:

- Run with the ball into open space
- Run with the ball at opponents in order to
    - move defenders and their defensive cover,
    - shield or screen the ball,
    - pass the ball between and behind defenders,
    - move past the defender with the ball, or
    - shoot.

Although these options all involve multiple techniques, it would appear to be more beneficial to coach combined techniques rather than coach isolated techniques. In the past, teaching players techniques has been reduced to teaching the elements of each isolated technique. As we mentioned earlier, the problems players have when playing the game occur at the juncture points of these techniques. That is when the player moves from one technique to another. If a player is moving with the ball and decides to run the ball at a defender and pass the ball into space behind them, they will probably have problems at the juncture between these two techniques, when the dribble ends and the pass is initiated. Early research into skill acquisition by Bryan and Harter (1899) found that the distinction between average and elite performers was due to the fact that elite performers were able to smoothly link together techniques (i.e. become a smooth performer). This work reinforces the idea that errors in sequence learning occur at the juncture points within a larger sequence of skilled action (see motor skill acquisition and the learning process in the bibliography for more recent research that supports the findings of Bryan and Harter). Therefore an efficient method of teaching soccer techniques that will be emphasized here is to consider the overall intention of the player's action within a game situation. In our example below, the intention while moving with the ball is to place the ball into the attacking space for cooperating players to run on to. The various methods that a player has to fulfill this intention are part of their overall repertoire of techniques. The problem for the coach is to give the player situations where choice is available. When progression is indicated, the practice should become more realistic and closer to game conditions, not in the fact that more pressure is applied to the player with the ball but in the production of longer sequences of action that are game related.

First, it would be instructive to outline our objectives using diagrams. A coaching session will then be outlined that fulfills these objectives.

Objectives

- A player should be able to move with the ball and
  - keep it within playing distance;
  - change direction and speed and
  - switch attention between the ball and the environment.

Diagram 1

- A player should be able to move with the ball into attacking space.

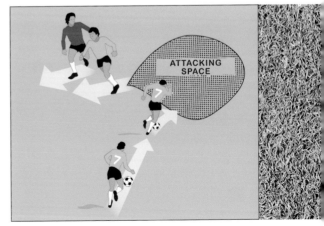

Diagram 2

Diagram 3

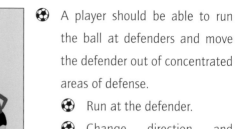

A player should be able to run the ball at defenders and move the defender out of concentrated areas of defense.

- Run at the defender.
- Change direction and move the ball to the side of defender.

Diagram 4

A player should be able to shield the ball away from a defender while moving.

Diagram 5

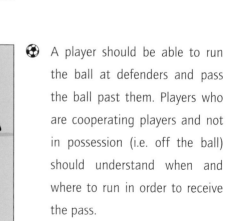

A player should be able to run the ball at defenders and pass the ball past them. Players who are cooperating players and not in possession (i.e. off the ball) should understand when and where to run in order to receive the pass.

⚽ A player should be able to run the ball at a defender and move *with* the ball past them.

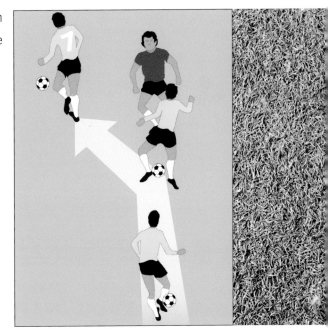

Diagram 6

⚽ A player should be able to run the ball at a defender, move into shooting position and take a shot.

Diagram 7

These are all objectives of dribbling. What follows are a series of practices that will assist the player in attaining these objectives.

PRACTICE A

Diagram 8

Diagram 9

Diagram 10

- ⚽ Use a coaching grid (the area and number of players occupying the area is variable and dependent upon the technical ability of the players) and have each player with ball. All players move anywhere in the area and are encouraged to:
  - ⚽ Keep ball within playing distance.

- ⚽ Use both inside and outside of feet to move ball.

- ⚽ Use both left and right feet.

Use the sole to stop the ball and pull the ball back.

Diagram 11

Keep the head up, looking around as much as possible.

Diagram 12

Change speed.

Diagram 13

Change direction quickly.

Diagram 14

⚽ Control body weight and body movements, creating balance. Correct balance will aid a player in changing direction.

Diagram 15

⚽ Coach can call "Stop!" to have players check if the ball is always within playing distance. If speed is increased and area is decreased, collisions will occur if players do not keep their heads up.

⚽ Use the same setup as above but remove two or three balls. Players without a ball are now defending players and try to win the ball off the other players in the area. When a ball has been taken from a player, that player must go to other players to win a ball.

Diagram 16

⚽ An elimination game can be used with the original setup. All players begin with a ball and two areas of equal size are designated for playing. All players begin in one area. Their objective is to kick another player's ball over the boundary lines and still maintain control of their own ball. When the ball goes out of the first area, the players dribble the ball and go to the second area and continue to practice as described above. The coach should be coaching players who are lacking in technique and are now in the second area. Never have eliminated players standing around watching the end of the first competition.

PRACTICE B

⚽ This activity uses one ball between two players. In diagram 17 below, X9 has to take the ball and place it under control on the target line T1. O5 has to take the ball from X9 and place it on target line T2.

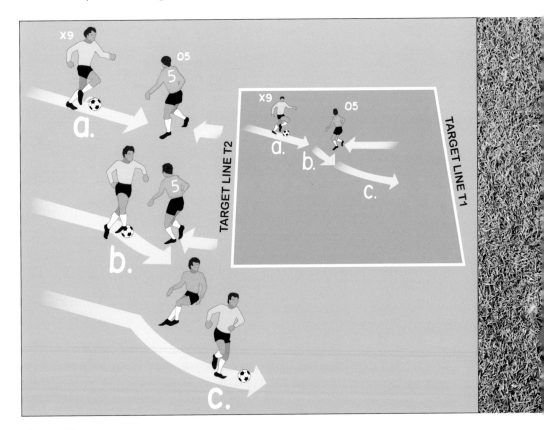

Diagram 17

⚽ Players always return to their respective target lines at the start of each practice.

Coaching Points

⚽ Vary the approach.

⚽ Bring the ball across the midline of the defender's body, causing the defender to distribute their weight in that direction.

⚽ Change speed when moving past defender.

⚽ This next practice is a 2-vs-1 situation and players can rotate position. One goalkeeper (O5) and one outfield defender (O4) are against an attacking player (X6) in a 10-by-15-meter grid (see diagram 18 below).

Diagram 18

⚽ Make the goals regulation size for the age group. In diagram 18, O5 is the goalkeeper while X6 is the attacker. O4 is the defender and cannot move back across the shooting line therefore this defender can only intercept or block shots. X6 must try to move O4 to one side with a body movement or a ball movement and then take the shot. X6 cannot move across the shooting line.

Coaching Points

⚽ Encourage the attacker O4 to move the defender by feinting to one side and then taking a shot.

⚽ Emphasize that the attacking player does not have to completely move around the defender to take the shot.

- Swerving shots around defenders (essentially using them as a screen) can be encouraged.

- Add one extra player to the practice above. One of the players moves into the goal while two attackers (X9 and X10 in diagram 19) play against one defender (O4). If the O team wins the ball, one of the X players then becomes a goalkeeper.

Diagram 19

Coaching Points

- Encourage dribbling toward the defender, thus giving an option of a pass or a shot for the attacker with the ball.

- The cooperating attacker is encouraged to make good attacking runs off the ball to either free themselves for a pass or take the defender away from a good defending position.

- Shooting is encouraged after the player has created a shooting opportunity by dribbling the ball forward into space.

⚽ Progress from above into a small-sided game of 3 vs 3 (two outfield players and one goalkeeper as in diagram 20). Use regulation size goals but do not allow shooting outside the attacking third of the small pitch (marked out in diagram 20). All coaching points previously made can be reiterated here.

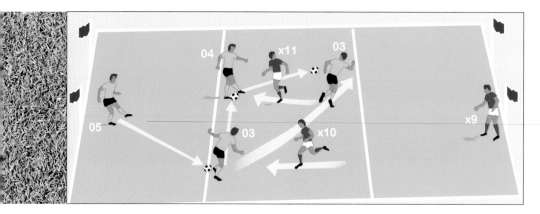

Diagram 20

⚽ To finish the dribbling practice a small-sided, 6-vs-6 game can be used to demonstrate where, within a larger game, dribbling can be of use. It is also important to illustrate to players when dribbling could be employed most efficiently in a tactical context. During small-sided games or practice games where 11 vs 11 is used, the following coaching points can be made as the situation arises.

Coaching Points
Dribbling can best be employed:

⚽ When defenders are equal to attackers numerically. It is necessary to gain numerical superiority by forcing your attackers to dribble at and past defenders.

⚽ In the attacking third of the field. It is dangerous to dribble in the defensive third of the field.

⚽ When players in your team are technically capable of dribbling.

⚽ When there is a slow attack building up.

⚽ When the defense outnumbers the attack. Your good dribbler should then be encouraged to run the ball at defenders and commit one or more defenders to the ball so as to create numerical superiority for the attackers in other areas of the field where the ball should ultimately be passed.

⚽ When opposing defensive players are uncontrolled and reckless tacklers. This could be a good source of free kicks in the attacking third of the field.

CHAPTER 9
RECEIVING THE BALL

The different levels of soccer abilities could be analytically distinguished by observing the speed at which the player can select and execute a given technique at the appropriate moment during the game and in a pressure situation. The technique that invariably highlights these differences is that of receiving the ball. Highly skilled players usually execute this technique more accurately and in a much shorter period of time than a poorly skilled player. It is therefore important that the coach provide the players with the basic components of receiving the ball in easy to understand point form information. These key factors of receiving are given below.

The player receiving the ball (high or low, slow or fast) should:

- Move as much of their body into the line of flight of the ball as possible, and as early as possible.
- Select which part of the body should be used to control the ball.
- Offer this control surface toward the ball.
- Withdraw this control surface on impact to cushion the ball.
- Move the ball into a playable position (highly skilled players complete the previous action and this action sometimes with only one touch of the ball).
- Look up, listen and get ready for the next action or, better still, have the next action prepared and under way.

It is important that the player does not practice receiving the ball without performing the next action. Players only receive the ball in order to complete another technique, be it shooting, passing or dribbling. The objective of the practices therefore must stress these combined techniques while stressing the key factors mentioned above. In each one of the following practices these key factors should be stressed and highlighted.

PRACTICE A

⚽ One ball between two players. The server uses varying heights and speeds of service and also varying distances between receiver and server.

⚽ The server varies service to receiver and then moves to right or left and only calls for a pass after receiver has controlled the ball.

RECEIVER

- - - - ▶ MOVEMENT OF PLAYER
———— ▶ PATH OF BALL

SERVER

Diagram 1

⚽ As in diagram 1, the server varies service to the receiver. The receiver has to control the ball and then take the ball with their feet to either of the squares beside them.

⚽ Same as above with the proviso that the server now indicates which square the ball must be taken to.

⚽ Using a grid area of 15 by 15 meters:

    ⚽ The server serves the ball away from the receiver who must move into the line of flight of the ball before controlling it.

    ⚽ After serving the ball, the player becomes active and moves to a corner of the grid and asks for a return pass.

PRACTICE B

- Using the 20-by-10-meter grid area as in diagram 2, the server can either throw or play the ball from the ground to the receiver.
- The player receiving the ball then controls the ball with the feet and moves to either corner of the grid.
- When the ball is served, opponent and defending player X1 becomes active and is allowed to try and take the ball before the receiver can reach the corner of the grid.

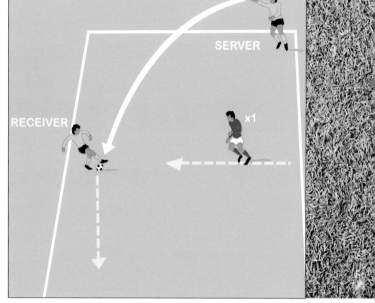

Diagram 2

Variations

- Distance of X1 from receiver
- Type of service to receiver
- Position of the server
- Position of receiver

PRACTICE C

In the following practice a more game-like situation is used to stress the key factors of receiving the ball.

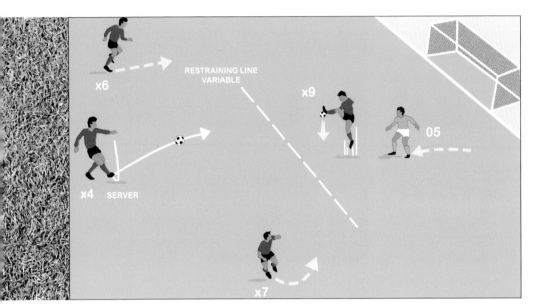

Diagram 3

- ⚽ In diagram 3, X4 serves in to X9. The distance between X4 and X9 can be varied to determine the type of pass X9 has to deal with.
- ⚽ O5 is a defender who becomes active once the ball is played to X9.
- ⚽ The distance of defender O5 from X9 can be varied dependent upon skill level of X9.
- ⚽ X9 cannot move back beyond the marked line toward X4. This condition forces the receiver to use good efficient control of the ball to move away from the defender.
- ⚽ Defender O5's objective is to win the ball and clear the area of play, preferably to the outside of the field.
- ⚽ Decisions that X9 has to make:
    - ⚽ X9 could hold and screen the ball, while waiting for X6 or X7 to move into an area where they can receive a pass. One or both of these cooperating players can be brought into play intermittently on the coach's command or whenever X4 decides it is appropriate.
    - ⚽ X9 could turn on the ball and attempt a shot on goal. In order to do this X9 can use the techniques learned in the chapter on dribbling.

This practice can be built into a functional practice where the coach will concentrate on the functional role of the receiver while progressing into a full game which starts from X4. More cooperating and opposing players may be added as the situation demands.

Coaching Points

⚽ The receiver should move towards the ball but not too soon. They must not drift into the space.

⚽ Early selection of the controlling body surface is now essential because of pressure from the defender.

⚽ Fast decision making from the options available is also essential. Either:

   ⚽ Hold and wait for cooperating attacking players.

   ⚽ Turn and try to get a shot at goal.

   ⚽ Pass (lay off) to cooperating players who are available. In this case a withdrawal of control surface may not be required, as a first-time pass is needed.

CHAPTER 10
PASSING

Throughout the history of soccer there have been many changes in tactical thinking. These changes have become more frequent over the last 30 years than in any other period. The changes in tactical philosophy have only been possible with an increase in personal technical ability of the players. Throughout the whole range of techniques this increase in skill level has become more evident in passing than in any other technique in the modern game.

The realization that ball possession is important for a team to score was in itself encouragement for players to work hard at improving the quality of passing. The philosophy of teams that stress the importance of ball possession is relatively simple.

⚽ Accuracy of passing is directly related to the distance over which the ball has to travel. Therefore the shorter the pass, the more probable it is that the ball will reach its required target and ball possession will be maintained. It therefore becomes necessary to have players in reasonably close proximity to the player with the ball.

⚽ Passes with a low probability of success should not be attempted in the defensive half of the field; only safe passes should be given in this area.

⚽ If play becomes very congested in advanced areas of the field (attacking third of the field), it may become necessary to move the ball back and come forward in less congested areas.

⚽ Players should be patient, composed and confident when in possession of the ball.

With this philosophy in mind it is important that the coach adapt the practice to help players utilize the technique of passing in realistic situations emphasizing the following key factors:

- Accuracy of the pass
- Correct force (or weight) of the pass
- Correct timing of release of the pass
- Deception of the pass

Coaching Points for Short Passing

- The percentage of success decreases when the passing distance is in excess of 15 meters.
- The early decision to pass and early selection of the target (i.e. where to pass) is important. This could mean that the passer decides to pass and selects the target before he receives the ball, which would result in a team playing a great deal of one-touch soccer.
- An error allowance should be taken into consideration before selecting the target (i.e. do not expect maximum results when passing to colleagues who are closely marked by a defending player).
- The receiver should show themselves as a wide target area to the passer and be moving towards the ball in the same line as the line of flight of the ball (i.e. do not always expect the passer to make an accurate pass to a receiver who is moving away from the passer).
- The force of the pass (weight of the pass) must be related to the distance over which the pass must travel; the urgency of the pass (are there any recovering defenders to consider?); the direct threat of pressuring defenders and the ground conditions.
- For a team to achieve maximum retention of ball possession, the passer must immediately reassess their position once they have executed the pass (pass, look and move). In certain situations it is helpful to players to try and follow their pass after making it.

PRACTICE A

Diagram 1

⚽ Diagram 1 illustrates that after X9 has passed the ball to O6 they move to another position. Only when they reach that position do they call for the pass from O6. It is important that the receiver X9 should then call for the pass and move toward the pass.

⚽ Pass then move in one grid area. Only pass when the receiver faces the passer and calls for the pass.

PRACTICE B

In this practice, the setup (shown in diagram 2) is the same as that of Practice A with the exception of increasing the number of pairs within a larger enclosed grid area. This should accomplish two objectives. First, the receiver has to find a gap between players to make the pass. Second, this gap has to be exploited quickly before it is no longer available. The receiver should find a space through which the passer can put the ball safely. The receiver should readjust their run if the passing channel is blocked, or the passer can withhold the intended pass.

The coach should emphasize pass, look then move.

Diagram 2

PRACTICE C

A series of 10-meter grids will be used for the next progressive practice.

Diagram 3

Keep Ball

Diagram 3 illustrates an area for three attackers versus one defender. The rules are very simple. The attackers score one point for every pass that is made. The defender scores two points for every intercepted pass and one point for every time the ball is played out of bounds by the attackers. There are several variables within this practice that can be adjusted to meet the skill requirements of the players.

Variations

- ⚽ Size of area (the area can be increased to 20 by 20 meters if the skill level is poor)
- ⚽ Number of attacking players (4 vs I can be used if the 3 vs I is difficult at the beginning)
- ⚽ Number of defending players (can be increased if 3 vs I is not challenging the players).
- ⚽ Other conditions can be used to bring out many of the points made earlier.

Conditions can be added to the practice. For example, the defender can be conditioned not to tackle the player in possession. This will increase time available for pass selection and execution early on in practice. Also the attacking players can be conditioned to one-touch, two-touch or three-touch play. This will increase the demands on decision making and good ball control, and also improve early support by cooperating attackers.

Coaching Points

⚽ Pass and follow the pass (maybe only one or two meters) to give early support to the player who has just received the pass.

⚽ Pass to a wide angle supporting player.

⚽ If a supporting player is moving into space, pass the ball to that space. The force of the pass determines its eventual accuracy such that the ball and the supporting player arrive at the same time.

⚽ Encourage the use of deception in passing.

⚽ Allow for players to experiment with various types of passes.

PRACTICE D

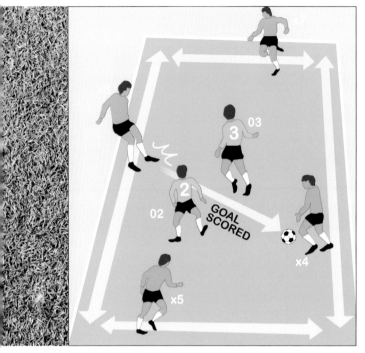

Diagram 4

The organization of this practice is 4 vs 2 as illustrated in diagram 4 below. Attacking X players should pass the ball between the O defenders to score a goal. Attackers can only move along the boundary lines. The defenders score by touching the ball or forcing the attackers to pass the ball out of the line markings.

Coaching Points

⚽ Players should be patient. If the player in possession cannot score by splitting the defenders with a pass, then they should change the point of the attack by passing to a cooperating and supporting player along the boundary line.

⚽ In order to make a penetrating pass between the two defenders, early selection of the pass should be made. It is likely that one-touch passes will split the defenders and make defensive covering positions difficult.

⚽ Supporting players should show themselves as a target early to show the passer a clear passing channel.

⚽ The supporting players should be continually moving to create the passing channel.

PRACTICE E

In order to emphasize the coaching points that were brought out in the previous practices, a small-sided conditioned game could be used (e.g. one- or two-touch soccer, overloading one side with attacking players to allow attackers to have enough supporting players as passing options).

Diagram 5

Diagram 5 illustrates the extra field markings that would condition this game. No players are allowed to wait in, or receive a pass in, the shaded area. A goal can only be scored within 15 meters of the goal.

These conditions encourage teams to flood (i.e. move many cooperating players into the area) areas on the flanks (sides of the field) with attacking players so as to retain possession. If it is not possible to move the ball forward, the team should try to bring the ball back and play along the opposite flank. This condition also encourages cooperating attacking players to make runs around the back of defenses on the opposite sides of the field to where possession is being maintained.

PRACTICE F

The line drills explained below are excellent for preliminary beginning activities leading to a practice that stresses the importance of passing. Diagram 6 outlines the organization of players. Many variations can be used with this practice. Diagram 6 shows X3 pass the ball to O1 and sprint to the back of the opposite line. O1 must then pass the ball to the next X player and sprint to the back of the opposite line, and so on.

Diagram 6

Variations

- ⚽ One touch or two touches of the ball.
- ⚽ The player receiving the ball can move out left or right away from the line, then ask for the pass.
- ⚽ Two attackers from one line move out to attack one defender from the opposite line. The aim is to pass the ball safely to the next player on the opposite line.
- ⚽ Goalkeepers can be included in this warm-up. They would field the ball and roll a pass out to the opposite line. They could also stop shots if the outfield player decides to shoot or go down at the feet of an on-rushing player.
- ⚽ Heading the ball can be incorporated instead of passing with the feet.
- ⚽ The distance between lines can be varied to enable different types of passes (e.g. short, long or chipped passes).

Diagram 7

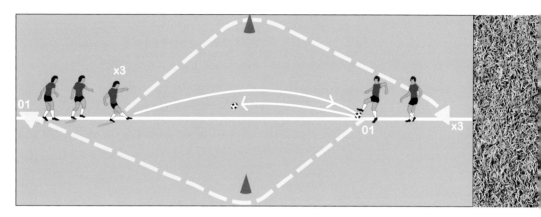

Diagram 8

- The distance the player who has just completed the pass runs can also be varied. This can be accomplished using a combination of cone placement as illustrated in diagrams 7 and 8.

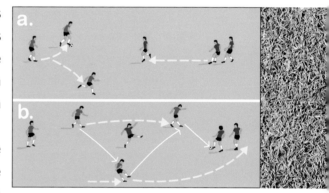

Diagram 9

- Add two attackers vs one defender from the opposite line as shown in diagram 9. These defenders can be conditioned not to tackle for the ball but only intercept a pass.

- Goalkeepers can be involved both defensively and offensively.

- Central goals can be introduced to the middle of the line as shown in diagram 10.

- Competition between the lines of players can be encouraged by the coach.

Diagram 10

PRACTICE G

This practice is termed a ghost game because the coach asks the players to play against a ghost team using their imagination. Even though there is no opposition, care should be taken with every pass and speed of play should not be compromised. Therefore, high standards of passing throughout the practice are still required. The diagram shows a 4-vs-0 setup (plus a goalkeeper) but this can also be done using an 11-vs-0 setup (plus a goalkeeper)

Coaching Points

- ⚽ Four players simulate game-like conditions.
- ⚽ The four players move and pass as they would in any 4-vs-4 small-sided game.
- ⚽ This is also excellent practice for goalkeepers to keep moving around their penalty and goal areas. It is also excellent practice for stopping shots.
- ⚽ Whenever a player moves into the attacking half of the field they can become a defender by raising a hand and shouting "Defender." This then makes the practice a 3-vs-1 game.
- ⚽ The defender now tries to win the ball from the three attackers.

- ⚽ When the ball goes out of play, the X team once again become a team of four players.
- ⚽ Variations on the number of defenders can change the conditions, and hence the complexity, of game.

Diagram 11

PRACTICE H

This practice is also a good preliminary practice and requires the following:

- One ball between six players.
- Players are arranged in two lines of three facing each other.
- The ball must travel up and down the line in a zigzag pattern and back again.
- Players are only allowed two touches of the ball. One touch to control the ball and one touch to pass the ball.

Coaching Points

- The player's body position should be open to enable them to give a pass straight or to the side.
- The coach should stress the accuracy of the pass.
- Receiving players should be ready to move into the line of flight of the pass.

Progression can be made by using one-touch play, speeding up the pass and making it competitive between groups of six players, each one trying to keep the passing sequence alive.

PRACTICE I

As a progression from Practice H, combine two groups of six players and arrange them into four lines of three players as shown in diagram 13. Alternatively this practice could be an extension of the line drill explained in Practice F. Indeed the practice begins as two line drills that intersect each other. Use two balls and have the players initially pass the ball to the opposite line and run to the back of the opposite line.

Diagram 13

Coaching Points

- ⚽ Stress the accuracy of each pass.
- ⚽ Players should look up before and after each pass to avoid interfering with the other line practice.
- ⚽ Receiving players should move forward to collect the pass and be in a good receiving position.

Progression 1

Introduce one-touch play for both groups and add a second ball to be played round the back of the lines by the last players in each line. The back player in each line should drop back approximately 3 meters and expect a pass around the back of the line until it is their turn to move forward. See diagram 14.

Coaching Points

⚽ The player at the back of the line has to be ready for a pass or to move forward.

⚽ It is important to retain awareness of both the passing and receiving at the front and back of the lines.

Progression 2

Ask the player at the back of the line to follow their pass to the line that received their last pass.

Diagram 14

Introduce two balls moving around the back of the lines and condition all play to one touch.

Coaching Points

⚽ Force and accuracy of the pass should be stressed.

⚽ Keep looking up and be aware of everything around that is changing especially when not in possession of the ball.

PRACTICE J

The organization of this practice is illustrated in diagram 15. Begin with one ball between six players (grouping can be continued from previous practice). There are three lines of two players forming a triangle. The ball is played to one line and the player then moves to the other line; the ball cannot be played to a line with only one player.

Diagram 15

Coaching Points

⚽ Think before passing.

⚽ Selection of where to pass becomes important.

⚽ Selection of where to run after the pass becomes important.

⚽ All processes of perception, decision making and action are stressed.

PRACTICE K

The same groups of six players that have been used in previous practices can be maintained for this practice. There should be four attacking players around a grid area of 10 by 10 meters (see diagram 16 below). One defender (substituted every minute by the spare player) should be positioned inside the grid. This second defender can make it 4 vs 2 as the attacking team improves their performance. The four attacking player's objective is to make ten consecutive passes before the defender intercepts. The four attacking players cannot cross the boundary lines to come inside the grid.

Diagram 16

Coaching Points

- ⚽ The coach should stress the correct timing of the release of the pass.
- ⚽ Deception of the pass should be encouraged.
- ⚽ The angle of the supporting player to receive the pass is critical to a successful pass.
- ⚽ Players must decide whether to make one or two touches.

PRACTICE L

One of the most effective aspects of attacking play is a long, penetrating pass that travels behind and between defenders into space or the long-cross field pass that switches play from one side of the field to the other. Because long passing is so important, it is critical that coaches stress the need for players to practice the long pass as often as possible.

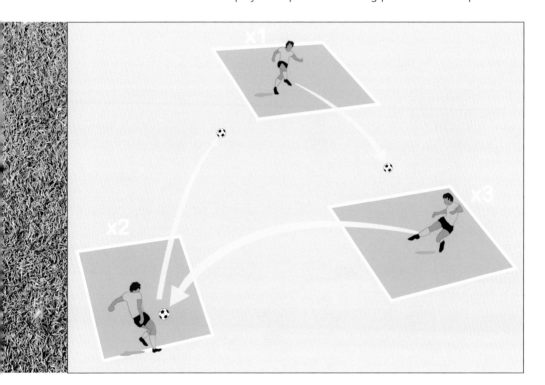

Diagram 17

- ⚽ The practice uses groups of two or three players (see diagram 17).
- ⚽ Ten-meter grids are marked by cones
- ⚽ The distance between the grids can be varied but should be at least 30 meters apart.
- ⚽ Obstacles may be placed in the areas between the grids to ensure the pass is lofted. Clearing the obstacle is a good response cue for the player.

- The task is for the pass to land inside the grid and be controlled on the first touch by the receiving player. This controlling reception must also set the player up for their own pass. Younger players may need two controlling touches before passing.

- The practice can progress by introducing two players per grid, one to control and pass (lay off) to the fellow attacker. Their job is to make a one-touch long pass. This is excellent realistic training for the goalkeeper who should be looking to play the ball in excess of 40 meters.

Coaching Points

- All points relating to receiving the ball (see chapter 9) should be reinforced, especially asking the player to move early into the line of flight of the ball.

- Contact with the instep of the foot (laces of the boot) should be made through the bottom half of the ball.

- The head should be steady with the eyes still and looking down at the ball. However, in order to keep the head down (as in a golf swing) a better response cue will be for the coach to ask the player to look at the grass underneath the ball. This should stop the player from anticipating where the ball will go with the eyes which results in moving the head upward too early.

CHAPTER 11
VOLLEYING

Volleying a ball by definition is to contact the ball whilst it is in the air. There are numerous occasions when this would occur and so it becomes necessary to practice the technique of volleying. This section will be divided into two segments: volleying with the feet to (a) score and (b) clear defensively.

These are probably the most difficult techniques to master, and call upon the player to fully concentrate upon the task and not be distracted by pressuring opposing players.

VOLLEYING TO SCORE

Key Factors

- ⚽ The player must get behind the line of flight of the ball and allow the ball to drop as low as the situation allows before making contact with the striking foot.
- ⚽ In order to make sure the ball goes below the goal's crossbar, it must be struck at or above the midline of the ball. This is mainly accomplished by keeping the knee of the striking leg above or level with the ball.
- ⚽ In order to get the ball between the goal posts, a good contact on the ball is required and the positioning of the non-kicking side of the body is vital. The shoulder of the non-kicking side points at the corner of the goal to be hit. If the shoulder is opened out too far, the ball will be pulled across the face of the goal or sliced wide of the target. If the shoulder is too closed, the leg swing is inhibited.

PRACTICE A

⚽ Throw the ball against a wall and volley the rebound back to a goal marked on the wall.

⚽ Practice as above but with a partner serving the ball from either side and also to the front of the shooter.

⚽ In the penalty area have a partner serve a high ball from the point where the goal area cuts the dead ball line. The receiving player stands near the penalty spot and moves toward the ball in order to volley past a goalkeeper who is initially conditioned to stay on the goal line. For a group practice, a fielder can be employed behind the goal line and places can rotate after several attempts. With large groups, improvised goals can be made from corner flags and along touch lines.

⚽ Using the setup above, defenders can be introduced as required. The defender should initially be stationed behind the player making the attempt to volley the ball, and the distance between defender and attacker should be varied.

Coaching Points

⚽ Movement toward the ball must be fast but controlled.

⚽ Selection of striking surface must be made early (e.g. head or feet).

⚽ Total concentration should be placed on the line of flight and point of contact on the ball throughout. It is important that the pressure of opposing players does not distract the attention of the striker.

⚽ The head should be kept still and the response cue "Eye on ball" can be used.

PRACTICE B

⚽ The players form two lines in front of the coach about 15 meters out from the penalty area.

⚽ The coach should be positioned at the top of the penalty area with a designated player whose role in the practice is to head the ball to the volleying player (possibly the team's centre forward). This player begins the practice behind the coach inside the penalty area (see diagram 1a).

⚽ One player (X9) in the line passes the ball to the coach and the coach plays the ball to either wing for the player to move onto.

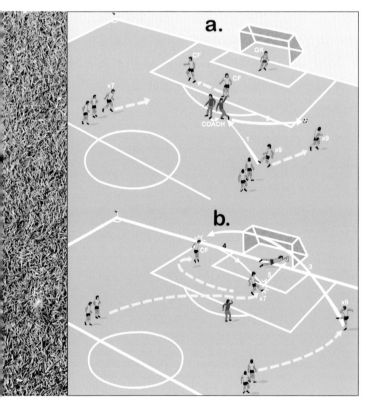

⚽ While one player X9 moves out to the wing in order to cross the ball, the designated forward player moves away from the player who has the ball toward the far post preparing to receive the cross.

⚽ When the far post cross is made, the forward player heads down a ball for X7 to shoot first time (see diagram 1B).

Diagram 1

PRACTICE C

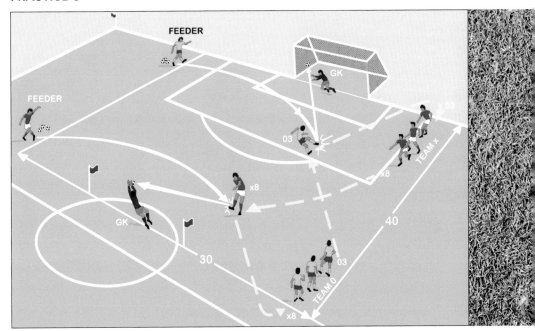

Diagram 2

- ⚽ Divide players into two teams of three or four per team, Os and Xs, as shown in diagram 2.
- ⚽ Play is started with a shot on goal X8 who moves to the back of the O team.
- ⚽ O3 then moves in to volley a shot from the cross of the feeder.
- ⚽ O3 then moves to the back of the X team.
- ⚽ The aim is to score goals from crosses using the volley technique.
- ⚽ After each attempt, the player changes lines and teams.

Coaching Points

- ⚽ Players should move toward the cross and try to take the cross on the volley.
- ⚽ Use the head or feet to make early contact with the ball.
- ⚽ While attempting to get a shot on target, try to volley the ball back in the direction of the cross; this is usually across the goal and into the side netting of the far post.

VOLLEYING TO CLEAR DEFENSIVELY

Key Factors

⚽ The player must move quickly to the line of flight of the ball (response cue "Be first to the ball").

⚽ Contact must be made as early as possible.

⚽ Contact should be made below the midline of ball to make the ball rise high and wide away from goal.

⚽ The ball must have height and distance after contact (in that order of importance).

PRACTICE D

⚽ Begin the practice with one ball between three players as illustrated in diagram 3. The distance between players is variable depending on the skill level of the players but preferably greater than 30 meters. The ball is continually played first time to each player.

⚽ This is a difficult skill and the coach may wish to simplify the practice by allowing the ball to bounce once before the players strike the ball.

– AREA BALL MUST LAND IN WITHOUT BOUNCING

Diagram 3

PRACTICE E

⚽ Organize a simple functional practice on a player (e.g. central defender O5 as illustrated in diagram 4) in the penalty area, where the central defender's starting position is on the penalty spot. Add players, opposing and cooperating, as skill improves. Vary the service from all servers S1, S2, S3 and S4 into O5 from different sides and down the middle of the field.

Diagram 4

⚽ This situation should be built to a full phase of game when success is achieved.

Coaching Points

⚽ Defending players in areas close to the goal must move quickly to attack the ball and make the clearance.

⚽ Selection of the contact area must be made quickly.

⚽ Players should maintain total concentration on the flight of ball (response cue "Eyes on the ball").

⚽ Judgment as to where the ball will drop should be made early.

CHAPTER 12
HEADING

The ball is in the air for a large proportion of the time during the adult game. It follows that the first selected area of contact of the ball will be the head. It does not matter how technically able a player is, unless the player can contact the ball before the opposing player, the technique is of little help. For this reason it is important that a team should be technically proficient in all aspects of heading. This message comes with a strong caveat. Since young children cannot raise the ball above head height, there seems little need to involve them in heading practice, and due to recent evidence concerning concussions in young athletes, we do not recommend practicing heading below the age of 10 years.

As with the previous chapter on volleying the general points concerning heading will be dealt with first and then two specialized aspects of heading will be illustrated: defensive heading for clearance and heading to score.

TECHNIQUE OF HEADING

Key Factors

- Keep the eyes on ball, although during contact the eyes usually close.
- The point of contact should be the flat part of forehead.
- Lean back before contacting the ball.
- Use the arms to propel the body forwards by moving them backward (a rowing action).
- Power comes mostly from the stomach and back muscles not from a flexion of the front neck muscles.
- The neck should stay relatively fixed (although in some instances this may not be possible).
- Pull the arms back just before contact to move the trunk forward.
- Give players the idea of heading through the ball to the target.
- Since the velocity of the trunk is maximum around a central point (see diagram 1), players should try to make contact just before or at this point.

Diagram 1

PRACTICE A

⚽ One ball between two or three players, one serving while the other heads the ball back. Have the player increase power by trying to head over the server and as far past them as possible.

⚽ To increase the power of using the trunk and also to improve timing of the heading technique, have the header of the ball sit on the ground (see diagram 2). The server comes closer and gives accurate service. The only way the header can now achieve a powerful contact is to use the arms correctly, lean back and use trunk correctly, keep the eyes on the ball and do not bend the neck. The timing of when to move forward is now imperative. A good response cue for the coach to give the player is to wait and move late and fast.

⚽ Have a group of three players rotate through the positions of server, header and receiver. This will make the player heading the ball redirect the path of the ball at an angle toward the receiver. This is done, not by a neck movement, but by a turn of the trunk toward the direction of the target.

Diagram 2

JUMPING TO HEAD THE BALL

Key Factors

⚽ Maximum height is achieved if:

   ⚽ The player is moving forward to meet the ball.

   ⚽ The take-off is from one foot.

   ⚽ The player should jump and lift one knee and the arms displacing as much weight as possible upwards. (This will give maximum height but it is not always possible for players to execute these aspects of jumping, because of situational factors.)

⚽ Whilst in the air, power comes from hip flexion and trunk, arm and shoulder extension.

⚽ The most frequent mistake in heading a high ball is the timing of when to jump to meet the ball. The majority of players find that they are jumping too early, hence they are on their way down when executing the technique. Once again a good response cue for the coach to use is for the player to jump late but fast. The extra speed forward will also give more height to their jump.

DEFENSIVE HEADING FOR CLEARANCE

PRACTICE B

- ⚽ One ball between three players (see diagram 3). Rotate after five attempts.
- ⚽ The server varies service and the attacking player (O10 and O9) varies the distance from the defending player who is heading.
- ⚽ Goals are needed in order to give direction to the practice.
- ⚽ Boundary lines and targets are used as goals for defenders to clear over or hit targets.
- ⚽ Attacking players should attempt to win ball and score.
- ⚽ Progression of this practice would be for the attacking players to be free to move anywhere before service and that the service is distributed anywhere into the set area. (This practice can be built up into functional practice on the defending player using cooperating and opposing players around the goal.)

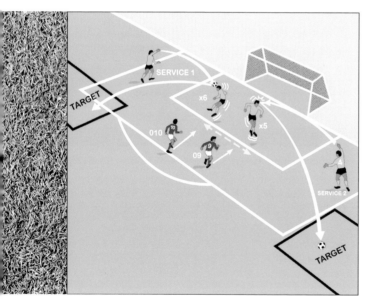

Diagram 3

Coaching Points

- ⚽ Maximum power will be obtained if the ball is headed back in the direction from which it came (hence optimal positioning of the headed ball should be as close to the position it came from but not giving it back to the opposition).
- ⚽ Priorities should be to head for height, distance and width of clearance, in that order.

HEADING TO SCORE

PRACTICE C

- ⚽ Use 10-meter grids with one ball for every two players.
- ⚽ Each player makes their own goal on a line of the grid using cones and face their partner.
- ⚽ One player serves the ball to themselves and attempts to score in the opposing player's goal (see diagram 4).
- ⚽ The opposing player acts as a goalkeeper.
- ⚽ After each attempt the roles are reversed.
- ⚽ The progression of this practice could be for the partner to serve the ball at varying heights to the opposing player who heads for goal with the first touch. Jumping to head and diving headers could be practiced here.

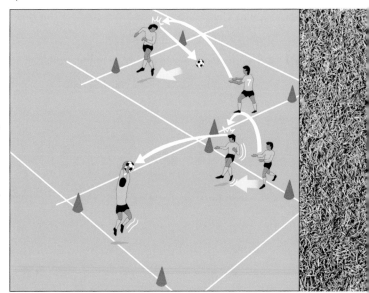

Diagram 4

PRACTICE D

- Using one ball between three players, the server serves a high ball from the side to the near or far upright posts of the goal.
- In diagram 5 attacker X9 should attempt to score.
- Defender O5 must win the ball and clear the boundary lines.

Coaching Points

- The ball should be headed down.
- Scoring chances will come from placing the ball into the near post corner back toward where the ball came from.
- It may be necessary to glance or redirect the ball into the far post corner area if the near post area is congested with players.

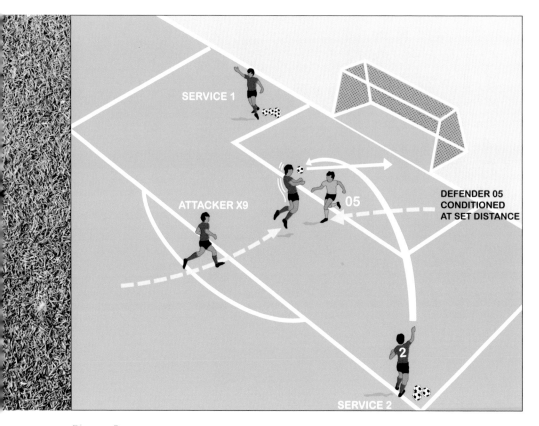

Diagram 5

PRACTICE E

⚽ Form two teams (e.g. 7 vs 7) with goalkeepers and full-size goals.

⚽ Field markings should be approximately 60-by-40 meters but is dependent upon the number of players.

⚽ Play a game of "Head and Catch."

   ⚽ No kicking the ball.

   ⚽ Goals can only be scored from headers.

   ⚽ Sequence must be either head to hand or head to head.

   ⚽ Interceptions must be in line with the attacking team's sequence.

   ⚽ Players only have three steps and three seconds when in possession of the ball.

CHAPTER 13
GOALKEEPING

Goalkeeping requires highly specialized technical development. It is because of this reason that a major emphasis should be placed upon goalkeeping technique during any team coaching situation. However, this same reason has caused many coaches to be apprehensive about imparting valuable information to goalkeepers. Coaches often feel that they have inadequate knowledge of goalkeeping because they have not played in that position themselves. Some clubs now offer specialized goalkeeper coaching from ex-goalkeepers. However there are certain important points related to team performance and basic technique that can be given by all coaches. Also the goalkeeper must be made to realize their importance as a member of the team and not as an individual with special isolated skills.

A goalkeeper is obviously one of the most important defensive players on the team, but they are also, potentially, one of the most valuable players in initiating attacks and could be an indispensable General at the back of the defensive unit.

In this section we will deal with goalkeeping in all aspects of the game.

The techniques of goalkeeping can be divided into 6 main areas:

- ⚽ Fielding and collecting the ball
- ⚽ Dealing with crosses
- ⚽ Movement around the penalty area and off the goal line
- ⚽ Shot stopping and diving
- ⚽ Distribution
- ⚽ Responsibility at set plays

FIELDING AND COLLECTING THE BALL

Fielding the ball is distinguishable from shot stopping in that the goalkeeper has time to move the body fully across to the line of flight of the ball before collecting; for example, a long pass from the opposition that the goalkeeper can reach before the on-rushing opposing forward reaches the ball.

Key Factors

The aim of a goalkeeper is to place as many surfaces as possible between the ball and the goal and to bring the ball quickly into possession. Once in possession the goalkeeper must think immediately of attacking possibilities.

The goalkeeper should:

- Move into line of flight of the ball early.
- Present a solid surface between the ball and goal. Usually both legs are placed close together though not so close as to prevent good balance and not so wide so as to leave a gap for the ball to go through.
- Move the second surface (the hands are a goalkeeper's collecting surface) down to the ball by bending at the waist. (Do not bend the knees too much as they obstruct the view of the ball and ease of collecting.)
- Allow the ball to run into palms of the hands.
- Bring the ball up below chin and cradle it there, giving full vision of play.
- Be ready to distribute to attacking players.

PRACTICE A

It is important in a coaching practice that the goalkeeper has a complete objective (i.e. collection of the ball, control of the ball, selection and distribution of the ball); see diagram 1 for an example.

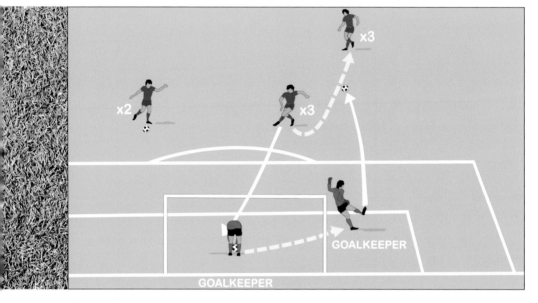

Diagram 1

Diagram 2

⚽ As in diagram 1, X players vary direction and speed of shot to goalkeeper. This player then moves for an accurate distribution from the goalkeeper or the player elects to tell the goalkeeper to kick long downfield.

⚽ Progression for X1 is to give the same service to the goalkeeper but, after playing the ball, to run in and challenge the goalkeeper while O1 attempts to find a space for the goalkeeper to pass the ball. If the goalkeeper cannot play an accurate pass to O1 they should be encouraged to kick long and deep into the opponent's half. Targets should be set up in the opponent's half for this possibility (see diagram 2).

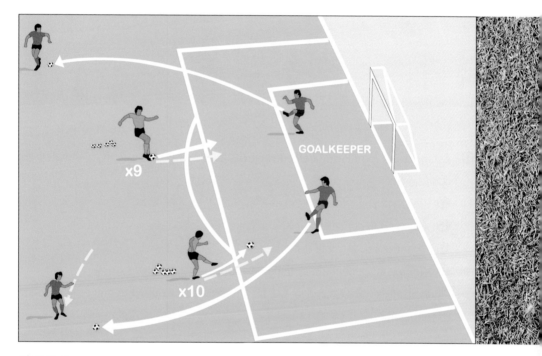

Diagram 3

⚽ The goalkeeper should use the correct method of fielding the ball under all circumstances. It is then necessary to implant this motor pattern using speed practice. In diagram 3, X9 and X10 are feeding the goalkeeper the ball at varying speeds and varying directions. The basic points made in technique should be constantly reinforced. It is important here that the servers give a service that allows the goalkeeper enough time to field the ball. It is not a shooting practice.

PRACTICE B

⚽ In diagram 4, X4, X5, X6 and X7 are servers who take it in turn to vary the type of shot. Without any opposition the goalkeeper should always collect the ball or find it necessary to palm it over the bar.

Diagram 4

⚽ As above but introducing defenders as the goalkeeper gains success. Defenders are conditioned:

   ⚽ To stand still and not move.

   ⚽ To stand in one area, allowed to jump for the ball.

   ⚽ To move but within a restricted area.

   ⚽ To free movement about the goalmouth.

⚽ Other attackers and defenders can be introduced as required to bring the situation close to game.

DEALING WITH CROSSES

One of the major problems facing many goalkeepers is how to deal with balls that are crossed into the penalty area from the sides of the field. Too many goalkeepers use these occasions to make spectacular clearances, punching or tipping over the bar, when the majority of times the goalkeeper could safely collect the ball with their hands. For a goalkeeper to correctly execute the technique of collecting crosses, two factors are important:

⚽ Early decision making.

⚽ Speed and agility in the goal area.

A goalkeeper possessing these two attributes can concentrate on the techniques involved in dealing with crosses.

PRACTICE C

⚽ See diagram 5 for the number of players and organization area on the field.

⚽ This could be duplicated from both right and left sides of the field.

Diagram 5

Coaching Points

- Very early in the flight of the ball, the goalkeeper should judge the line of flight and the area where the ball will be dropping. The more time they have to make the decision the more accurate the decision will be.

- If it is possible for a goalkeeper to reach a cross, then they should do so. However if they feel they cannot collect the cross, then they should stay in their goal. Goalkeepers should not move into a position that is between the goal line and the cross path due to indecision.

- If the ball is too far out from the goal for the goalkeeper to reach, then they should elect to stay close to their goal line and be ready for the next play. Depending upon individual speed and height, goalkeepers should usually be responsible for everything that is landing within their goal area (6-yard box).

- Once the goalkeeper has elected to go out to the ball they should make another early decision about whether it is safe to catch the ball or whether it is better to punch the ball clear. This decision would be taken in light of the following two factors:

  - The number of players between themselves and the ball.

  - If the ball is dropping just under the cross bar. The goalkeeper in this case would palm the ball over the bar. Using the opposite arm and leg, he should push the ball vertically and then guide it over the bar. Pushing the ball up vertically first, prevents the goalkeeper from palming the ball into their own goal.

- More height is gained if the goalkeeper can jump after a forward movement. It should always be emphasized that the goalkeeper is moving forward toward the ball (even if it entails only one or two steps).

- The more body weight that can be lifted as high as possible the more height will be attained. For this reason the goalkeeper should jump off one leg, lifting the other as high as possible and bending at the knee, and lift the arms and hands in a ready position.

- The ball should be taken at the highest possible point. This would emphasize the advantage which the goalkeeper has over other players. The fault of many goalkeepers at this stage of the technique is that they have arrived too early, which would necessitate either moving backwards for the ball or allowing it to go over their outstretched hands. Once again a good response cue for goalkeepers would be to decide early but move forward late and fast.
- At this point in the technique the goalkeeper will either:
  - *Catch the ball*
  - Move the hands out in front of the body, not behind. The ball should be visible all the way into the hands.
  - The fingers spread to receive the ball from the back.
  - Elbows should be slightly bent to allow the arms to cushion the force of the ball (but not hyperextended).
  - Goalkeepers should then bring the ball down into a cradle position just below the chin, sliding the hands and arms around to protect the ball.

  - *Punch the ball*
  - Because of the pressure of opposing players, the goalkeeper may elect to punch.
  - They should punch for height, distance and width, in that order.
  - It is important that this decision is made early so as to enable the goalkeeper to exert the full power of their body momentum into the punch.
  - More accuracy and safety comes from using two fists moving through the ball together. However in very difficult situations punching with one hand can be used.
  - The fists must come together early in the movement forward to the ball. The ball is contacted in the middle of the range of movement not at the end. This will give maximum velocity to the ball.
- If the ball has been punched, the goalkeeper should then move back and readjust their position immediately.
- If the ball has been collected they should prepare to distribute the ball as soon as possible.

MOVEMENT OFF THE LINE AND AROUND THE PENALTY AREA

Goalkeepers have often felt that the only time during the game that they are concerned with play is when the ball is within shooting distance. However, a successful goalkeeper should be continually aware of where the ball is on the field all the time during the match, whether the ball is with the opposing goalkeeper or with the opposing front striker. The goalkeeper's movement about the penalty area should always be in relation to the position of the ball on the field. There are occasions when the coach should even encourage the goalkeeper to move out of the penalty area and move up in support of their own defensive players. This would more likely be when the ball is in their team's attacking third of the field. In certain professional teams goalkeepers are used as the back line of outfield defenders or as an extra outfield player. In this role the goalkeeper often comes out of the penalty area to intercept a long pass that goes behind the team's defenders.

The importance of the goalkeeper's movement in their penalty area can be easily brought out in a game situation, where a continuous monitoring of the goalkeeper and their position with respect to the ball can take place. A coach could place themselves behind the touch line beside the goal and be continually prompting the goalkeeper to the exclusion of all the other players. The coach will be concerned solely with the goalkeeper's movement in relation to play and with communication they have with the other players on the team.

The goalkeeper should understand that the best chance of stopping shots is to reduce the amount of goal which the opponent has to aim at. This becomes of vital importance when outfield defenders are completely beaten and an opponent with the ball has a clear run at goal. Movement around the penalty area throughout the game allows the goalkeeper to anticipate early the angle of approach they should make to the on-rushing forward. Here are some key factors for goalkeepers to consider when faced with an on rushing opposing attacker.

Key Factors

- The goalkeeper should move off the goal line quickly but under control.

- The goalkeeper should realize the danger that exists at the near post; they should not allow the attacking player to see too much room to shoot on that side.

- The goalkeeper should try to apply defensive pressure to the oncoming attacker.

- The goalkeeper should stand up and try not to dive in anticipation of the shot.

- If the near-post shot is covered sufficiently the probability is that there will be only one direction to dive towards, that being the far post (making opposing players predictable).

- A wide barrier should be presented as the shot is made (i.e. diving at right angles to the shot and not forward or backward toward or away from the goal).

- Adjustment should be made immediately after the shot is collected or knocked away by the goalkeeper. If the shot is collected the goalkeeper should protect the ball using their arms and body and then distribute the ball. If the shot is knocked away, the goalkeeper should readjust position.

- Young players should be given indications when to move away from their starting position thus eliminating any indecision on their part. The distance the attacking player is from goal determines when the goalkeeper should begin to move. A good simple marker for junior goalkeepers to move away from goal is when the attacking player is about to cross the edge of the penalty area. This assumes the goalkeeper has the correct starting position, on an arc 3 to 4 meters from the goal line.

- The goalkeeper should be still as the attacker is about to shoot. This keeps the head steady so that the eyes can focus on the ball and allows for an efficient dive or stop. Keep the head steady while moving out (response cue). Many goals are scored and shots taken when goalkeepers are moving toward the attacker. It is worth giving up distance toward the ball in order to have a controlled dive.

PRACTICE D

⚽ In diagram 6, X9, X10, X11 and X7 are attackers whose target is to score. O5, O6, O4 and O3 are defenders who are recovering back to their position, goal-side of their opposing players. They are conditioned to a certain position behind X attackers (giving the attackers the advantage).

⚽ One attacker (X player) at a time tries to take the ball and score. The defenders have targets of clearing the ball over a touchline or putting it through goals A or B.

⚽ Play does not stop until the ball is in the goals or over the touchline.

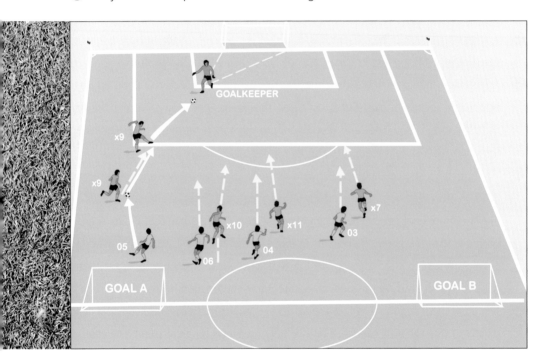

Diagram 6

SHOT STOPPING AND DIVING

A thrust upwards and to the side is required for shots that are wide of the goalkeeper.

Key Factors
- Height is important in obtaining maximum dive length.
- The goalkeeper should keep the ball in view all the time and bring as much of their body behind the ball as possible. A good response cue would be "Keep the head steady!"
- The hands move to complete the save and try to pull the ball into the body. If the shot is difficult to catch, then the ball should be pushed away from goal to the side with a firm wrist.

PRACTICE E
- Practice diving in a coaching grid using two goalkeepers. In diagram 7, G1 places the shot so as to vary the movement of G2 and then G2 takes the shot at G1. Distance between goals can be varied depending on the age of the players.
- Using a similar practice, have another player squat down to the side of G1 (or place a soft barrier) and cause G1 to dive over the obstacle before making the save. This will improve the height of the dive.
- Have the shooting player place some shots closer to the side of the goalkeeper. If the shot is not wide (i.e. requiring a full dive) and is placed just to the side of the goalkeeper then the goalkeeper should get their body to the floor as quickly as possible and therefore offer a solid barrier to the shot. In order to accomplish this, a good response cue for the goalkeeper is "Kick the standing legs out from underneath them and to the side." This will allow gravity to pull the body to the floor. This technique of dropping to the floor and not diving requires a good deal of practice.

GOALKEEPER

GOALKEEPER

Diagram 7

DISTRIBUTION OF THE BALL

The goalkeeper is potentially the most effective attacking player on the team. They can deliver an accurate short pass to defensive players and also deliver the most penetrating pass to the front strikers, usually without pressure from opposing players. It is for this reason that the goalkeeper should be made aware of the responsibility to the attacking possibilities of the team. The most efficient methods of distribution should be provided. The coach should help the goalkeeper understand when and how to distribute the ball.

Rolling the ball
The ball is rolled underarm along the ground. This is used when a supporting player moves in near support of the goalkeeper and is not under pressure by any opposing players. Sure possession is gained from this pass and an attack can be initiated quickly from the outfield player. An example is given in diagram 8. (This technique, however, should not be used over a long distance.)

Diagram 8

Throwing the ball
The most accurate and safe methods of throwing the ball is the javelin throw (as used in throwing a javelin) and the overarm bowl (as used in bowling a cricket ball).

Key Factors
- ⚽ Foot of the non-throwing side is planted forwards in the direction of the throw.
- ⚽ Bring the ball back by the ear.

- The throwing hand is spread and behind the ball.
- Eyes are on the target.
- Weight is distributed over the back leg.
- As the throwing arm moves toward the target:
    - weight transfers to the front leg,
    - eyes stay on the target,
    - the non-throwing arm swings out and back to increase body rotation
    - the fingers release the ball and
    - the wrist follows through in the direction of the target.

This method is used when the player who is receiving the ball is not being pressured and when the ball can reach them in time to allow for safe control of the ball before a challenge from the defender. The goalkeeper must realize the limitations when throwing. It must be in a safe situation, unless the goalkeeper can deliver the ball long distances (over the halfway line) to on-rushing forwards. Diagram 9 illustrates where this could be used.

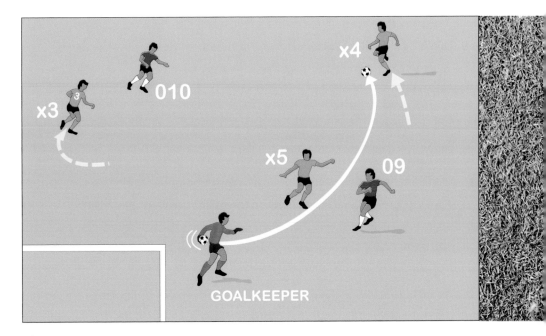

Diagram 9

Kicking the Ball

Two main methods of kicking the ball are the volley (or the punt), and the half volley (or the dropkick).

(1) The Punt

The ball is kicked while in the air. This will deliver a long, high clearance if the team are under pressure, or a long, high pass to the front strikers. This is often used to test the capabilities of the opposing rear defenders in clearing a high, penetrating kick. Practicing the arrangement of front players and midfield players to accept and get control of such a pass is extremely beneficial for retaining possession in the front third of the field. Front strikers should know where the kick will likely land (after much practice) and challenge for the ball. Midfield players should use the front players as markers to ensure that if the ball is played back or if a defender wins the challenge they are in a good position to gain control of the second ball or knock down. This can be practiced similar to a set play.

(2) The Drop Kick

The ball is kicked just as it hits the floor from the goalkeeper's hands. This will give a lower trajectory than the punt but will be a longer and possibly more accurate pass. This is a more difficult skill to master. It arrives at the target (front striker or winger) much more quickly than the punt and therefore is perhaps more beneficial in transition play for fast breaks.

Illustrations of when the kick is used are given in diagram 10. In deciding the priorities of distribution, the goalkeeper must keep in mind the following 3 factors:

- ⚽ The team should try to regain or retain possession of the ball by working hard to move supporting players in and around the ball as quickly as possible.
- ⚽ Safety is a major concern. When the goalkeeper has the ball, it is in the defending third of the field and any lost possession in this area can result in a goal being conceded.
- ⚽ The more penetrating the pass, and the faster the attacking players can move into their front third of the field, the higher the likelihood that a shooting opportunity can be created.

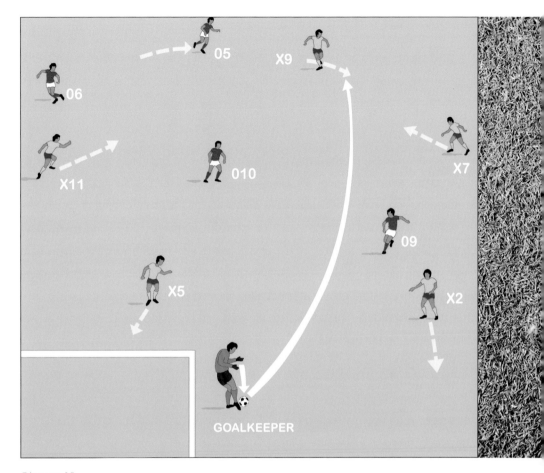

Diagram 10

RESPONSIBILITY AT SET PLAYS

The goalkeeper should be aware of their role at set plays just as every other player on the team. The following is a list of factors the goalkeeper should keep in mind when faced with a "set play" situation.

Attacking goal kicks

Many young goalkeepers shy away from taking their own goal kicks and have another player take them. This is poor attacking play. It would create a numerical advantage for the opposing team and hence make it easy for this team to defend. It would also necessitate the player taking the kick to sprint an additional 20-25 meters to move up with teammates in support of the attack (while also making sure the player does play opposing players onside). A goalkeeper should practice and perfect the goal-kicking technique with constant encouragement and coaching points. This practice can be done after the end of regular practice with many balls and targets (cones or even one or two players) set up on the full field.

Setting up a wall at free kicks outside the penalty area

The wall should be set in position by an outfield player with the brief support of the goalkeeper. A goalkeeper setting the wall has to move to a post in order to line up the wall, and by doing this leaves the whole of the goal open. The goalkeeper should position themselves to the side of the wall to give a direct view of the ball, but not too far over because of the possibility of the ball being chipped over the wall into the opposite corner of the net. If the referee insists the opposing team wait for the whistle to start play, then the goalkeeper will have time to check the wall is adequately covering the near post.

Position of a corner kick

The goalkeeper has to be aware of the possibility of:

⚽ A hard-driven, in-swinging corner kick to the near post.

⚽ The problem of moving across the goal through a densely populated area.

For these reasons modern tactics demand the goalkeeper should not be positioned on the far post. The goalkeeper should take up a position at least half way across the goal and possibly just in the front half of the goal. Also the goalkeeper should move off their goal line by approximately 0,5 meters to allow them to move toward the ball. It is also important for two outfield players to be situated just inside the goalpost. Many goals are scored because these covering post players were not positioned to block the shot and make the goal smaller for the goalkeeper. These players should also remain in these post positions until the ball is cleared away from the penalty area.

Position at long throw-ins that are aimed at the goal area

⚽ The goalkeeper should move to attack these throws and be responsible for balls dropping in the goal area since they have a greater advantage of reaching the ball than any other players. If the goalkeeper knows they cannot reach the ball they should remain on their goal line.

CHAPTER 14
SHOOTING

In the first chapter of this book we discussed events that lead to the scoring of goals and suggested that some events consistently result in shots being taken and goals being scored. If there are such consistencies in soccer, then it should be possible to isolate key factors that lead to the scoring of goals and analyze them in detail. Information from this analysis should therefore logically lead to the development of coaching practices that help players understand these key factors of successful performance. For example, we have shown that the ratio of the number of shots taken to the number of goals scored has consistently approximated 10:1. By way of example, let us use the analysis from one of the FIFA World Cup competitions we have analyzed, the 1994 World Cup (other World Cups yield similar trends). In this particular World Cup, 1,458 shots were taken and 141 goals were scored, giving again a ratio of approximately 10:1. The relevance of this fact becomes apparent when the number of missed shooting opportunities is tallied. For the 1994 World Cup, 153 opportunities to shoot were not taken. If these opportunities were taken it would translate into approximately 15 goals given the previous ratio of shots to goals. Fifteen goals is a significant portion (10%) of the total number of goals scored in that competition.

Players who score goals recognize the shooting opportunity early and produce on-target shots. Of the 1,458 shots taken 315 were blocked. The vast majority of these blocked shots was due to the fact that the shot was taken too late, allowing the defender to block the shot. Also 612 shots were off-target, with the majority being shot over the height of the cross bar. Therefore, only 531 shots (36%) required the goalkeeper to make a save or score a goal.

This type of information gives coaches an excellent basis from which to identify certain key factors for shooting. The problem for the coach is twofold. How can we create a shooting opportunity and how can we improve the player's technique of shooting once they decide to take that opportunity?

First and foremost the environment for shooting practice must be realistic. An interesting exercise for a coach would be to analyze the shooting practice itself and then ask the question "Is it realistic?" "Are the players faced with the same situations that arise in competition?" "Are the players practicing hitting or missing the target?" and finally, "After the practice, do the players understand the key factors of successful shooting?"

Key Factors

- Players should understand that not every shot will result in a goal.
- Players should recognize a shooting opportunity.
- Early shots pay dividends. Late shots might never happen and might be blocked.
- Shots should be on target.
- Shots that move away from the goalkeeper cause more trouble than shots that move toward the goalkeeper.
- Shots that swerve and dip cause problems for goalkeepers (but also have the higher probability of missing the target).
- Accurate contact on the ball is a critical component of a successful shot.

As you can see there is nothing very complicated or technically demanding about these key factors. However, if players are to maximize their team's ability to score goals, understanding these key factors of shooting becomes important.

SHOOTING PRACTICE

Taking shots on goal has always been one of the most attractive aspects of football. The immediate visual feedback, the simple and easily understandable objective of the task at hand—putting the ball in the net—is the overall objective of the whole game. However, one of the major areas of concern in soccer is the lack of goals. At the highest level in the game, defensive strategy over recent years has become increasingly more efficient with the result that putting the ball in the net has become increasingly more difficult. On examination it would appear that tight marking defensive systems are denying the front players the opportunity to shoot in and around the penalty area. The coach should therefore be concerned with the task of producing players who have the ability to be quick, controlled, courageous, technically proficient and totally committed in tight marking situations that often arise in possible scoring positions around their opponent's goal.

One of the problems in coaching players the technique of shooting is to ensure that players keep their shots below the goal height. Nothing can result from a shot that is too high, but many events can lead from shots that are wide of the goal. In practice situations the priority ordering should be first to take the shooting opportunities, then try to ensure the shot is on target. Finally the coach should ensure that other attacking players are ready inside the penalty area for unexpected results from the shots that are taken.

The following practice situations should vary such aspects of play as the angle of the approaching ball to the attacker, the distance the attacking player is away from goal, the number of players (attackers and defenders) in and around the ball and the way in which the shooting opportunity arose. These coaching practices and games are aimed at improving shooting in the game.

SHOOTING INSIDE THE PENALTY AREA

PRACTICE A

This practice (shown in diagram 1) is designed to improve shooting when the player receives the ball with their back to goal.

Diagram 1

- ⚽ X9 turns and shoots.
- ⚽ The X feeder varies service.
- ⚽ O5 and O4 can be brought in after X9 achieves success.

Coaching Points

- ⚽ Keep eyes on ball throughout the service and shot.
- ⚽ Try to make a good contact as early as possible.
- ⚽ Turn and fall away to shoot.
- ⚽ Placement of the non-kicking foot usually restricts the movement of the body. The foot should be turned outward and planted early.
- ⚽ Knee position should be high and over the ball.
- ⚽ Strike through the top half of the ball to keep the shot down.

Progression 1

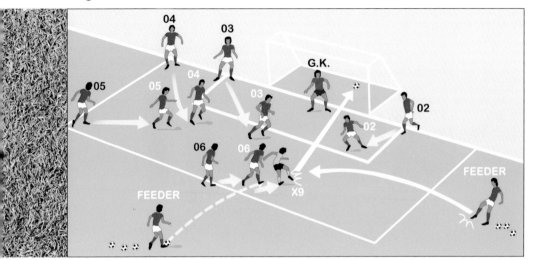

Diagram 2

- 🌐 Pressuring defenders O2, O3, O4, O5 and O6 can be brought in when required and can have varied starting positions (see diagram 2).
- 🌐 Two X feeders vary service from in front of X9 to crosses, high, low, half volley etc.
- 🌐 X9 must contact the ball early and score.

Coaching Points

- 🌐 Contact the ball as early as possible (attack the ball).
- 🌐 For a crossed service the player should contact the volley with near foot.
- 🌐 Pick corners and try to hit low shots.
- 🌐 Consider the coaching points made in the chapter that details volleying to score.

PRACTICE B

⚽ Diagram 3A illustrates the practice. No opposition to the shooting player at first with the ball being served in at varying heights from feeder.

⚽ The ball can be played into any of the X players.

⚽ Diagram 3B illustrates the progression. If the ball is played into X9, players X7, X8 and X10 become defending players and try to prevent the shot and clear the ball away from goal. Instant shooting is a technique important for X9 who must shoot quickly. This can be used as a competitive game with goals being accumulated by each player.

⚽ Players use skills acquired in the previous practice (practice A).

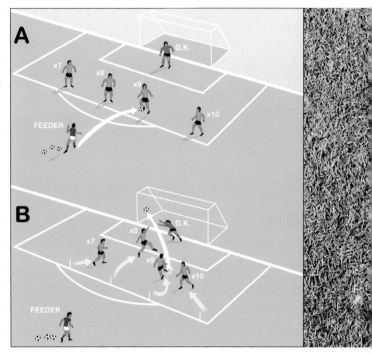

Diagram 3

SHOOTING OUTSIDE THE PENALTY AREA

PRACTICE C

⚽ O5 feeds the ball to X9 (varying the height of service) as shown in diagram 4.

Diagram 4

⚽ X9 is encouraged to:
  - ⚽ Move forward toward the ball.
  - ⚽ Take the ball down, forward and to the side away from the defender O5.
  - ⚽ Make the second touch of the ball a shot (if the ball can be shot towards goal with the first touch, then the coach should encourage this).
⚽ After service, O5 becomes a defender and tries to block X9's shot.

Coaching Points
⚽ Stress the first technique of playing the ball down into the space away from O5 and into a shooting channel.
⚽ During the practice if more defenders are brought into the penalty area the technique of shooting using the technique of a dipping volley could be coached.

PRACTICE D

Diagram 5

- Players pair off with one ball between two players.
- Use two goals if more than 10 players are involved to avoid long lines. Two goals and two goalkeepers can be used for squads of 16 to 20 players.
- The coach or feeder places themselves with their back to goal on the edge of the D outside the penalty area.
- The goalkeepers can take up any position they wish off the goal line.
- The distance between the players and coach is about 15 meters.
- Two players start together.
- The player with the ball hits a hard, low drive into the feet of the coach and then moves forward for the coach to pass the return ball.
- The other supporting player must also run for the expected lay-off pass from the coach because the coach can pass to either player.
- The lay-off pass from the coach can be varied from slow and low to high and fast.
- The player who does not receive the lay-off pass must follow the shot in and try to shoot any rebounds the goalkeeper may give up.
- The shots are made from approximately 20 meters out and are always hit first time.

Coaching Points

- Players should not try to hit the ball as hard as possible. They should strive for controlled accuracy and make the shot hit the target.
- Because it is more difficult to aim for space than it is to aim for a target, the players should initially be asked to aim for the goalkeeper. This will ensure on-target shots and could produce many rebound situations. After success they can then be asked to aim for the sides and corners of the goal.
- The key factor of shooting is to keep the head steady and the eyes on the ball when striking.
- When players have mastered the technique of getting their shots on target, the coach should ask players to try and hit the ball with swerve or late swerve. Late swerve is gained when the ball is struck just to the side of center with the follow through going straight. A ball that is swerving away from the target (goalkeeper) will hopefully cause problems for the goalkeeper.

Progression 1

- Introduce stationary players into the penalty area. These players can only stick out a leg to block a shot.
- Shooting players must now try to shoot just above knee height. A ball travelling at this height is more difficult for defenders to control or block.
- Shooting players should also be aware of deflected rebounds off defenders in the penalty area.
- This practice is also useful in testing goalkeepers on screened shots. That is, screened shots that may also be deflected by defenders.

CREATING THE SHOOTING OPPORTUNITY

PRACTICE E

Diagram 6

- ⚽ In diagram 6, X9 is the attacker and O5 is the defender and the goalkeeper maintains a correct starting position.
- ⚽ Both players begin the practice on the edge of the 6-meter goal area. O5's position can be conditioned to the goal line to give X9 more time. But as the practice progresses O5 can begin from anywhere inside the goal area.
- ⚽ If O5 wins the ball the objective is to clear the ball from the penalty area. The game is still alive until the ball is out of play or in the goal.
- ⚽ When X9 begins the practice any of the six balls placed outside the area can be played.
- ⚽ X9 moves out to control any of the balls and O5 moves out to defend.
- ⚽ X9 must score or try to shoot on target.
- ⚽ After each play the number of balls that X9 can select is reduced by one until X9 has only one ball left. This then becomes much more predictable for O5 to defend.
- ⚽ A competition can be set up between the two players when O5 becomes the attacker.

Coaching Points

- ⚽ When X9 moves on to the ball he must try to turn on it as quickly as possible.
- ⚽ X9 should not try to screen the ball and finish with back to goal. This will slow the play down and in the game allow the defending players to recover.
- ⚽ When X9 is turned to face O5 and the defender moves directly in to tackle for the ball, X9 should try to push it past the defender and shoot.
- ⚽ Once X9 has possession of the ball, the attacker should try to set up for a shot with the minimum number of ball contacts.
- ⚽ One technique available for X9 would be to feint to one side, push the ball to the other side of the defender and then take the shot. It is not necessary to completely move around the defender before taking the shot. In fact, it is possible for X9 to use the defender to screen the goalkeeper and bend a shot around O5.
- ⚽ Another technique would be for the attacker to be composed and patient, even be able to stand on the ball and anchor the defender momentarily before moving and shooting. This will increase the unpredictability of the situation for the defender.

Progression 1

Add another defender O6 who is always conditioned to begin their run from the goal line. This means the attacker now has to shoot past two defenders.

Additional Coaching Point

If the extra defender O6 covers to the left of X9, then X9 should fake a move towards the covering defender and push the ball to the non-covering side and then shoot as shown in diagram 7.

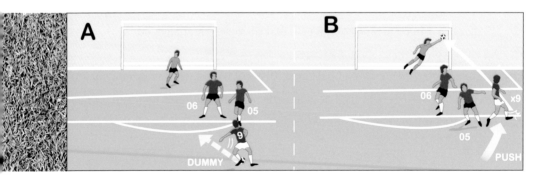

Diagram 7

PRACTICE F

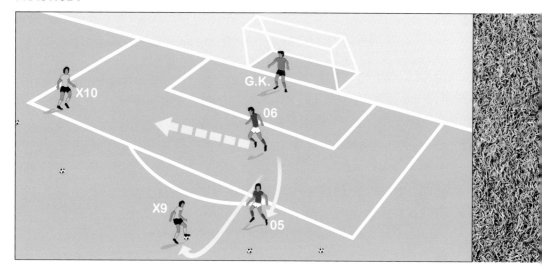

Diagram 8

- This practice extends the previous practice.
- X10 is brought in to assist X9 and always begins from the edge of the penalty area (see diagram 8).
- Now X9 has the option of shooting or passing to X10.
- X10 can return the pass for X9 to shoot or can shoot themselves.
- One-touch play is encouraged after the initial turn. This ensures that the attackers do not spend unrealistic amounts of time preparing to shoot.

Coaching Points

- X10 must be close enough to allow a fast, accurate combined play such as a wall pass.
- The accuracy of the pass to X10 from X9 and the accuracy of X10's return pass is important.
- All previous coaching points are reinforced.

Progression 1

⚽ Add an extra defender O4 to defend against X10 and allow X10 to start with X9 in the goal area. Either X10 or X9 can move for the ball to begin the practice.

Additional Coaching Points

⚽ If X9 moves for the ball, X10 should try to present themselves as an early target for the pass.

⚽ X10's position should be away from goal side of X9 in order to draw the covering defender away from the shooting angle, and allow the return pass to be given into central areas.

⚽ X10's pass back into central areas may be given with spin moving towards goal (if the pass from X9 is delivered with enough force) because:

     ⚽ The ball when spinning toward goal will be hit with spin hence the shot will tend to go down and not be shot over the crossbar.

     ⚽ The defender O5 will find it difficult to judge the path of the ball, while X9 will be able to move on to it quickly.

     ⚽ This type of pass can be given quickly.

⚽ X10 can either give this return pass inside to X9 or turn with the ball outside of O4 and shoot as shown in diagram 9.

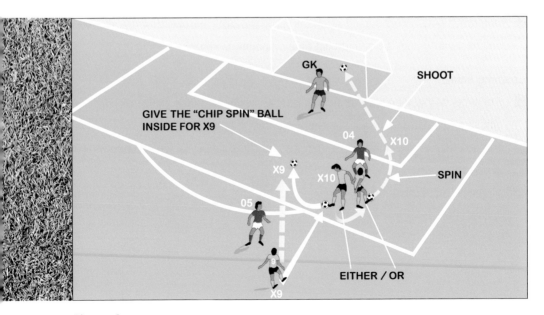

Diagram 9

PRACTICE G

Diagram 10

- The setup is the same as in practice E (see diagram 7B), but the balls are set up 30 meters away from the goal.
- When X9 is turned on the ball facing the goal, they play the ball to X10 and take the return.
- X10 returns the pass and then moves away on a run to find attacking space behind defender O4.
- X9 then has to play the ball into space for X10 to move onto.

Coaching Points

- The type of run away from the ball by X10 is of critical importance. The first dummy run takes the defender O4 in one direction, then the real run to receive the ball back from X9 brings X10 inside of the defender O4.
- If another attacker X11 is brought into the practice either they or X10 can receive the pass from X9 and they should try and move themselves into attacking space by making runs which take defenders away from the ball.

PRACTICE H

Diagram 11

- ⚽ As illustrated in diagram 11, XF feed balls in from either side (varied service).
- ⚽ As soon as the ball is fed to the striker X10 or X9, O5 comes into play from the starting position of anywhere inside the goal area.
- ⚽ X10 and X9 are limited to two touches of the ball.
- ⚽ O5 must try and clear the ball from the penalty area.

Coaching Points
- ⚽ The players receiving the service must affect instant control of the ball.
- ⚽ The attacker who does not receive the ball should try to move into a supporting position where the ball can be played to them with a first touch.
- ⚽ Ideally X9 should move slightly behind X10 and be moving toward X9, partially facing the goal, in order to shoot immediately as he receives the ball.

Progression 1

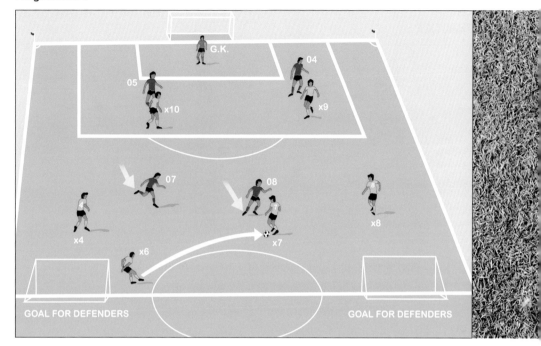

Diagram 12

⚽ This practice can progress to the situation illustrated in diagram 12, which is 4 vs 2 in the midfield area and 2 vs 2 in the penalty area. The reason for this overload of attackers is to ensure each attempt yields a pass into the penalty area.

⚽ Progression from this would be to add an extra defender in the penalty area and an extra midfield defender.

Coaching Point

X10 and X9 must work together to assure quick shooting possibilities. These combined plays would include such techniques as cross-over play, lay-off pass, spin off defender and shoot, wall pass etc. (see chapter detailing combined attacking play).

GAMES TO IMPROVE SHOOTING

PRACTICE I

Diagram 13

⚽ As shown in diagram 13 two goalkeepers are used to defend the same goal in a 7-vs-7 game within the penalty area (this number can be varied but many bodies create a realistic and fun environment within the penalty area).

⚽ Each team is allowed 2 minutes to score as many goals as possible.

⚽ The defending team tries to retain possession and keep the ball away from attackers for the 2-minute period or to play the ball out of the penalty area.

⚽ If a ball goes out of the penalty area the coach feeds the next ball in quickly and keeps a continuous game going.

⚽ If the ball is kicked out of area, the player last touching it must retrieve it by hand and place it in the D in front of the coach, meanwhile the coach plays the next ball in. This would bring a numerical advantage to one of the teams.

PRACTICE J

⚽ As illustrated in diagram 14, X9 and O7 try to score in their respective goals (which can be increased or decreased in size depending upon the technical ability of the players).

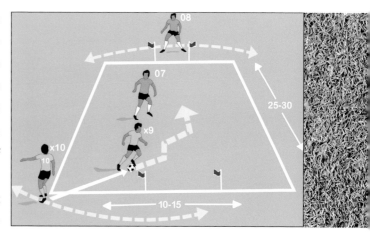

Diagram 14

⚽ X10 and O8 are not allowed into the playing area (10 by 30 meters) and are only allowed to use half of the area surrounding the boundaries. They should keep the game continuous with a supply of balls. If the ball goes over the boundary line or through a goal, X10 or O8 should recover the ball and find their respective team members with an accurate pass to feet or into space.

⚽ X9 and O7 should not leave the field of play.

⚽ After 2 minutes the players switch roles. The game can be continuous for as long as the coach desires.

Progression 1

⚽ The organization is the same as above with the addition of another retrieving player (two players retrieving [X11 and X10] and one player playing [X9]).

⚽ X9 and O7 now have the option to use these assisting players with a short pass if the marking from the defender is too close. X10 and X11 may also pass to each other so as to set up X9. (These assisting players are still not allowed to enter the field of play but may pass the ball to each other through and around the field of play.) They are only allowed two touches of the ball.

Progression 2

The setup remains as above but introduces a second striker, so that the game now becomes 2 vs 2 with two assisting players (on the outside of the grid) per team.

PRACTICE K

Diagram 15

- ⚽ Diagram 15 illustrates a 4-vs-4 instant shooting game that can take place inside the penalty area with a portable goal moved to the D of the penalty area.
- ⚽ Each team is conditioned to two touches before the ball has to be shot at goal.
- ⚽ The goalkeepers serve the ball into their own team with varying service:
- ⚽ Ball rolled out
- ⚽ Ball thrown out at thigh or waist height
- ⚽ Ball thrown hard at players

Coaching Points
- ⚽ All players should be ready to shoot.
- ⚽ All players should be encouraged to shoot by coach and colleagues.
- ⚽ Knock-downs and lay-off passes will be used most often if passing is required.
- ⚽ Players receiving the ball should be half turned in a ready-to-shoot position.
- ⚽ The body shape of players when shooting is important to make the correct contact on the ball.

WHAT IS AN EFFECTIVE GOAL SCORER?

Here is a quote from the late Allen Wade, a former Director of Coaching for the English Football Association.

"An effective goal scorer:

- Always expects the ball to come.
- Is prepared and alert.
- Sights the target, re-sights and adjusts position constantly.
- Prepares feet and body positions constantly.
- Keeps the head still during the shot.
- Concentrates attention on a precise point of impact.
- Swings through the impact point of the ball towards the target for as long as possible.
- Is prepared to miss (but hates it!).
- Shoots for the far corner of the goal.
- Sometimes passes the ball past the goalkeeper.
- Swerves or spins the shots, making them difficult to hold.
- Can see (imagine) 'channels' from feet to target area even in unlikely positions."

CHAPTER 15
COMBINED AND IMPROVISED
TECHNIQUES

COMBINED TECHNIQUES

Since the game is a continuous flow of many techniques from all players it is important that we try to organize our practices so as to involve a combination of techniques. An example of combined techniques could involve dribbling, passing and shooting with a rotation of players so each perform these tasks. The quality of each technique within this combined whole will be stressed to achieve the total aim of the practice. Initially the technical practice should be unopposed so as to allow the players to concentrate on quality performance. It is important to relate these unopposed drills to a game-like situation where the quality of technical performance is stressed within a game setting.

Unopposed work to improve technical excellence is important if players are to become complete performers. However after considerable practice the players should be asked to perform these tasks under pressure from defenders, the essential factor being the application of these techniques within a game. If the players move from technique work into a contrived or conditioned game, the qualities learned in the unopposed setting have to be stressed in the game. This gives purpose and realism to the practice progression.

PRACTICE A: Chip—Lay Off—Drive

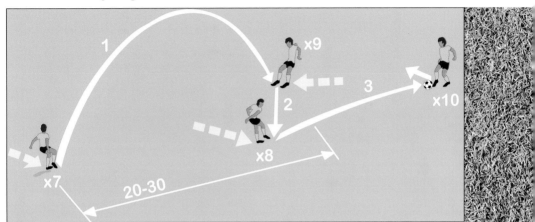

Diagram 1

- One ball between four players as illustrated in diagram 1.
- X7 starts the practice by tossing up the ball and then pushing the ball one touch to the side and then chipping the ball to X9.
- X9 moves to the ball, trying to make contact just before it lands to lay off the ball to the side of X8.
- X8 moves onto the ball to drive the ball to the feet of XlO with their first touch.
- X10's first touch puts the ball to the side ready to chip a ball to X8 and then the practice continues.

Coaching Points

- The chip pass must have back spin and be fading into the feet of X9.
- The lay-off pass should allow X8 to play the ball first touch. This means the ball will be stopping as it reaches X8. This is accomplished by X9 cushioning the ball as it is received.
- The low drive pass should be played in hard and low to the feet of X10. This is accomplished by keeping the head down and steady as well as the body being well balanced (the player should not be stretching or falling).
- Position of receiver for the low drive is in line with the pass. They should be ready to pull back the controlling surface and move the ball into playing position (within 2 meters of the receiver).

PRACTICE B: Conditioned Game

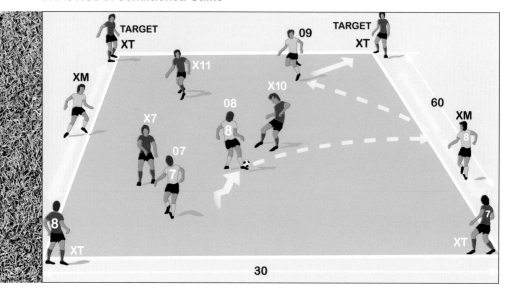

Diagram 2

- ⚽ Diagram 2 illustrates the 3-vs-3 practice taking place inside a 30-by-60-meter area.
- ⚽ The two players marked XM (X midfield players) are included to assist only the attackers and cannot come into area.
- ⚽ The four players marked XT are target players and are intended to be goals of the attacking team. Passes to these players score a goal.
- ⚽ If the O team is attacking, the aim is to get the ball past the X team and also play to an XT. The XT then transfers (with two touches) the ball to the opposite XT who in turn drives a ball into one of the O players, who then become attackers going to the opposite end. If needed, the XT can pass to XM who lays off a pass to an attacking team member (see diagram 3 for an example).
- ⚽ If the X team wins the ball, they then attack the opposite end.
- ⚽ Six players who are inside the area play for ten minutes then switch with outside players.

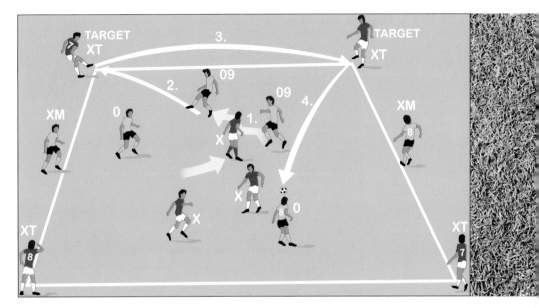

Diagram 3

Coaching Points

⚽ The quality of all techniques (e.g. chip, lay off, drive) is stressed.

⚽ The use of supporting XMs to get a pass behind defenders is encouraged (the game should be 5 vs 3 if these midfield players are used to full advantage).

⚽ The speed with which attackers change direction and look for the through drive from XT players is stressed.

PRACTICE C: Phase of Play Stressing Techniques

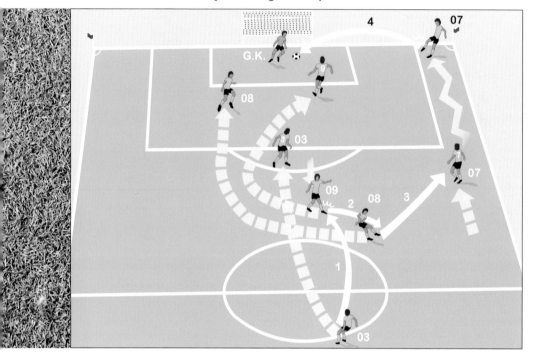

Diagram 4

- ⚽ Diagram 4 illustrates how O3 begins the practice by chipping the ball to O9.
- ⚽ O9 then lays the ball off to O8.
- ⚽ O8 drives the ball out to flank player O7.
- ⚽ O7 dribbles down flank and is only allowed two touches before crossing a far post chip or passing to a near post space depending on which area they find themselves in at the end of the dribble (see the chapter dealing with crosses).
- ⚽ O9, O8 and O3 move into predetermined areas that are recommended for the cross and they try to score against a goalkeeper.

Coaching Points

⚽ Quality of technique should be stressed.

⚽ The movement of players after the performance of the technique and their movement toward areas of importance for the cross are critical for the coach to stress.

⚽ Re-emphasize the key factors of crossing.

⚽ Scoring the goal using good shooting technique is also important.

Progression 1

Conditioned defenders can be introduced to pressure the application of technique and then become unconditioned defenders who defend their goal.

IMPROVISED TECHNIQUE

Exciting football has been evident within the game when individuals produce the unpredictable and seemingly impossible maneuver against high-quality opposition. The names of truly world-class players are few and the names of world-class players who can produce the seemingly impossible are even fewer. The excitement produced by players such as Shackleton, Best, Pele, Cruyff, Ronaldo and Messi can be lasting memories in the minds of many spectators of all ages. The influence that these players have upon the young developing players is immeasurable, especially with the media coverage afforded to today's stars. Imitation of the moves that these great players made is a natural consequence of this exposure. Young players will attempt to perfect the technically difficult moves that they have seen. Although all young players cannot completely replicate the moves, a vast majority of young players can reproduce the once assumed impossible untested maneuvers. With the kernel of the idea implanted, a handful of talented young players will also produce their own version of the move and hence develop something new.

The final stage in the creative process is the ultimate pinnacle in the coaching progression. While some critics of coaching would say that coaching produces stereotypical players, effective coaching should produce truly creative players. The process of creation is possible if the coach is open minded and does not limit players during practice and game situations. Young developing players should be allowed to experiment with their own techniques and not be afraid to fail. Likewise the coach should encourage the players to attempt technically demanding moves.

The coach can do this by:

- ⚽ presenting the kernel of a complex combination of techniques;
- ⚽ presenting situations that demand seemingly untested and difficult maneuvers for the players;
- ⚽ making players aware of the physical principles of moving bodies (e.g. spin, swerve etc.);
- ⚽ allowing experimentation in 1-vs-1 situations; and
- ⚽ encouraging the players to practice this special skill once they have initially mastered it.

The first method of challenging the players to produce advanced techniques is one of advanced selection. These are players who can select the unpredictable yet simplistic move in a tight pressured situation. A very simple practice can develop this advanced selection and execution.

PRACTICE D

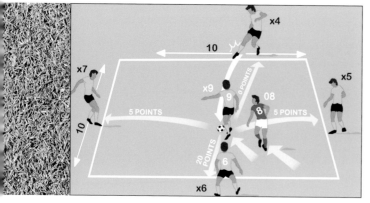

Diagram 5

⚽ Four players (X4, X5, X6 and X7) play outside the grid as illustrated in diagram 5. These players cannot enter the grid.

⚽ Inside the grid, X9 and O8 play 1 vs 1, with X9 being the attacking player.

⚽ X9 is restricted to one touch while the outside players are allowed two touches.

⚽ If the defender O8 touches the ball then this player gets 10 points, and the ball is passed to an outside player.

⚽ The outside players can pass to each other in addition to serving X9.

⚽ If X9 plays the ball back to the server, they get zero points. If X9 plays the ball to the side supporting players (in the diagram these are X5 and X7), they get 5 points. If X9 can play the ball to the player immediately behind them (X6 in the diagram) they get 20 points.

⚽ Play is limited to 3 minutes per player in the middle and then they switch. Points can be used as a motivating factor.

⚽ Outside players should try to test the inside player by giving them varied services, passes that are high, hard, low, soft, etc.

⚽ While the coach may indicate some methods of achieving a high score, their main job will be to emphasize that the inside player should try to go for the 20-point play and also to praise and be positive about original and potentially useful moves.

The second method of encouraging players to experiment concerns the complex combination of techniques that the player may already have in their repertoire. An example of such a combination of techniques is given below.

PRACTICE E: Chest Control With a Volley on Goal

⚽ The ball is served to the receiving player to above chest level (see diagram 6).

⚽ The receiving player moves into line of flight and pushes the ball directly upwards with the chest. This gives the receiving player more time on the ball.

Diagram 6

⚽ The receiving player moves back and volleys back to server before the ball touches the ground.

Progression I

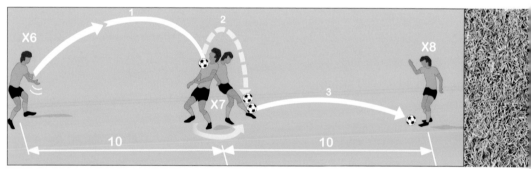

Diagram 7

⚽ Three players are involved in this progression. X6 still serves the ball by hand while X7 chests the ball directly up (see diagram 7).

⚽ X7 then moves around the ball and volleys it to X8.

Coaching Points

⚽ The player receiving the ball should keep the head steady and eyes on the ball throughout the skill.

⚽ The ball should be pushed up from the chest. This gives the player time to move around the ball.

⚽ X7 may have to fall away from ball to contact the middle of the ball.

Progression 2

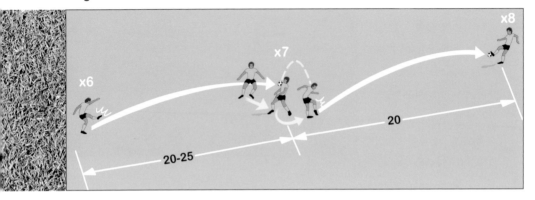

Diagram 8

⚽ The service from X6 is now a driven pass to chest height (not a lofted pass) as shown in diagram 8.

⚽ X7 must now move into a good contact position as the driven pass is not as accurate as the service from hand. Also the distance over which the volley must travel has increased to 20 meters.

Coaching Points

⚽ If the foot is wiped up the ball when volleying then the ball should dip due to increased spin on the ball later in flight.

⚽ Dipping volleys cause problems for the goalkeeper if this is used as a shooting technique.

Progression 3

Diagram 9

- ⚽ Players align themselves near the goal with the final volley being a shot on goal (see diagram 9).
- ⚽ The ball is driven into the edge of the penalty area where the receiving player is tightly marked. This player (O8) can be conditioned not to intercept early on but later can become more active.
- ⚽ The chest is used to push the ball directly up and the receiver moves around the ball protecting it from the defender.
- ⚽ A falling side-volley can then be used to shoot on goal. (If the service is not to the chest, then any areas can be used to raise the ball directly up to allow the volley to be used as a shot on goal).

DIPPING VOLLEY

The principles of physics are directly concerned with soccer techniques. Laws that govern the resultant movements of spheres when forces are applied also govern what happens to a soccer ball when it is kicked. Although detailed scientific knowledge is not required when applying a force to the soccer ball, an understanding of what is possible can aid players in producing the unpredictable. An example of how the physical laws have affected the game is well illustrated by the way in which the change in the composition of the ball has caused increasing problems for goalkeepers due to the change in flight path of the ball. The coach is recommended to visit the many websites (some are highlighted in the bibliography) now available that examine the physics of ball motion as it relates to soccer. All players should be allowed to experiment with techniques that result in the ball dipping and swerving. The two shooting examples that are given below deal with a dipping and swerving ball.

PRACTICE F

Diagram 10

⚽ Players drop the ball from two hands and volley directly into the goal as shown in diagram 10. This can be also good goalkeeping practice for diving.

⚽ Players are then asked to wipe the foot up the ball, with the knee being raised quickly upon contact. This action will cause the ball to have top spin. Depending upon the type of force, the contact will determine how fast and late the dip will occur.

⚽ While the ball is being dropped from hand, the players can be asked to wipe the foot up the ball at different angles trying to apply both swerve and dip (see diagram 11).

Diagram 11

Action of Wipe (Facing the Ball)

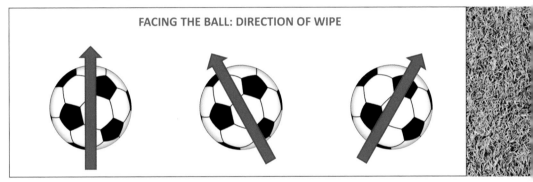

FACING THE BALL: DIRECTION OF WIPE

Diagram 12

Progression 1: Free Kick

⚽ X7 lifts the ball up for X8 to produce a dipping volley toward goal.

⚽ Area of kick placement is just outside the penalty area as shown in diagram 13.

⚽ When the players can produce this skill, they should practice the skill many times.

Diagram 13

SWERVING SHOT

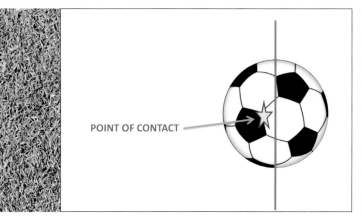

Diagram 14

This type of shot is quite common in the modern game (perhaps because of the changing nature of the ball). Contact is made across the intended line of flight. The swerve is almost immediate with the follow through at an angle to the intended flight path. However in order to produce a ball that swerves late in flight the player should impart more force on the ball and make contact slightly off center as shown in diagram 14.

The follow through is toward the target. This will cause the ball to rotate slowly at first but during flight the difference in pressure build-up causes more rapid rotation, and hence swerve. A similar phenomenon occurs when driving a golf ball. The ball looks as if it is going straight to the green when it suddenly bends away into the rough.

Flight of Ball

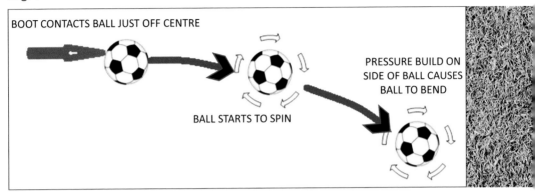

Diagram 15

Since many players already induce early swerve, the key factor is to forget about inducing swerve since the follow through is toward the target. The key is to make contact just off center.

PRACTICE G

Diagram 16

⚽ The practice organization is shown in diagram 16 with the intention of the players being to deceive the goalkeeper by applying late swerve.

⚽ Allow the players to experiment with all types of swerve but have them pay attention to the way in which the ball turns after contact is made and during flight. The design on the ball is very useful in giving feedback to the players about the movement of the ball. If it is possible a video recording and close up of the kick and ball flight would be helpful for players. Also if possible take a video of the kick from the position of the goalkeeper to show the details and timing of the swerve.

DRIBBLING PAST DEFENDERS

The ways in which attackers dribble past defenders in a 1-vs-1 game situation are many and varied. With the exception of shooting on goal this is possibly the most exciting aspect of the game and for players the most rewarding. Most top-class players develop their own personal style and are successful with only slight variations on a main theme. However the truly great players have surprised many good defenders with a completely different way of taking the ball past them. Many examples come to mind for instance Cruyff for Holland against England in 1972, Tony Currie for Leeds, Gento for Real Madrid, Garrincha for Brazil, George Best for Manchester United, Pele for Santos, Ronaldo for Real Madrid and Messi for Barcelona.

If the players are given an idea of the simple mechanics behind these moves, they may then develop their own new and unique methods of dribbling past defenders. It is then for the coach to encourage the player to practice this technique and use it in competition and not criticize if it fails. However, the coach should also make it very clear when and where this experimentation can take place during the game.

PRACTICE H

Diagram 17

🖤 For this practical session the coach should arrange several 1-vs-1 situations just outside the penalty area with the instructions to dribble past the defender and then produce a shot on target.

🖤 The aim of the defenders is to be relatively passive until the new technique is well laid down.

🖤 The coach should demonstrate the mechanics of one or two unusual moves that have been used in the past. The players can then use the ones demonstrated or create their own. If their own move is created, the players should be encouraged to practice this one move and improve this special skill.

PART 5
BEGINNING AND ENDING OF PRACTICE

CHAPTER 16
BEGINNING ACTIVITIES

Warm-up sessions are an integral part of nearly every modern sports training practice. It is generally accepted to be necessary by sports science practitioners, physiotherapists and coaches. This chapter will not provide details on the many aspects of warm-up activities for soccer as they are covered in many other excellent texts (see bibliography for an example). However, some general principles should be followed in order to properly prepare the body for the ensuing physical bout of exercise.

The main goal of any warm-up is to increase the temperature in the muscles that will be used in the sport. To prepare the body for maximal physical efforts, it has been suggested that the ideal warm-up for a soccer game or practice lasting from 90 minutes to 2 hours would be approximately 15 minutes at a maximum intensity of 70% heart rate. Several studies have suggested this would help improve physical performance in both sprint times and vertical jumps (see reviews by Bishop).

Some simple basic guidelines to abide by follow:

- Start slowly and progress to faster speeds.
- Include four directional movements (forward, backward, side to side, diagonals).
- Incorporate jumping, landing and cutting (changing direction).
- Use the ball whenever possible.
- Include dynamic stretching and movements that take the pertinent joints in the body through a range of motion that will happen in the game or practice.
- Fifteen minutes is a reasonable duration for the warm-up, but timing will depend on ambient temperature (colder temperatures = longer time periods).
- Finish the warm-up with some sprints or relay races with or without the ball.
- Use the ball in a competitive but fun way to improve player interest and encourage the players to end the bout with some short, maximal exertions.

Many sports including soccer are now using the warm-up to incorporate some preventative injury programs or prehab exercises in order to decrease the incidence of non-contact injuries such as ACL (anterior cruciate ligament) tears in the knee. The FIFA 11+ Warm-Up is a helpful resource that can provide some ideas for exercises and warm up structure (see bibliography for website). FIFA 11+ is divided into three parts: it begins with running exercises (part I), moves on to six exercises with three levels of increasing difficulty to improve strength, balance, muscle control and core stability (part II), and concludes with further running exercises (part III). The different levels of difficulty increase the programme's effectiveness and allow coaches and players to individually select and adapt their specific programme. These warm-up exercises take between 15 and 20 minutes to complete for senior players and replaces the usual warm-up before training. Prior to playing a match, only the running exercises are performed and for no more than 10 minutes.

One important consideration for coaches is to remember that the effects of the warm-up quickly dissipate if the warmed-up player is inactive (e.g. standing and listening to the coach talking) for 7 minutes or more after the exercise. It is important therefore to plan the pre-practice meetings before the warm-up begins, and try to be succinct and to the point with coaching points throughout the training session.

The beginning activities detailed in the following chapter are designed with the expectation that the flexibility and mobility exercises specific to soccer that are needed to bring the body to physical readiness have already been completed (although some could be used within the above warm-up session). Despite the importance and benefits of warming up, the coach is warned against spending large amounts of time (greater than 20 minutes before a 2-hour practice) at the start of each practice engaged in activities that are not game or ball related. The sooner the player engages in a ball-related practice the better. To avoid confusion of terminology, we have used the term *beginning activities and not warm-up activities*.

One major problem coaches have with beginning activities is that of organization. They take time and effort to plan so that the correct permutations of players, space, balls and progressions meet the requirements of a good beginning activity. The following gives the coach some organizational frameworks to work within. Also these practice sessions accommodate for both progression and adaptability. They also allow for some coaching points to be given to players, although the aim of the activity should be to keep players active with little if any standing and listening.

ACTIVITY 1

- ⚽ A low ratio of balls to players. Ideally it would be preferable if all players had one ball each to begin the session.
- ⚽ Individualized. The first practice should allow the players to begin on their own. All players need not be present.
- ⚽ Self-evaluating and ongoing. Self-testing practices require the player to improve upon their own previous test performance. Daily records can be kept by the coach or the player. It is hoped that this will be self-motivating.

A technique circuit can be set up by the coach prior to each session. Certain areas of the field should be marked out and designated for a different technique practice. Something along the lines of a national skill award program could be used with additions of techniques such as shooting, goalkeeping and heading etc. Use could be made here of such things as the pendulum ball, adequately marked shooting walls (or boards) and sand pits for keepers etc.

The following activities are designed with regard to the need for each player to be involved in all the processes of perceiving, decision making and action. Other warm-up sessions usually stress only the physical readiness of the player (i.e. the response side). Of equal importance are the two preceding processes. Perception and decision-making processes are somewhat underplayed in most warm-up sessions and these beginning activities should require the players to look and listen, make decisions and perform the act efficiently and accurately.

ACTIVITY 2

- The playing area should be 20-by-20-meter area grids with cone markers.
- One ball per player.
- All players (including goalkeepers) work within the total grid area.
- All players should be facing the coach inside the grid, with the ball at their feet.
- The players use the coach as the mirror with all players in front of the mirror.
- The coach will progressively give more alternatives and instructions to players.
- When the mirror (coach) moves, the players reflect their image.
  - The mirror moves forward; players pull the ball back (always facing mirror).
  - The mirror moves right; players move left pulling ball sideways.
  - The mirror moves back; the players dribble the ball forward.
  - The mirror moves left; the players pull ball to right.
  - The coach varies speed and intersperses stopping into the above four movements.

Coaching Points

- When stationary, players must be ready to move with the ball.
  - Be on their toes
  - Keep knees slightly flexed
  - Keep ball in playing distance
- Keep head up and match the mirror image.
- Keep ball within playing distance.
- Use sole of foot to drag ball back.

Additional Instructions

In addition to the above:

- When the coach moves both arms to the right side, players roll over the ball and pick it up on their left side.
- When the coach moves the arms to the left side, players roll right.
- When the coach points toward the players, players perform a backward roll taking the ball with them.
- When the coach points backwards, players perform a forward roll taking the ball with them.

Coaching Point

Don't look for gymnastic expertise, just the efficiency and speed with which the player can go down, get up and be ready to perform.

Additional Instructions

In addition to the above, when the coach puts both hands in the air, pointing straight up, players turn and dribble to the farthest back line of the grid and return to face the mirror wherever it may be (coach is encouraged to move so players have to look up and find the coach).

The decisions are now quite complex and testing. Do not fatigue players too early, too soon. Use the stop commands to give the brief coaching point. This practice can be adjusted to suit any response requirements. That is, any instruction can be translated into any technique or activity. The coach must demand a high standard of concentration and efficiency from the players. A great deal of encouragement will be needed from the coach.

From this point on in the coaching session, consideration should be given to the technical theme that has been outlined in the coaching plan of the session. Activities should converge on the specific technique that has been identified by the coach. The aim is to move through relevant progressions, and not to jump from practice to practice without thought to the overall theme of the coaching session. Before giving an example of a particular progression, certain guidelines relating to how to progress can be specified:

- Keep the practices relatively unopposed depending upon skill of level of the players.
- Keep all players active.
- Offer few, if any, brief coaching points.
- Keep the ratio of balls to players low.
- Progress with as little organizational rearrangement as possible (e.g. do not move from five players per one ball to three players per one ball or have to rearrange areas while players stand still and wait).
- Progress with regard to decisions as to on- or off-the-ball behaviour (e.g. while off the ball, players should be thinking of the probability of being involved directly in play, receiving a pass or offering indirect support).

The following practice is an example of how to progress toward the combined technique of the lay-off pass (details can be found in the chapter on combined attacking play).

ACTIVITY 3

⚽ Use a 15-by-15-meter area grid and cone markers.

⚽ One ball per two players.

⚽ All players work within the total grid bounded by the cones.

⚽ Goalkeepers will be involved without a ball. If there are two goalkeepers, each goalkeeper will operate in one half of the area. The area can be enlarged and split up to accommodate more goalkeepers.

⚽ Players are asked to pass the ball between each other.

⚽ Goalkeepers try to intercept passes (with hands) and roll the ball back to players.

Diagram 1

Coaching Points

⚽ Ball should have top spin to keep it hugging the ground.

⚽ Players should wipe the foot up the ball with each pass.

⚽ Use the inside of laces part of the boot. Stress the importance of laces part of the boot as a contact area and its versatility and speed as a passing technique.

⚽ The ball should be hit with correct force (well weighted) to prevent interception.

Additional Instructions and Demonstration

- ⚽ Player (X9) with the ball dribbles with the ball (see diagram 2a).

- ⚽ Player without ball (X10) who has just passed, runs away from the ball to any area of the grid.

- ⚽ Player without ball (X10) then checks back down the line of the intended pass from X9 showing a full target (see diagram 2b).

- ⚽ Player with ball (X9) gives a well-weighted pass as soon as the player without the ball (X10) checks back.

Diagram 2

- ⚽ If interception is likely, the player with the ball (X9) fakes a pass and moves off to another area for another possible pass.

- ⚽ The player without the ball (X10) checks back out again.

Coaching Points

- ⚽ After passing the ball, move off at speed (change of pace).
- ⚽ Change pace when checking back for a pass.
- ⚽ Check back down the channels between defenders toward the passer.
- ⚽ Always be ready to adjust the run if interception is likely.
- ⚽ Receive and move off quickly in another direction.
- ⚽ Pass the ball early over distances in excess of 6 meters.

Additional Instructions

Diagram 3

- The goalkeeper can now not only intercept but is encouraged to go down at a player's feet to win the ball.
- After the player with the ball (X9) makes the pass, they move towards the player that has just passed to (X10) (right or left side) in order to receive a one-touch lay-off pass from X10 (see diagram 3a).
- The player receiving the return pass (X9) then moves off with the ball (see diagram 3b).
- X10 moves to another area of grid and then checks back to give another lay-off pass.
- After five lay-off passes, players switch roles.

Coaching Points

- After making a pass the player must move either to the right or left immediately to give the player receiving the pass an early indication of where to play the lay-off pass.
- The player giving the lay-off pass should be ready to take some of the weight off the ball (reduce the force of the pass), and play it back into the path of the oncoming player.
- Player receiving the return pass should play the ball forward within playing distance with their first touch of the ball.

Additional Instructions and Demonstration

- A period of time should now be given to allow the players experimentation.
  - Balls chipped up for a headed lay-off pass.
  - Forceful driven passes.
  - Passes played into either foot.
  - The lay-off pass chipped up and curling into path of player (with the inside, outside or laces part of the boot).
- Demonstrations should be given frequently to encourage individuals to experiment.
- Reorganization with respect to specific elements of the lay-off pass can then be continued.
- An approximate time allocation of 15 minutes is given for these first three beginning activities.

ACTIVITY 4

Diagram 4

- ⚽ Set up no more than seven players in a circle within an appropriate-sized grid area.
- ⚽ Players pass and move to another position on the circle.
- ⚽ Variations that could be used include:
  - ⚽ Distance of players from each other
  - ⚽ Size of area
  - ⚽ Movement of players
  - ⚽ Number of balls. For example, two balls per group as shown in diagram 6.

Coaching Points

- ⚽ Pass and follow your pass.
- ⚽ Pass and change position with another player who is not receiving the pass.
- ⚽ Two players who are not directly involved in play can interchange position.
- ⚽ In diagram 5, X2 passes to X5. When the pass is being made, X3, X4 and X6 know they are off the ball and not involved directly in play. At that time, while the ball is moving, two players interchange position (in this case X3 and X4). X6 must now realize that they are the most likely to receive the next pass.

Progression

Any combination of these variables can make the development of this practice as complex as desired.

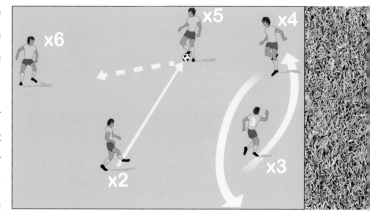

Diagram 5

- ⚽ Employ the goalkeeper in the middle to intercept passes or as a member of the circle. Outfield players should then be encouraged to vary the type of pass given to the keeper.
- ⚽ Dribble the ball to the player.
- ⚽ Passes may be headed or a combination of techniques could be used.
- ⚽ Shooting within the circle at goalkeepers can also be encouraged.

Diagram 6

- ⚽ A triangle consisting of three goals can be placed inside the circle. The goalkeeper's task would be to guard all three and move around to each one as the ball is passed amongst the outfield players. The balls can be passed around or shot through one or two goals. A tally of goals can be kept. Players can be encouraged not shoot from within 8 meters of the goal.

ACTIVITY 5

Diagram 7

⚽ Players face each other approximately 5 meters away and pass the ball between them (see diagram 7). Variations that could be used include:

    ⚽ Type of pass (instep [laces], volley, head, hands [goalkeeper]).

    ⚽ One or two touches by the receiving player. Play the ball to the side with the first touch and then pass with the second.

    ⚽ Keep the ball off the ground.

    ⚽ Movement of both players. Movement direction can also be varied (e.g. receive ball moving onto pass and also moving to the side).

    ⚽ Movement of one player.

    ⚽ Number of touches between partners.

    ⚽ Experimentation can be encouraged between players.

⚽ In diagram 8 the ball is played up to O9. Then O9 controls the ball and moves backwards leaving the ball for X10 to move onto and pass back to O9. Service can vary from hands, feet or from head.

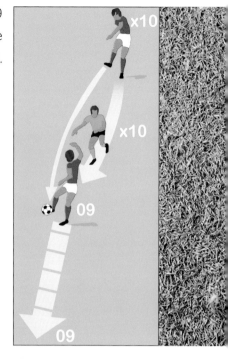

Diagram 8

⚽ In diagram 9, player O9 keeps varying the distance by moving back and forth. This requires X10 to vary the weighting (force) of the pass.

Diagram 9

ACTIVITY 6

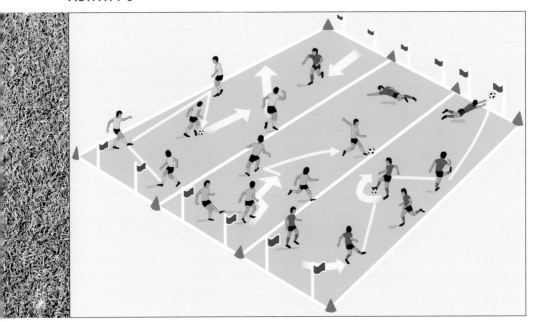

Diagram 10

- ⚽ Three small-sided game areas (30 by 10 meters).
- ⚽ No more than five players plus one goalkeeper to a group as in diagram 10.
- ⚽ Three games of five outfield players vs one goalkeeper.
- ⚽ This can be termed a simulation (i.e. ghost) game.
- ⚽ The team of five players should try to simulate exactly what it would be like playing against five imaginary opponents.
- ⚽ All moves should be as realistic as possible.
- ⚽ Goalkeepers should concentrate on correct movements as though defending players were actually there.
- ⚽ Goalkeepers should be exposed to shots from no less than 10 meters from goal.

Progression 1

- ⚽ If one player wishes, they can raise their arm and shout "Defender one!" This means that until the ball is out of play, the game becomes 4 vs 2 (one outfield player plus one goalkeeper). The four attackers still play as though there is a game of equal numbers underway.
- ⚽ Two or three players could be allowed to become defenders at will.

It is hoped that these organizational tips have given the coach a basic framework and an example of variables that can be adjusted. The coach is now advised to design their own beginning activities for their own team. No one person knows more about the idiosyncrasies of their players than the coach. Therefore the coach's design will take into account all the factors that make their team different.

CHAPTER 17
ENDING A PRACTICE WITH CONDITIONED AND FUN GAMES

EXAMPLES OF CONDITIONED GAMES

Any game that has a condition placed upon it and rules to enforce that condition can be considered a conditioned game. In many ways, the use of the conditioned game in soccer has been abused by coaches in the past. Coaches who wish to fill in time and still appear to be coaching often call out to the players to begin a game of Two Touch and give little thought to what benefits this particular restriction has. Other coaches give a conditioned game and then step back and become a referee and feel there is no more coaching to be done, and that the condition in the game will bring out all the coaching points in itself.

The conditioned game is a means of isolating one or two skills within a particular game, and concentrating upon their development within a game like context. The major benefit of using a condition is that all the players in the game are encouraged to use the skill(s) under coaching consideration. The conditioned game should be used in context with the main theme of the coaching session and hence the conditions are pre-planned with respect to certain skills.

A coach has further problems to consider when applying conditions to a small-sided game. In order to assist the coach in selecting and implementing a conditioned game here are some guidelines.

⚽ Do not make the conditions too artificial. Transfer of training may not take place under extremely artificial situations.

⚽ Be strict concerning enforcement of the condition.

⚽ Use small-sided games as much as possible. Remember, in an 11-a-side game, the time a player is in contact with the ball is reduced.

The games outlined below list the skills and techniques that are considered in each game. Coaches should try to make up their own conditioned games to facilitate their own practice sessions.

ONE TOUCH, TWO TOUCH, ETC.

Games that limit the number of times a player may contact the ball while in possession are probably the most commonly used conditioned games. Any game beyond Three Touch becomes very difficult to monitor and is of limited value.

One Touch

This game should emphasize the following:

- ⚽ The fast pace of the game
- ⚽ Player's movement off the ball as the key to a successful attack
- ⚽ Player's awareness of space
- ⚽ Close and quick attacking support to player on the ball
- ⚽ Support for the next pass
- ⚽ Ability to lay off a pass quickly
- ⚽ Communication from supporting players
- ⚽ Quick shooting
- ⚽ Application of pressure on opposing players as the pass is on its way

Two Touch

This game emphasizes all the points made above for One Touch with the addition of concentrating on a player's ability to receive the ball and bring it under control quickly with the first touch. "Don't get the ball stuck under your feet" (response cue). Consider the first touch as a pass to one's self.

Three Touch

This game can be used with players who lack the skill to compete in the Two Touch game.

DRIBBLING PAST ONE OPPONENT

Before players can pass or shoot they must first take the ball past one or more opposing players.

This game should emphasize the following:

- ⚽ Taking on and dribbling past opponents
- ⚽ Improving the player's ability to turn with the ball if they receive a pass with their back to their opposing goal

EVERY SECOND PASS

In this game, every second pass has to be either a long pass or a shot on goal. This game should emphasize the following:

- ⚽ Accurate use of the long pass
- ⚽ Movement of front strikers into the space the ball is to be played
- ⚽ Creation of a good early target for a pass
- ⚽ Ability to control a long ball played from the defensive or middle third of the field
- ⚽ Quick shooting once the ball is in the attacking third of the field

DEFENSIVE PRESSURE ON THE PLAYER IN POSSESSION

This game requires the defending player nearest the player in possession to apply pressure. This game should emphasize the following:

- ⚽ Application of defensive pressure to the opposition when defending
- ⚽ Early attacking support (options for a pass)
- ⚽ High levels of physical work rate

PASS TO FEET

This game requires every player to pass the ball to a colleague's feet. It should emphasize the following:

- Accurate passes and maintenance of possession
- Creation of good targets for a pass
- Screening the ball
- Support positions from cooperating players

CROSS TO SCORE

This game requires that only balls crossed from the sides can be used to score goals. It should emphasize the following:

- Accurate crosses
- Heading and volleying for goal
- Build-up of play to utilize width of the field and wing play

EVERY SECOND BALL

This game could become a little artificial but does encourage the players to head and challenge for a ball early. This sometimes is a fun game that could be employed at the end of a practice.

SHORT PASSES

Every pass must be a short pass unless the player is shooting on goal. This game should use a small field area and emphasize the following:

- Close support
- Short, accurate passing
- Retaining possession

OTHER GAMES

Split Squad Game

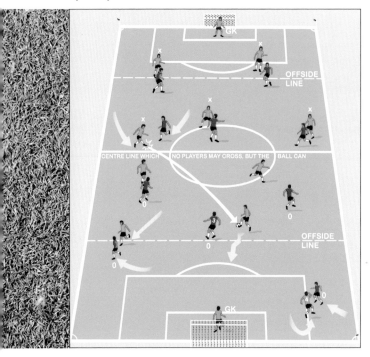

In diagram 1, Xs and Os cannot cross the halfway line. Only when the ball comes into their half of the field can they begin to play (one side attacking and one defending). A line where players are offside is drawn on each half. This game may involve as many players as the coach wishes (e.g. 7 vs 7 in one half and 7 vs 7 in other half).

Diagram 1

This game should emphasize the following:

⚽ Improvement of defensive pressure by forward players while in the opponent's half of the field

⚽ Tight marking by back defensive players

Ghost Game

Many variations of this game can be improvised by the coach. Using the full field, eleven players will play against an imaginary opposition. The play continues as if the attacking players are being pressured by imaginary defenders. Upon the whistle or call from the coach, designated players (usually six of the front and midfield players) turn and become opposing players and attack their own goal. This creates a 5-vs-6 situation of possibly attack vs defense. When a goal is scored, when the ball goes out of play or when another call is given by the coach, the game reverts back to 11 vs 0.

This game should emphasize the following:

- ⚽ Creation of imaginative players using the full potential of passing possibilities
- ⚽ Creativity among players
- ⚽ Quick reversal from attack to defense

Games That Use Two or More Balls

Any game, full size or small sided, can be used to introduce a second ball to play with. More than two usually creates much fun but the game has little reality. For example the Split Squad game outlined above can be used effectively if using 2 balls.

This game should emphasize the following:

- ⚽ Speed of decision making
- ⚽ Awareness of the total situation around players
- ⚽ Fun

Games That Use Four Goals

Diagram 2 illustrates that team X defend goals A and B while Team O defend goals C and D.

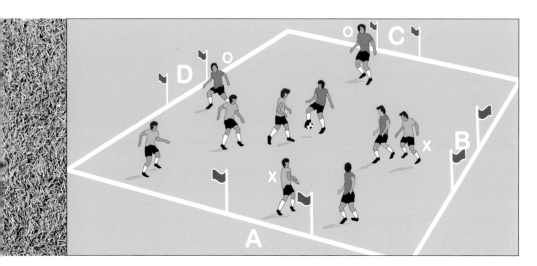

Diagram 2

Small-sided games should be used because many defensive principles become distorted when relating to four goals. For this reason this game has limited value other than being enjoyable.

This game should emphasize the following:

⚽ Awareness of all attacking possibilities

⚽ Increase of defensive responsibility for the team

⚽ Fun

Number Soccer

Diagram 3 illustrates the organization behind this game.

Diagram 3

- ⚽ Players on team X are given numbers as are players on team O.
- ⚽ Each team lines up on their own goal line.
- ⚽ The goal is extended to fit the number of players and all can become goalkeepers for this practice, but they are not able to use their hands.
- ⚽ When the coach calls a number, those numbers on each team come out and play against each other.
- ⚽ These called numbers could produce a 1-vs-1 game or, if the coach calls two numbers, a 2-vs-2 game, etc.
- ⚽ When the coach calls another number, the ball must immediately be left alone by the players and they return to their line and the newly called players sprint to the ball and continue the game until a goal is scored or the ball is played out of the designated area.

This game should emphasize the following:

- ⚽ Quick utilization of opportunities
- ⚽ High work rate for short periods of time
- ⚽ Fun

Piggy-Back Soccer

Players pair off. They play all the rules of soccer while carrying their partner on their backs. The use of a small area is essential to make the game practical. Frequent change of partner position is necessary.

This game should emphasize the following:

- ⚽ Fun
- ⚽ Muscular endurance

Three-Legged Soccer

Partners tie one leg together and play soccer as one pair of players. This game should emphasize fun.

Group Soccer

Any number of players links arms and plays soccer. This can be used as a progressive game. For example, begin a normal game with each player as an individual. Then pair players up making the game 5 pairs vs 5 pairs (goalkeepers remain individual). Then combine the pairs into fours. Then the entire team can be linked as a 10-person unit playing with linked arms.

This game should emphasize fun.

Walking Soccer

This game can be played with small-sided games in a reduced-size field. Players may only walk and are penalized for running. This game should emphasize the following:

- ⚽ Fun
- ⚽ Tactics
- ⚽ Awareness of position on the field and space available

It is important that a well-planned session allows some time for the players to come together and have fun in a light-hearted manner. The end of a hard session is an excellent place to introduce such games.

PART 6
THE COACHING PROCESS

It has long been established that coaches play a significant role in the facilitation of all players' sporting abilities. Recent research relating to coach-player interaction has led many authors to define the coaching process and what constitutes effective coaching practice. Consequently the analysis of planning, management, instruction and observation is becoming increasingly popular as sports scientists attempt to classify coaching effectiveness. We believe that effective instruction is crucial to the pursuit of optimal sporting performance as the more effective the instruction, the more fully the instructor's role will benefit athlete performance.

The coaching process plays a vital role in performance sport, and can be described as the relationship between the coach and player(s), with the aim of facilitating an improvement in sporting performance. Significantly, the process impacts all aspects of performance from the development of essential skills through to the refinement of tactics and game plans. Many view the coaching process as being coordinated and integrated rather than an unsystematic aggregation of isolated training episodes. Within this process there is a continuous refinement and development of the player as they encounter new environments and circumstances.

The essence of the coaching process is to instigate observable changes in behaviour. The coaching and teaching of skill depends heavily upon analysis to effect an improvement in athletic performance. Informed and accurate measures of performance are necessary for effective feedback and improvement of that performance. In most athletic events, analysis of the performance is guided by a series of qualitative assessments made by the coach. In diagram 1 we outline a simple flow chart of the coaching process. This describes the coaching process in its observational, analytical and planning phase. The game is watched and the coach will form an opinion of positive and negative aspects of the performance. Often the results from previous games, as well as performances in practice, are considered before planning the preparation of the next match. The next game is played and the process repeats itself.

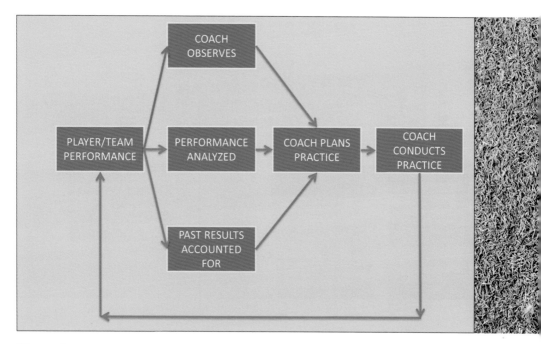

Diagram 1

As mentioned earlier, it is very difficult for an observer to view and assimilate all the action taking place across the whole playing area. Coaches are only able to view parts of a game at any one particular time and much of the peripheral play is lost. Therefore coaches are often limited to basing their post-match feedback on partial information about a team's or an individual's performance. During a game, many occurrences stand out as distinctive features, ranging from controversial decisions given by officials to exceptional technical achievements by individual players. While these are easily remembered, they tend to distort the coach's assessment of the total game. Most of the remembered features of a game are those that can be associated with highlighted features of play. Events that occur only once in the game are not easily remembered and can be rapidly forgotten. Furthermore, emotions and personal biases are significant factors affecting memory storage and retrieval. Therefore the feedback from the coach may be inadequate and an opportunity is missed to optimize the performances of players and teams.

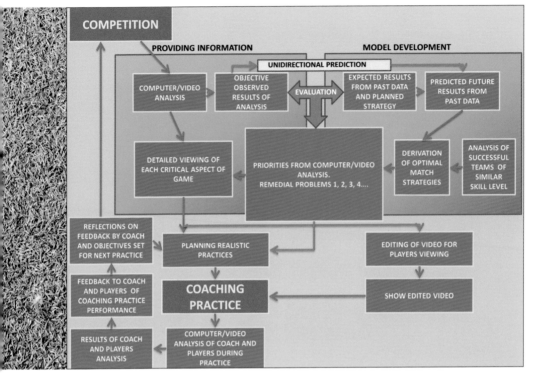

Diagram 2

Objectivity in observation can be obtained through the use of a sport analysis system. Hand notation systems (pencil and paper checklists) are in general very accurate but have disadvantages (e.g. the more complex ones involve considerable learning time. The introduction of computerized notation systems has enabled the problem of data processing to be tackled positively. Used in real-time or with video playback in post-event analyses, they enable immediate and easy data access as well as allowing the opportunity to present data in graphical and other pictorial forms. The increasing sophistication and reduced cost of video systems has greatly enhanced post-event feedback (termed *providing information* in diagram 2), from playback with subjective analysis by a coach to detailed objective analysis by means of computer interactive video systems. Database development will also enable predictive modelling (termed *model development* in diagram 2) which subsequently leads to the enhancement of future training. With the adoption of such a match analysis system the coach can now be intricately involved in the expanded coaching process flow chart described in diagram 2.

Using such a system of coaching (as indicated in diagram 2) allows the coach to formally organize the process of coaching by:

- ⚽ Providing information to the player(s) via video and summary graphics of performance.
- ⚽ Developing a predictive model of performance based upon past results and results from successful teams at the same level of skill, allowing for the creation of optimal match strategies.
- ⚽ Prioritizing remedial problems for improvement during the next coaching practice.
- ⚽ Planning realistic practices based upon previous game events, allowing players to view these selected highlights before practice.
- ⚽ Analyzing the coaching practice in order to allow both player and coach to review their performance from practice.
- ⚽ Providing feedback to coach and players of their performance during practice.

All coaches who have previously struggled with recalling the memory of events when talking to players about performance errors during practice or when planning the next practice should consider the powerful educational medium of video and analysis described above. Consider the situation where the coach can show players particular game events and make salient points about strategy, tactics or techniques after which players go out and practice in realistic situations, these practice environments having been derived from watching the competition. Furthermore while these players are practicing and the coach is instructing and delivering feedback, a video recording is being compiled of their practice. The players then end the practice by comparing the practice performance with the previously recorded competition performance. With the advent of relatively inexpensive portable video technology this scenario is within the reach of most coaches. It only requires a concerted administrative effort on behalf of a few individuals. The problem for coaches is to determine what aspect of the recorded game is the most important since only one or two points should be addressed per practice. Showing the entire video of the game to players may actually retard performance because of information overload. Information about the key factors of successful performance (*predicted future behaviour in diagram 2*) will not only give a good quantitative description of performance, but will also guide the coach in choosing the key elements that have to be addressed in practice and edited out of the competition recording. This type of detailed analysis can be achieved if the coach adopts such a systematic match analysis system.

CHAPTER 18
MODEL DEVELOPMENT
AND PREDICTION

When planning a coaching practice not only is it important to assess how the players have performed in their last game, it is also important to consider their accumulation of previous performances, as well as some general idea of the perfect performance for their level of expertise. This is highlighted on the right side of the flow chart in diagram 2 in the previous chapter. Trying to predict future performance on the basis of data from previous performances is an important goal for coaches and research analysts alike. This is known as performance modelling and can be attempted in a number of ways. Typically the basis for any prediction model is that performance is repeatable to some degree. In other words, events that have previously occurred will occur again in some predictable manner in the future. This is also the basis for scouting a team that your team will eventually face. Will the performance you have just seen, and perhaps analyzed, be similar to the next performance? If this was not the case, then any predictions would be severely limited causing one to question the usefulness of scouting reports. The question therefore arises as to what extent performances are repeated in sport competition.

Consider two examples: in a team sport like soccer there are 22 players interacting and performing a high number of different actions in different areas of the pitch. This complex situation is not likely to provide easily recognizable, repeated situations. The game of squash on the other hand involves just two players (discounting the game of doubles) in a relatively small court area with a more limited number of actions (i.e. shots) available. Scientists have thus, unsurprisingly, tried to assess repeatability of performance in sports like squash before considering sports like soccer. In the early 1990s Dr. Tim McGarry (a sport scientist working out of the lab at UBC) found a limited number of repeatable events, or invariant behavioural responses, that would be capable of describing an individual performance between different pairs of opponents. It was possible to predict performance using matches against the same opponents. One possible reason for this problem was that perhaps the complexity of the analysis had not matched the complexity of the sporting situations examined. It may also be the case that elite sports players adapt their style of play to different opposition, creating a complex pattern which is far more difficult to ascertain.

In 2000 Magnus Magnusson developed software called Theme (www.noldus.com) which is seemingly able to recognize complex repeated patterns (called T-patterns) from within complex data streams. These patterns are now possible to obtain given the sophistication of soccer analysis systems. A T-pattern was defined in a paper by Andy Borrie and colleagues as "a combination of events in which the same events occur in the same order with the real-time differences between consecutive pattern components remaining relatively invariant." The published work that has used Theme so far been primarily focused on animal behaviour with the exception of Andy Borrie and colleagues who looked at on-the-ball behaviours in soccer. They identified some patterns within teams; for example, one pattern, which occurred three times during the first half of a European Championship qualifying match in 1998, consisted of the ball being passed through four (of 18) pitch zones. They suggested that this type of pattern was not easily discernible without using Theme, and concluded that many temporal patterns exist in soccer which may go undetected. Further research is now underway in several labs to overcome the problems of modelling complex systems such as those found in soccer. Some of this recent work is detailed in the *Routledge Handbook of Sports Performance Analysis* that was edited by Tim McGarry and colleagues (see bibliography).

The difficulty of assessing complex sporting performance for consistent patterns of play has led some researchers to re-evaluate the methodologies used. One such approach is to consider the sporting contest as a dynamical system. This term is used to describe a system whose inherent behaviours have self-organizing properties (i.e. regularity is thought to be as a result of changes within the system as opposed to being imposed by external influences), the classic example being the gait patterns (walk, trot and gallop) exhibited by quadrupeds at different speeds. Thus the system (the legs in this instance) exhibits a stable pattern of behaviour at a given speed. This behaviour is disrupted or perturbed when a different speed is required. After this disruption the system reorganizes itself and becomes stable once again, albeit displaying a different structural pattern.

Most of the work in this area has examined racket sports where perturbations (i.e. transitions in the system between stability and instability) can be examined more clearly. However, the application to team sports such as soccer is intriguing as it may uncover invariant behaviours during the game. For example, should we be examining changes in system stability (perturbations) that lead to shots or shooting opportunities rather than accumulating statistics on passes, possessions, set plays etc.? Can we describe what a perturbation in soccer looks like? Mike Hughes and his colleagues described perturbations as incidents that change the rhythmic flow of attacking and defending in soccer. For example, a perturbation could be a decisive pass or dribble or an unexpected loss of possession. They suggested that there were, on average, 88 unsuccessful perturbations (those that did not end up as a shot on goal) per match during a sample of 15 matches in the European Championships and approximately 30 successful perturbations that *did* lead to shots. The theory behind the existence of perturbations and the change of system state between variance and invariance has a number of followers, although the existence of a decisive action (perturbation) does not. Interestingly expert coaches in racquet sports can predict the onset of a perturbation or change in stability (leading to a winner, error or let) and there is some anecdotal evidence that a similar prediction can be made by expert coaches in soccer. For example, an expert observer in soccer can detect when a particular change in possession will result in a shooting opportunity, even one that is sequentially (in time) removed from the immediate play. Perhaps fast transitions (breakaways) during games will play a role in defining important critical phases in play. It may then be possible to develop a strategy to optimize certain aspects of the team's strengths and exploit the upcoming opposition's weaknesses. It is clear more work is needed in this area of match analysis to examine the nature of perturbations as they do appear to be a defining element within such a complex system as a soccer match. Some of the research studies into data modelling have been novel attempts to consider soccer matches in a different way. Instead of treating all behaviours equally, the idea that some perturbations are perhaps more important than others is proposed. Findings from this type of investigation challenge researchers and coaches to consider how relationships between opponents and within teams develop.

Since soccer involves many facets (e.g. tactics, motor skills, strategy), scientists' attempts to understand, model and make predictions about how all of these components fit together to produce the finished product have involved many different approaches. We have sought to comment on some of these methods but do not claim it to be exhaustive. Indeed new approaches are developed constantly, usually borrowing methods and ideas from other disciplines. These new techniques can appear both complex and sometimes rather obtuse. However, the potential for these new methods to rationalize our understanding of complex situations should not be disregarded. One relatively new method for sports analysis whose objective is to arrive at a definite conclusion from complex and ambiguous decision making is called fuzzy logic. Originally conceived as a way of processing data by allowing partial set membership rather than absolute set membership or non-membership, it was only in the 1970s when computers became available to process vast quantities of data that this rule-based solution became useful in many different contexts. Recently these techniques have been applied to sports. A weakness of fuzzy logic systems is the need for the analyst, probably in conjunction with coaches or other experts in the sport, to define the rules for group (set) membership. Although the strength of the method is the ability to handle different rules for different criteria, the rules still need to be formulated by the scientist. A computational model which takes this process one stage further is known as an artificial neural network (ANN). Developed on the principles of nerve cells and their interactions, Jergen Perl suggests this type of model has the ability to identify new relationships based on previously encountered ones. This new, at least in the sporting context, technique has great potential, but for the near future is likely to remain an academic research tool rather than one used for coaching. Indeed Roger Bartlett, commenting on such approaches to modelling predictions as fuzzy logic, ANN and most recent genetic programs, concluded that whilst the potential remains high, actual research output remains low. One of the reasons he gave was the relatively high costs associated with developing such systems compared to the lower amount of research money available to academics working in sports research.

CHAPTER 19
ANALYSIS OF THE
COACHING PRACTICE

Let us now turn our attention to the coaching practice itself. In the expanded coaching process described earlier, we have seen that it may be possible to use similar analysis techniques in practice to those we use in competition. The question of importance therefore would be "What are the ingredients of a successful coaching practice?" To answer this question we must first describe what happens during a practice session. Diagram 1 provides a general overview of the events that occur during a normal coaching practice.

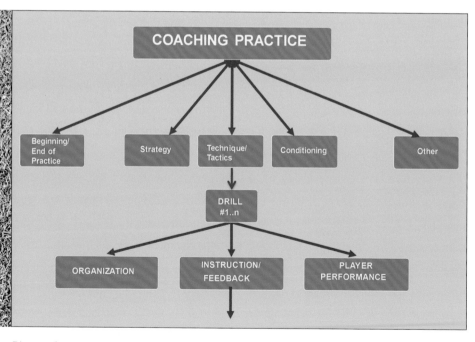

Diagram 1

Although we accept that conditioning is of vital importance to players, it is beyond the scope of this book to adequately deal with all the physiological aspects of soccer performance. Also, we have dealt with examples of beginning and ending activities in previous chapters. Therefore, since the majority of time spent in a practice involves tactical and technical aspects of soccer, our emphasis here will focus upon these elements of the practice. The player's performance has been the focus of the book so far, and now we turn our attention to the behaviours of the coach during practice. Coaches organize the practice and then deliver instruction to the players. Let us examine general recommendations and best practices for organizing the practice and then detail how we can measure and hopefully improve the delivery of instruction and feedback to players. The following components of a practice can be used as a recommended guide to coaches who wish to optimize the organizational aspects of a practice. The coach may wish to review the coaching session and ask themselves "Was each component of organization present in the practice?"

ORGANIZATION

Enjoyment

Most players began playing soccer because of their enjoyment of the game itself. Soccer is the most popular team game in the world and as such it has several intangible attributes that make the game intrinsically motivating to players of all ages and all ability levels. Many psychologists tell us that if a human being experiences pleasure during the performance of an action they are more likely to repeat the task or return to the task setting. The key is therefore to make the practice enjoyable. However, if the young player is exposed to limited ball time and has memories of only sit-ups, push-ups and wind sprints, they will be less likely to return to the practice for the same punishment. Practice sessions are in existence to encourage the development of soccer skills. However it is important that players realize that if they are to improve, practice is the key, and that for young players, the number of hours they spend playing with the ball at their feet is positively correlated with the level of skill they will attain. Physical practice therefore is critically important. If the practice environment (not necessarily coaching feedback) can provide the player with useable feedback about errors, then the more practice the better. This is why the player should strive to practice every day and the coach should provide the player with practices that can be done at home and alone if needed. Although practice does not make perfect, a perfectly enjoyable practice goes a long way to making the skill perfect.

Realism

How can we achieve a realistic practice environment? The following elements maximize the potential for a realistic practice.

Playing Area

The playing area can take the form of many organizational set ups. Ten-by-ten-meter grids can be marked out with anything from pylons to coats or bags. A full-size soccer field can be adapted to provide two mini soccer fields with practice areas in each corner. Central goals where two games share the same goal can be used for many purposes to organize practices relative to individual technique (see below for more detail on possible playing areas).

Opposing Players

Opposing players need to be active during all stages of skill acquisition. However, placing conditions on defenders to be passive to a certain degree can be used to achieve success. These conditions can be gradually removed the player performing the technique becomes more competent.

Cooperating Players

Soccer is a team game and requires interplay with other members of the team whether the players are directly involved with play (the players passing and receiving the ball) or indirectly involved (the player moving into space to receive a pass). Most techniques should be practiced with cooperating players.

Objectives

Each session should have a clear goal for each player, by which we don't always mean a physical soccer goal. The goal or objective can be the number of consecutive passes made by a team, the player having to control the ball on a target line, or the player being able to pass the ball to a specified target player. All of these are valid goals for players.

Activity and Order of Events

If the coaching sessions are well planned and are realistic, players should be active throughout each progression of the skill practice. The order of events for each drill should take into account the fact that any information provided by the coach must be relevant to the existing knowledge base of the player. Usually if the coach is introducing a new technique and practice set-up, the players have no reference point at the outset of the session by which to accept verbal technical information. They have not tried it for themselves! A meaningful and relevant approach would be to organize each skill practice as outlined below:

- Set up the playing environment.
    - Define the boundary of the space needed.
    - *Briefly* describe the objectives of the practice to the players (no coaching points necessary at this time).
    - Set up cooperating and opposing players that are necessary for the practice.
    - Be clear about what the targets are for both cooperating and opposing players.
    - This environment should bring out the technique or skill to be coached and allow appropriately directed instruction and feedback (skill-related comments).
- Set the players to work in the environment. Players will make predictable errors which will prepare them to accept corrective feedback and instruction.
- Demonstrate the skill, using one of the many methods we have outlined in the book if necessary, and remember that a picture is worth a thousand words. Then give only one or two coaching points that are key factors of skill performance.
- Send players back to practice in order to implement these coaching points. Remember, physical practice of the skill in a realistic setting is extremely important.
- Change the playing environment with the aim to progress within the skill being coached.
- The important point to remember is that the environment must be set with an aim to keep the players active, involved and successful.

Progress

A further characteristic of a well-organized coaching practice that should be evident in all coaching sessions is one of progress. It is possible for the coach to move the players along a skill continuum. That is, make the skill problem more difficult such as increasing the pressure from opposing players. It is also feasible to make the situation more simplistic if the players are having trouble with the original practice set up. Reducing the complexity of the coaching situation is a method that many coaches do not use and yet is probably as important as increasing complexity. The main question for the coach is "When do I progress and change practice requirements?" The answer should be driven by either success or failure at the skill. If a player finds the situation too complex and continues to fail in achieving the goals that have been set, it may be necessary to reduce the complexity until the goal is attainable. Alternatively if the players find the situation too easy (i.e. they always achieve the goal) then a move toward the more complex and demanding practice would be required. The goals set should be self-rewarding, that is, attainment of the goal should positively reward the player. This principle of progress through success should not be viewed in its narrowest terms. For example, when a player cannot perform a technique he or she should not be kept at the same practice until they find success. There are many paths to the successful performance of a technique. Perhaps a new coaching environment may achieve the success required. In addition to the situation being self-rewarding, the coach is also needs to add external reinforcement such as "Well done! That's it! Good!" Some coaches are continually searching for errors. In their attempt at making the team better they try to eliminate errors by saying "No! That's not it!" Although skill learning can take place by directing the player away from errors using negative feedback, perhaps a more effective method would be for the coach to search out good elements of a player's performance and praise these. It is also sometimes helpful to allow the player to make errors in the performance. As long as the player knows the performance was in error and has the ability to correct the error, then errors can be beneficial to the skill-learning process. However, when praising good performance the coach should be discerning. Too much praise devalues the reinforcement they give. Make a player work for the praise, but when they have earned it, the coach should give it with gusto!

Skill

The priority of the coach must be to devote a major portion of time to the development of highly skilled and imaginative players. The coaching session should reflect a concern for skill improvement. General priorities regarding responsibilities during a game will allow the player more freedom to apply the skillful technique. Adherence to general principles of team play (not systems of play) will offer players more chance to adapt to all phases of play in all areas of the field.

Adaptability

The practice that the coach plans and implements is the vehicle by which the player improves skill and as such the practice should be challenging to the player, but not too complex. Coaches should coach to the level of players they are working with and be continually aware of how the player is performing under the constraints of the environment that has been set out for them. Every coach should constantly check the way in which their players react to the practice and be able to adapt a practice or change to an alternate practice if the practice is too simple or too complex, or just not suited to the players they have. This would require that within the coaching plan the coach should make provision for alternative practices that will bring about similar end results. The more aware a coach becomes of the players' abilities, the less likely the coach will be to use alternatives. This is of course presupposing that there was a correct initial selection of a coaching plan.

Persistence

Coaches of soccer skills should always encourage players to persist with a particular skill or technique despite the fact that it might take long periods of time to master. In most team games the attitude historically has been that realistic practice of the individual skills is a minor concern and that the game and its tactics are much more important. Athletes in individual sports such as golf, tennis, swimming and gymnastics spend long hours every day perfecting their technique. There is no reason why soccer players should be exempt from a training regime that requires mastery of the techniques within the game. Extended time practicing techniques such as shooting, short and long passing, dribbling etc. should be part of every player's day in addition to the team's tactical practice.

Individual Coaching

Homogeneous groupings, via age categories and skill level, are the basis for our competitive organizations. Because of this it is expected that all our players are at a similar developmental stage. This however is never the case, even at a professional level. Individual differences are a characteristic of all players and it would be folly to expect all players to react in a similar way to each practice. Whereas each practice should involve at least one coaching point, along with this coaching point should come the flexibility for a player to select his or her own interpretation and elaborate upon the main theme. Players should be encouraged to experiment with the techniques they have available. The coach should also realize the player's limitations and play down the weak points while building up the strong points. With this emphasis on coaching individuals comes the responsibility of giving individuals specific feedback that pertains to them. Coaches (even during half-time talks) should direct specific information to players and avoid too many generalities. Players will often avoid taking responsibility for a general statement directed at too many players.

Goalkeeping

Goalkeepers have invariably been abandoned at practice because of the numerical superiority of the outfield players. Along with every plan should be attached a series of specific practices for the goalkeeper; it is hoped that the goalkeeper will be involved as much as possible in the coaching sessions with his or her teammates. However, goalkeepers do need specialized training and provisions should be made for this within the coaching session. These activities should not be just time-filling exercises, but carefully prepared progressions (see the goalkeeping chapter in this book).

Punctuality

The coach should always arrive at the training ground early and dressed to perform. If the players arrive and they see the coach waiting for them with the balls laid out, cones placed in correct positions and corner flags placed in as goals, then the players' expectations are raised and they become inquisitive about the ensuing practice. The coach should then begin the practice on time despite late arrivals. It will be made quite clear that the practice begins just as the game begins, with everyone dressed and ready to play on time. The players who arrive early should have a self-evaluating general warm-up to be practicing before all of the other players arrive. These extra practice minutes will become a regular occurrence for all players towards the end of the season.

Coaching Theme

The coaching practice should be structured so that it is possible to relay information to players. A successful way of achieving this would be to maintain a common theme throughout the practice and also to work progressively through the season with an outline or plan of what is to be achieved during the year. With young players (8-12 years) it may be necessary to cover all aspects of play within the season and during each session concentrate upon technical improvement. It is especially important with very young players (8-10 years) that the skills of receiving the ball, dribbling and shooting are taught and practiced. Players who possess good technical ability can be integrated into any team formation. Older players (12+) may also respond well to coaching that is developed through team analysis. The coach may well have a general outline of the topics they wish to cover but the coach's personal plan must be adaptable to meet the problems that arise from analysis of games and practices. Since this book is aimed at coaches working at all levels, the planning must be flexible and left to the individual coach. Each chapter has been designed so as to provide a progression through a common theme and many alternate practices around that theme have been given. The coach should first choose their personal priorities. When this has been decided, the next step should be to plan a coaching session that will fulfill these prioritized objectives.

Administration

The volunteer coach devotes their time and effort to the players, and the frequency of practice often becomes a compromise between availability of players, game-day schedule and availability of the coach. A possible minimum of two coaching practices per week excluding game day would be advisable. For young players it is a mistake to begin these practice sessions too late in the evening. However, your practice time may be dictated by the community in which the players live. The length of practice is nearly always controlled by the coach. Many coaching practices extend well beyond the attention span of most young players. Younger players become tired, inattentive and generally disruptive. When motivational levels are low, it is worthless to proceed with a practice any further. Practices which are short, enjoyable and active are much more preferable as long as the coach can provide the players with practices they can use at home. One of the most time-consuming aspects of coaching players is the initial organization of the practice, and it is the small details of this organization that can make the difference between a good and an average coaching session. The following is an example of a checklist of items that are already available or potentially available to the team.

- Balls: correct size; large number
- Training vests: two sets of different colours
- Cones: at least 12 for marking areas
- Corner flags: over 5 feet tall, also used to make temporary goals
- Nets or portable or mini goals: pegs may be needed for the nets
- Watch: stopwatch with second hand may be required for some timed games in the practice
- First aid kit with bags of ice or cold packs: essential to have at all games and practices
- Analysis equipment: computer, video etc.

A smooth progression from one stage to the next should be evident in each coaching practice. This allows the player to understand how each part of the coaching session fits together. The transition between practices must try to maintain numerical groupings where possible (e.g. when players are in groups of three, the next step should try to move to groups of six). Playing areas should be adaptable with the least amount of movement of equipment. Coaches should try to avoid moving full-sized goals from one area to another or completely redesigning the space of playing area. Player grouping should be designated before practice, and the coach should know who is going where.

Playing Area

More attention should be paid to playing facilities. A greater control over field markings should be exerted over parks and recreation departments if at all possible. The 11-a-side field marking has limited use for a small number of players. There are many alternative field markings. For example here are some modified from an excellent earlier text, Teaching Soccer by William Thomson (1980; see bibliography).

Grid System

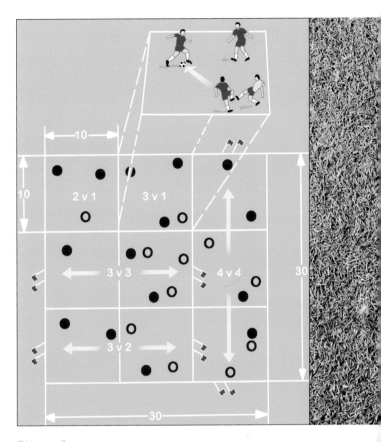

Diagram 2

Central Goals

Diagram 3

Mini Soccer

Diagram 4

Adapted Field Markings

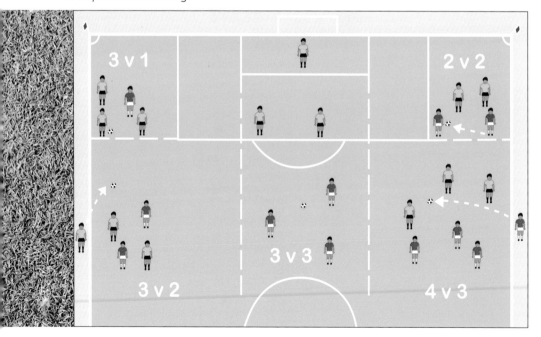

Diagram 5

In summary, the organization of a successful coaching session should include several vital ingredients to ensure transfer of training, satisfaction and intrinsic reinforcement. These include:

- Enjoyment
- Realism
- Activity and order of events
- Progress
- Skill
- Adaptability
- Persistence
- Individual coaching
- Goalkeeping
- Punctuality
- Coaching theme
- Administration
- Playing area

INSTRUCTION

Given that the coach has organized the practice with optimum planning and preparation, they must then provide the best possible instruction and feedback. Much of the early research into the effectiveness of coaching instruction mirrored the experimental designs used to investigate classroom teaching behaviours. From this research it became clear that teachers should have their teaching observed and analyzed in order to receive regular feedback with a view to modifying and improving their performance. Therefore, just as players can improve soccer performance by receiving accurate and objective feedback through objective analysis, so too can the coach improve their own performance if they are provided with adequate feedback.

In 1970 Flanders developed the Flanders Interaction Analysis System, which was one of the first observational instruments to systematically examine teacher-student interactions in the classroom. However, it wasn't until 1989 that Metzler used a computer-aided instrument to investigate the instructional behaviours of teachers and students within the physical education and sport setting. Although these instruments had identified the nature of verbal coaching behaviours, they did not fully describe the instructional style that coaches used in a soccer practice environment. These early systems failed to recognize the complexity of effective instruction and would therefore be limited to the scope of the original instrument. However, in the late 1980s and early 1990s Ken More (while working at UBC's Centre for Sport Analysis) developed a computer-aided coaching analysis instrument (CAI) specifically designed to quantitatively analyze the instructional profile of each and every verbal comment made during an observed coaching practice. The recording of comments into the computer was synchronized with a video recording of the coaching session, allowing the analyst to recall the image of the previously recorded behaviour, or search for any specific or group of behaviours. The instrument's architecture used by More is outlined in diagram 6.

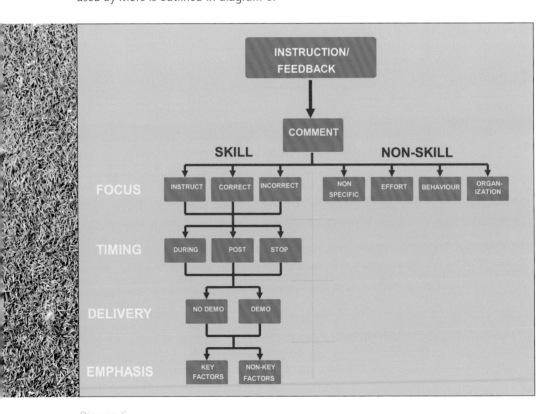

Diagram 6

While this structure was originally mapped onto the keyboard of a computer, its most recent application has been through performance analysis software FocusX2 (www. performanceinnovation.net; see bibliography). This software maintains the integrity of the data being logged on each comment, but permits instant compilation and display of summary data, and instant interactive access to the video associated with the data. This has very recently been updated with the launch of Focus X2i, a fully interactive video analysis and visual feedback app for the iPad.

After each comment the analyst uses the instrument to fully describe the comment. Questions the analyst should answer in a systematic manner revolve around whether a comment is about a skill or a non-skill event. For example if the comment was a non-skill comment it may be described as being concerned with the player's effort, the player's non-soccer-related behaviour, or organization of the practice, or is a non-specific comment. When the comment is directed toward a skill then several qualifying questions need answering: What was the focus of the comment? When was it delivered? Did the comment involve some form of demonstration? Was the comment directed to a key factor that was part of the original practice plan? The reasoning behind these descriptors of instruction and feedback was based upon best practice coaching behaviours. These are behaviours that would be expected of successful coaches.

Skill and Non-Skill Comments

Effective coaches spend more time instructing and providing feedback on the proposed content of the session than they do commenting on other unrelated aspects of the practice. The coach is concerned with the technique under consideration. If the coaching practice has been organized correctly at the outset and everyone understands the instruction and objective then there is less chance that coaches will spend time on non-skill items. While the occasional motivating comment to athletes can engage the attention, these comments should be used sparingly.

Focus of a Skill Comment

The focus of the comment could be on instruction or in the form of feedback. If adequate instruction has been provided at the start of practice then the remaining comments should be brief and provide feedback about the skill just performed. It is also preferable for players to receive a majority of positive feedback. The coach should be searching for good performance in addition to errors in performance. Coaches must try to balance feedback between correct and incorrect performance and be aware of age and ability when giving this feedback.

Timing of a Skill Comment

Consideration should be given to the timing of instruction and feedback. This timing is usually task specific. That is, when dealing with a complex skill the player may not be able to absorb feedback that is provided during the performance of the technique. Perhaps it would be more appropriate for the coach to wait until after the technique has been completed before offering any information. Also, if the player understands the errors they have made, then perhaps summary feedback should be provided after they have finished several attempts at the skill. Stopping or freezing play is a very effective method in coaching tactical aspects of teamwork (see the earlier chapter on defending for a good example of when freezing play can be used most effectively). When all players in the practice are frozen, the point made will be transmitted to all players and therefore involve them all in decision making.

Delivery of a Skill Comment

As discussed earlier in the book, demonstrations are an excellent method of providing information to players about past and potentially successful future performance (self-modeling). It is important however to remember that the demonstration (in whatever form it's delivered) must accurately portray the critical features of performance. Also each demonstration should be accompanied by clear and concise verbal instructions that ensure the athlete's attention is directed to the key factors of performance. We also recognize that it is unrealistic to require demonstrations as part of each comment. Verbal comments will still provide the majority of feedback, however where possible it is highly recommended to introduce a demonstration.

Emphasis of a Comment

The emphasis of the comments should be directed toward the key factors of performance that were outlined in the plan of the practice. As can be seen from the many practices described in this book, players use multiple techniques to achieve the goals set out for them. If the plan is to improve crossing ability, then the fey factors of crossing are the coach's main concern. For example, if during this crossing practice the defending players are making errors, the coach should not spend time commenting on their poor performance.

Providing Feedback to Coaches

This computer analysis instrument has been used previously by Ken More to describe the behaviours of coaches during a coaching practice and then to quantify the modification of these behaviours using the criteria set out above. More's results supported earlier work by Lawrence Locke who in 1984 stated that behaviour modification can occur through the use of data as direct feedback and information that provides recommendations for behaviour change. Coaches in More's study changed their coaching behaviour to approach best practice coaching behaviours. By way of example, diagram 7 illustrates the data sheets from one coaching practice. Included in these sheets are feedback notes that More used at the end of each coaching session along with video highlights of that session. Both quantitative data and video feedback were provided to the coach along with comments and recommendations from the analyst.

C OMMENT SUMMARY

Number of Drills	:2
Total Number of Comments	:129
Number of Skill Comments	:115
Number of Non- Skill Comments	:14

Analysis of 115 Skill Comments

Analyst notes

Focus of Skill Comments	Instruction	50	
	Correct	35	Great progress since last practice.
	Incorrect	30	
Timing of Skill Comments	During	65	Try to reduce comments made during an activity. Players don't pay attention. Show coach video examples of several comments that were not needed.
	Post	35	
	Stopped (Freeze)	15	
Delivery of Skill Comments	Number of Demonstrations	17	Try to vary the type of demonstration used.
Emphasis of Skill Comments	Key Factors	84	Excellent keep increasing this number.
	Non-key Factors	31	

Analysis of 14 Skill Comments

Non-Specific	6	This is good, keep these to a minimum especially the Non-Specific Comments.
Effort	0	
Behaviour	1	
Organization	7	

Diagram 7

After reviewing and discussing these data sheets with the analyst, the coach was then advised to write down their own reflections of the practice and the feedback they received. Before the next practice the coach would then set out coach behaviour objectives they would need to meet in the following training session. Making coaches aware of their behvioural traits during the practice is an important component of the entire coaching process.

SUMMARY

Throughout this book we have stressed the need to include objective match analysis within the coaching process, and diagram 2 outlines the many innovations that make the process more effective at changing players' and coaches' behaviours. The coaching practice is where learning and behaviour change occurs. Although we do accept that the coach fills many roles (from nutritionist to public relations spokesperson), providing instruction and feedback to the player during practice remains a priority. Effective instruction by the coach maximizes the potential for an optimal performance. Instruction requires the application of skills that range from planning and organizing the practice to presenting feedback and instruction to players. Simply stated, the coach is responsible for teaching the athlete what to do, how to do it and hopefully how to do it well. If we accept that players can benefit from information about their performance then it follows that coaches can also benefit from information about their performance. And since their performance on the training ground during practice is the most crucial aspect of their job, then it would be logical to not only analyze players' behaviours during practice but also the coach's behaviours. In this chapter we have highlighted several best practice behaviours that can assist the coach in improving their performance. It is possible to modify the coach's behaviours using the systematic analysis described here. Both players and coaches can benefit from the objective analysis of performance during the coaching practice.

PART 7
BIBLIOGRAPHY

MATCH ANALYSIS (PART 1)

Books

Anderson, C. & Sally, D. (2013). *The Numbers Game: Why Everything You Know About Football is Wrong.* London. UK: Penguin.

Carling, C., Williams, A. M. & Reilly, T. (2005). *Handbook of soccer match analysis: A systematic approach to improving performance.* Abingdon, Oxon: Routledge.

Hughes, C. (1980). *Soccer tactics and skills.* London: BBC/Queen Anne Press.

Kuper, S. & Szymanski, S. (2014) *Soccernomics: Why England Loses, Why Spain, Germany, and Brazil Win, and Why the U.S., Japan, Australia—And Even Iraq—Are Destined to become kings of the world's most popular sport.* New York. NY: Nation Books.

Reilly, T. (Ed), (1997). *Science and Soccer.* London: E. and F.N. Spon.

Reilly,T., Clarys, J. & Stibbe, A. (1993). *Science and Football II.* London: E. and F.N. Spon.

Reilly, T., Bangsbo, J. & Hughes, M. (Eds.), (1997). *Science and Football III.* London: E. and F. N. Spon.

Reilly, T., Lees, A., Davids, K. & Murphy, W. (Eds.), (1988). *Science and Football.* London: E. and F. N. Spon.

Wilson, J. (2010) *Inverting the Pyramid: The History of Football Tactics.* UK: Hachette.

Review articles

Bartlett, R. M. (2001). Performance analysis: can bringing together biomechanics and notational analysis benefit coaches? *International Journal of Performance Analysis in Sport, 1,* 122-126.

Bate, R. (1988). Football chance: tactics and strategy. In T. Reilly, A. Lees, K. Davids and W. Murphy (Eds.), *Science and Football.* London: E. and F. Spon, pp. 293-302.

Coutts, A.J. (2014) Evolution of football match analysis research, *Journal of Sports Sciences, 32,* 1829-1830.

Franks, I. M. (1988). Analysis of Association Football. *Soccer Journal,* Sept-Oct, 35-43.

Franks, I. M. & McGarry, T. (1996). The science of match analysis. In T. Reilly (Ed.) *Science and Soccer.* London: E. and F. N. Spon, 363-377.

Hughes, M. (1993). Notational analysis of football. In T. Reilly, J. Clarys & A. Stibbe (Eds.) *Science and Football II.* London: E. and F. N. Spon, pp. 151-159.

Hughes, M. & Sykes, I. (1994), Computerised notational analysis of the effects of the law changes in soccer upon patterns of play. *Journal of Sports Sciences, 12,* 180.

Medeiros, J. (2014). The winning formula: data analytics has become the latest tool keeping football teams one step ahead. *WIRED.CO.UK.* (23rd January), www.wired.co.uk/magazine/archive/2014/01/features/the-winning-formula

Nevill, A., Atkinson, G. & Hughes, M. (2008). Twenty five years of sports performance research in the Journal of Sports Science. *Journal of Sports Sciences, 26,* 413-426.

Sarmento, H., et al. (2014). Match analysis in football: a systematic review. *Journal of Sports Sciences, 32,* 1831-1843,

Original research

Ali, A. H. (1988) A statistical analysis of tactical movement patterns in soccer. In T. Reilly, A. Lees, K. Davids & W. Murphy (Eds.), *Science and Football.* London: E. & F. Spon.

Ali, A. H. (1992) Analysis of patterns of play of an international soccer team. In T. Reilly (Ed.), *Science and Football II.* London: E. & F. Spon.

Armatas, V., Yiannakos, A. & Sileloglou, P. (2007) Relationship between time and goal scoring in soccer games: Analysis of three World Cups. *International Journal of Performance Analysis in Sport, 7,* 48-58.

De Baranda, P., Ortega, E. & Palao, J. (2008). Analysis of goalkeeper's defense in the World Cup in Korea and Japan in 2002. *European Journal of Sport Science, 8,* 127-134.

Bradley, P.S., Lago-Peñas, C., Rey, E. & Sampaio, J. (2014). The influence of situational variables on ball possession in the English Premier League. *Journal of Sports Sciences, 32,* 1867-1873.

Carling, C. (2011). Influence of opposition team formation on physical and skill-related performance in a professional soccer team. *European Journal of Sport Science, 11,* 155-164.

Church, S. & Hughes, M. (1986). Patterns of play in Association Football: A computerised analysis. Paper presented at The First World Congress of Science and Football, Liverpool, 13th-17th April.

Franks, I. M. (1982). Quantitative Analysis of Team Games. In L. Wankel and R. Wilberg (Eds), *Psychology of Sport and Motor Behavior: Research and Practice.* Edmonton: University of Alberta Press, pp. 150-157.

Franks, I. M. & Goodman, D. (1986). Computer-assisted technical analysis of sport. *Coaching Review,* May-June, 58-64.

Franks, I. M., Goodman, D. & Miller, G. (1983). Human factors in sport systems: An empirical investigation of events in team games. *Proceedings of the Human Factors Society: 27th Annual meeting,* 383-386.

Franks, I. M., McGarry, T. & Hanvey, T. (1999). From notation to training: analysis of the penalty kick. *Insight: F. A. Coaches Association Journal, 2,* 24-26.

Franks, I. M. & Hanvey, T. (1997). Cues for goalkeepers: High-tech methods used to measure penalty shot response. *Soccer Journal, 42,* 30-33.

Garganta, J. & Goncalves, G. (1996). Comparison of successful attacking play in male and female Portuguese national soccer teams. In M. Hughes (Ed.) *Notational Analysis of Sport – I and II.* Cardiff: University of Wales Institute Cardiff, pp. 79-85.

Garganta, J., Maia, J. & Basto, F. (1997). Analysis of goal scoring patterns of European top level soccer teams. In T. Reilly, J. Bangsbo, and M. Hughes, (Eds.) *Science and Football III.* London: E. and F. N. Spon, pp. 246-250.

Grant, A., Reilly, T., Williams, M. & Borrie, A. (1998). Analysis of the goals scored in the 1998 World Cup. *Insight: The FA Coaches Association Journal, 2,* 18-22.

Harris, S. % Reilly, T. (1988) Space, teamwork and attacking success in soccer. In T. Reilly, A. Lees, K. Davids & W. Murphy (Eds.). *Science and Football.* London: E. & F. Spon.

Hughes, M. D. (2005). Notational analysis. In: R. Bartlett, C. Gratton, and C. G. Rolf (Eds.). *Encyclopaedia of International Sports Studies.* London: Routledge, pp. 1-7.

Hughes, M. & Bartlett, R. (2002). The use of performance indicators in performance analysis. *Journal of Sports Science, 20,* 739-754.

Hughes, M., Dawkins, N., David, R. & Mills, J. (1998). The perturbation effect and goal opportunities in soccer. *Journal of Sports Sciences, 16,* 20.

Hughes M. and Franks, I. M. (2005) Analysis of passing sequences, shots and goals in soccer. *Journal of Sports Sciences, 23,* 509-514.

Hughes, M. & Probert, G. (2006). A technical analysis of elite male soccer players by position and success. In H. Dancs, M. Hughes, and P. O'Donoghue, (Eds.) *Notational Analysis of Sport – VII.* Cardiff: University of Wales Institute Cardiff, pp. 76-91.

Hughes, M., Robertson, K. & Nicholson, A. (1988). An Analysis of 1984 World Cup of Association Football. In T. Reilly, A. Lees, K. Davids and W. Murphy (Eds.). *Science and Football.* London: E. and F. N. Spon, 363-368.

Hughes, M. & Wells, J. (2002). Analysis of penalties taken in shoot-outs. *International Journal of Performance Analysis of Sport, 2,* 55-72.

James, N., Mellalieu, S. & Hollely, C. (2002). Analysis of strategies in soccer as a function of European and domestic competition. *International Journal of Performance Analysis in Sport, 2,* 85-103.

Jinshan, X., Xiaoke, C., Yamanaka, K. & Matsumoto, M. (1993). Analysis of the goals in the 14th World Cup. In. T. Reilly, J. Clarys and A. Stibbe (Eds.). *Science and Football II.* London: E. & F. N. Spon, pp.203-205.

Jones, P. D., James, N. & Mellalieu, S. D. (2004). Possession as a performance indicator in soccer. *International Journal of Performance Analysis in Sport, 4,* 98-102.

Kempe, M., Memmert, D., Nopp, S. & Volgelbein, M. (2014). Possession vs. Direct Play: Evaluating Tactical Behavior in Elite Soccer. *International Journal of Sport Science, 4,* 35-41.

Lago, C. & Martín, R. (2007). Determinants of possession of the ball in soccer. *Journal of Sports Sciences, 25,* 969-974.

Lago-Ballesteros, J. & Lago-Peñas, C. (2010). Performance in team sports: Identifying the keys to success in soccer. *Journal of Human Kinetics, 25,* 85-91.

Lago-Peñas, C. & Dellal, A. (2010). Ball possession strategies in elite soccer according to the evolution of the match-score: The influence of situational variables. *Journal of Human Kinetics, 25,* 93-100.

Lago-Penas, C. & Lago-Ballesteros, J. (2011). Game location and team quality effects on performance profiles in professional soccer. *Journal of Sports Science and Medicine, 10,* 465-471.

Lewis, M. & Hughes, M. D. (1988). Attacking play in the 1986 World Cup of Association Football. *Journal of Sport Science, 6,* 169.

Lewis, M. & Hughes, M. (1988) Attacking play in the 1986 World Cup of Association Football. *Journal of Sport Science, 6,* 169.

Luhtanen, P. H., Korhonen, V. & Ilkka, A. (1997). A new notational analysis system with special reference to the comparison of Brazil and its opponents in the World Cup 1994. In T. Reilly, J. Bangsbo & M. Hughes (Eds.). *Science and Football III.* London: E. & F. N. Spon, pp.229-232.

Luhtanen, P., Belinskij, A., Häyrinen, M. & Vänttinen, T. (2002) A computer aided team analysis of Euro 2000 in soccer. *International Journal of Performance Analysis of Sport, 1,* 74-83.

Marqués-Bruna,P., Lees A. & Paul Grimshaw, P. (2007). Development of technique in soccer. *International Journal of Coaching Science, 1,* 51-62.

McGarry, T. & Franks, I. M. (2000). On winning the penalty shoot-out in soccer. *Journal of Sports Sciences, 18,* 401-409.

Noel, B., Furley, P., van der Kamp, J., Dicks, M. & Memmert, D. (2015). The development of a method for identifying penalty kick strategies in association football. *Journal of Sports Sciences, 33,* 1-10.

Odetoyinbo, K., Sapsford, P. & Thomas, S. (1997). Analysis of the effects for the 1994 FIFA experiment on semi-professional soccer. *Journal of Sport Sciences, 5,* 20.

Olsen, E. & Larsen, O. (1997). Use of match analysis by coaches. In T. Reilly, J. Bangsbo and M. Hughes (Eds.). *Science and Football III.* London: E. & F. N. Spon, pp. 209-220.

Papadimitriou, K., Taxildaris, K., Alexopulos, P., Mavromatis, G. & Papas, M. (2001). Defensive actions of finalist soccer teams in 18th World Cup in France. *Journal of Human Movement Studies, 41,* 125-139.

Partridge, D. & Franks, I. M. (1989). A detailed analysis of crossing opportunities from the 1986 World Cup. (Part I). *Soccer Journal. May-June,* 47-50.

Partridge, D. & Franks, I. M. (1989). A detailed analysis of crossing opportunities from the 1986 World Cup. (Part II). *Soccer Journal. June-July,* 45-48.

Partridge, D. & Franks, I. M. (1993). Computer-aided analysis of sport performance: An example from soccer. *The Physical Educator, 50,* 208-215.

Partridge, D. & Franks, I. M. (1990). A comparative analysis of technical performance: USA and West Germany in the 1990 World Cup Finals. *Soccer Journal, Nov-Dec,* 57-62.

Pollard, R. & Pollard, G. (2005). Long term trends in home advantage in professional team sports in North America and England (1876-2003). *Journal of Sports Sciences, 23,* 337-350.

Reep C. (1989). Charles Reep. *The Punter (The Scottish Football Association).* Sept, 31-37.

Scoulding, A., James, N. & Taylor, J. (2004). Passing in the soccer World Cup 2002. *International Journal of Performance Analysis in Sport, 4,* 36-41.

Silva, P., Duarte, R., Sampaio, J., Aguiar, P., Davids, K., Araújo, D. & Garganta, J. (2014). Field dimension and skill level constrain team tactical behaviours in small-sided and conditioned games in football. *Journal of Sports Sciences, 32,* 1888-1896.

Tenga, A., Holme, I., Ronglan, L. T. & Bahr, R. (2010a). Effect of playing tactics on achieving score-box possessions in a random series of team possessions from Norwegian professional soccer matches. *Journal of Sports Sciences, 28,* 245-255.

Tenga, A., Holme, I., Ronglan, L. T. & Bahr, R. (2010b). Effect of playing tactics on goal scoring in Norwegian professional soccer. *Journal of Sports Sciences, 28,* 237-244.

Yamanaka, K., Hughes, M. & Lott, M. (1993). An analysis of playing patterns in the 1990 World Cup for Association Football. In T. Reilly, J. Clarys and A. Stibbe (Eds.) *Science and Football II.* London: E. and F. N. Spon, pp. 206-214.

TIME/MOTION ANALYSIS OF SOCCER PLAYERS (PART 1)

Books

Carling, C., Reilly, T. & Williams, A. (Eds.). (2009). *Performance assessment for field sports.* London: Routledge.

Review articles

Castellano, J., Blanco-Villaseñor, A. & Álvarez, D. (2011). Contextual variables and time-motion analysis in soccer. *International Journal of Sports Medicine, 32,* 415-421.

Drust, B., Atkinson, G. & Reilly, T. (2007). Future perspectives in the evaluation of the physiological demands of soccer. *Sports Medicine, 37,* 783-805.

Drust, B. & Green, M. (2013). Science and football: Evaluating the influence of science on performance. *Journal of Sports Sciences, 31,* 1377-1382.

Reilly, T. (1990). Football. In T. Reilly, N. Secher, P. Snell, and C. Williams (Eds.). *Physiology of Sports.* London: E & FN Spon. Ch. 13, pp. 328-376.

Strudwick, T. (2012, May 14-16). Contemporary issues in the physical preparation of elite male soccer players. In *Proceedings of the 3rd World Conference of Science and Soccer.* Ghent: Ghent University Press, p. 113.

Original research

Barros, R., et al. (2007). Analysis of the distances covered by first division Brazilian soccer players obtained with an automatic tracking method. *Journal of Sports Science and Medicine, 6,* 233-242.

Bradley, P., Di Mascio, M., Peart, D., Olsen, P. & Sheldon, B. (2010). High-intensity activity profiles of elite soccer players at different performance levels. *Journal of Strength and Conditioning Research, 24,* 2343-2351.

Bradley, P. S., Sheldon, W., Wooster, B., Olsen, P., Boanas, P. & Krustrup, P. (2009). High-intensity running in English FA Premier League soccer matches. *Journal of Sports Sciences, 27,* 159-168.

Brooke, J. D. & Knowles, J. E. (1974). A movement analysis of player behaviour in soccer match performance. *Proceedings of British Sport Psychology Conference,* pp.246-256.

Buchheit, M., Allen, A., Poon, T. K., Modonutti, M., Gregson, W. & Di Salvo, V. (2014). Integrating different tracking systems in football: multiple camera semi-automatic system, local position measurement and GPS technologies. *Journal of Sports Sciences, 32,* 1844-1857.

Carling, C. (2010). Analysis of physical activity profiles when running with the ball in a professional soccer team. *Journal of Sports Sciences, 28,* 319-326.

Carling, C. & Bloomfield, J. (2010). The effect of an early dismissal on player work-rate in a professional soccer match. *Journal of Science and Medicine in Sport, 3,* 126-128.

Carling, C. & Dupont, G. (2011). Are declines in physical performance associated with a reduction in skill-related performance during professional soccer match-play? *Journal of Sports Sciences, 29,* 63-71.

Dellal, A., et al. (2011). Comparison of physical and technical performance in European soccer match-play: FA Premier League and La Liga. *European Journal of Sport Science, 11,* 51-59.

Dellal, A., Wong, D. P., Moalla, W. & Chamari, K. (2010). Physical and technical activity of soccer players in the French First League: With special reference to their playing position. *International Sportmed Journal, 11,* 278-290.

Di Salvo, V., Baron, R., González-Haro, C., Gormasz, C., Pigozzi, F. & Bachl, N. (2010). Sprinting analysis of elite soccer players during European Champions League and UEFA Cup matches. *Journal of Sports Sciences, 28,* 1489-1494.

Di Salvo, V., Baron, R., Tschan, H., Calderon Montero, F., Bachl, N. & Pigozzi, F. (2007). Performance characteristics according to playing position in elite soccer. *International Journal of Sports Medicine, 28,* 222-227.

Di Salvo, V., Benito, P., Calderon, F., Di Salvo, M. & Pigozzi, F. (2008). Activity profile of elite goalkeepers during football match-play. *Journal of Sports Medicine and Physical Fitness, 48,* 443-446.

Di Salvo, V., Gregson, W., Atkinson, G., Tordoff, P. and Drust, B. (2009). Analysis of high intensity activity in Premier League Soccer. *International Journal of Sports Medicine, 30,* 205-212.

Gregson, W., Drust, B., Atkinson, G. & Di Salvo, V. (2010). Match-to-match variability of high-speed activities in Premier League soccer. *International Journal of Sports Medicine, 31,* 237-242.

Kaplan, T., Erkmen, N. & Taskin, H. (2009). The evaluation of the running speed and agility performance in professional and amateur soccer players. *Journal of Strength and Conditioning Research, 23,* 774-778.

Leser, R. (2012). A wireless position tracking system for measuring sports performance in game sports. In *Book of Abstracts of the 3rd World Conference on Science and Soccer,* p. 68.

Leser, R., Schleindlhuber, A., Baca, A. & Keith, L. (2014). Accuracy of an UWB-based position tracking system used for time-motion analyses in game sports. *European Journal of Sport Science, 14,* 635-642.

Mayhew, S. R. & Wenger, H. A. (1985). Time-motion analysis of professional soccer. *Journal of Human Movement Studies, 11,* 49-52.

Nedergaard, N. J., Kersting, U. & Lake, M. (2014). Using accelerometry to quantify deceleration during a high-intensity soccer turning manoeuvre. *Journal of Sports Sciences, 32,* 1897-1905.

O'Donoghue, P., Boyd, M., Lawlor, J. & Bleakley, E. (2001). Time-motion analysis of elite, semi-professional and amateur soccer competition. *Journal of Human Movement Studies, 41,* 1-12.

Reilly, T. & Thomas, V. (1976). A motion analysis of work-rate in different positional roles in professional football match-play. *Journal of Human Movement Studies, 2,* 87-97.

Rico, J. & Bangsbo, J. (1996). Coding system to evaluate actions with the ball during a soccer match. In M. Hughes (Ed.). *Notational Analysis of Sport – I & II.* Cardiff: UWIC, pp. 90-95.

Varley, M. C., Gabbett, T. & Aughey, R. J. (2014). Activity profiles of professional soccer, rugby league and Australian football match play. *Journal of Sports Sciences, 32,* 1858-1866.

Withers, R. T., Maricic, Z., Wasilewski, S. & Kelly, L. (1982). Match analyses of Australian professional soccer players. *Journal of Human Movement Studies, 8,* 158-176.

METHODS AND TECHNIQUES OF MATCH ANALYSIS (PART 1)

Books

Baca, A. (Ed.) (2015). *Computer Science in Sport. Research and Practice.* London: Routledge.

Hughes, M. & Franks, I. M. (1997). *Notational Analysis of Sport.* E. and F. N. Spon. London.

Hughes, M. & Franks, I. M. (2004). *Notational Analysis of Sport II – Improving Coaching and Performance in Sport.* E. and F. N. Spon. London.

Hughes, M. & Franks, I. M. (2008). *Essentials of Performance Analysis.* London: E. and F. N. Spon.

Hughes, M. & Franks, I. M. (2015). *Essentials of Performance Analysis (2nd ed.).* London: Routledge/Taylor and Francis.

Taylor, J. (2014). *The Science of Soccer: A Bouncing Ball and a Banana Kick.* South Korea: University of New Mexico Press.

Review articles

Franks, I. M. & Goodman, D. (1984). A hierarchical approach to performance analysis. *SPORTS, June,* 4pp.

Franks, I. M. & Goodman, D. (1986). A systematic approach to analyzing sports performance, *Journal of Sports Sciences, 4,* 49-59.

Franks, I. M., Goodman, D. & Paterson, D. (1986). The real time analysis of sport: an overview. *Canadian Journal of Sports Sciences, 11,* 55-57.

Franks, I. M. & Nagelkerke, P. (1988). The Use of Computer Interactive Video Technology in Sport Analysis. *Ergonomics, 31,* 1593-1603.

Gerisch, G. & Reichelt, M. (1993). Computer and video-aided analysis of football games, In T. Reilly, J. Clarys and A. Stibbe (Eds.) *Science and Football II.* London: E. and F. N. Spon, pp. 167-173.

Gréhaigne, J. & Mahut, B. (2001). Qualitative observation tools to analyse soccer. *International Journal of Performance Analysis in Sport, 1,* 52-61.

Hughes, M. (1988). Computerised notation analysis in field games. *Ergonomics, 31,* 1585-1592.

Hughes, M. & Bartlett, R. (2002). The use of performance indicators in performance analysis. *Journal of Sports Sciences, 20,* 739-754.

Hughes, M. & Franks, I. M. (1991) A time-motion analysis of squash players using a mixed-image video tracking system. *Ergonomics, 37,* 23-29.

Lees, A. (2002). Technique analysis in sports: A critical review. *Journal of Sports Sciences, 20,* 813-828.

Lees, A. & Nolan, L. (1998). The biomechanics of soccer: A review. *Journal of Sports Sciences, 16,* 211-234.

Liebermann, D. G., Katz, L., Hughes, M., Bartlett, R. M., McClements, J. & Franks, I. M. (2002). Advances in the application of information technology to sport performance. *Journal of Sports Sciences, 20,* 755-769

Nevill, A. M., Atkinson, G., Hughes, M. & Cooper, S. M. (2002). Statistical methods for analysing sport performance and notational analysis data. *Journal of Sports Sciences, 20,* 829-844.

Partridge, D., Mosher, R. E. & Franks, I. M. (1992). A computer assisted analysis of technical performance, In T. Reilly, J. P. Clarys & A. B. Stibbe (Eds.). *Science and Football II.* London: E. & F. N. Spon, pp. 221-232.

Sampaio, J. & Maçãs, V. (2012). Measuring tactical behaviour in football. *International Journal of Sports Medicine, 33,* 395-401.

Original research

Atkinson, G. & Nevill, A. M. (2001). Selected issues in the design and analysis of sport performance research. *Journal of Sports Sciences, 19,* 811-827.

Castellano, J., Blanco-Villasenor, A. & Alvarez, D. (2011). Contextual variables and time-motion analysis in soccer. *International Journal of Sports Medicine, 32,* 415-421.

Ferreira, P. F., Volossovitch, A. & Gonçalves, I. (2003). Methodological and Dynamic Perspective to Determine Critical Moments in Sport Games. *International Journal of Computer Science in Sport, 2,* 119-122.

O'Donoghue, P. (2005). Normative profiles of sports performance. *International Journal of Performance Analysis in Sport, 4,* 67-76.

O'Donoghue, P. (2007). Reliability Issues in Performance Analysis. *International Journal of Performance Analysis in Sport, 7,* 35-48.

O'Donoghue, P. G, Dubitzky, W., Lopes, P., Berrar, D., Lagan, K., Hassan, D., Bairner, A. & Darby, P. (2003). An Evaluation of Quantitative and Qualitative Methods of Predicting the 2002 FIFA World Cup. *Proceedings of the World Congress of Science and Football V.* Lisbon, Portugal, pp. 44-45.

DECISION MAKING (PART 2)

Books

Broadbent, D. E. (1971). *Decision and Stress.* London: Academic Press.

Durso, F. T. (Ed.) (2007). *Handbook of Applied Cognition (2nd ed.).* Chichester, UK: John Wiley & Sons.

Lee, T. D. (2011). *Motor Control in Everyday Actions.* Champaign, IL: Human Kinetics.

Legge, D. & Barber, P. J. (1976). *Information and Skill.* London: Methuen.

Schmidt, R. A. & Lee, T. D. (2011). *Motor Control and Learning: A Behavioral Emphasis (5th ed.).* Champaign, IL: Human Kinetics.

Schmidt, R. A. & Lee, T. D. (2015). *Motor learning and performance: From principles to application. (5th ed.).* Champaign, IL: Human Kinetics.

Review articles

Abernathy, B. (1991). Visual-search strategies and decision-making in sport. *International Journal of Sport Psychology, 22,* 189-210.

Araújo, D., Davids, K. & Hristovski, R. (2006). The ecological dynamics of decision making in sport, *Psychology of Sport and Exercise, 7,* 653-676

Baker, J., Cote, J. & Abernethy, B. (2003). Sport-Specific Practice and the Development of Expert Decision-Making in Team Ball Sports. *Journal of Applied Sport Psychology, 15,* 12-25.

Gréhaigne, J.-F., Godbout, P. & Bouthier, D. (2001). The teaching and learning of decision making in team sports. *Quest, 53,* 59-76.

Johnson, J. G. (2006). Cognitive modeling of decision making in sports. *Psychology of Sport and Exercise, 7,* 631-652.

Moran, A. (2009). Cognitive psychology in sport: Progress and prospects. *Psychology of Sport and Exercise, 10,* 420-426.

Ripoll, H., Kerlirzin, Y., Stein, J. F. & Reine, B. (1995). Analysis of information processing, decision-making, and visual search strategies in complex problem solving sport situations. *Human Movement Science, 14,* 325-349.

Rulence-Pâques, P., Fruchart, E., Dru, V. & Mullet, E. (2005). Decision-making in a soccer game: a developmental perspective. *European Review of Applied Psychology, 55,* 131-136.

Williams, A. M. (2000). Perceptual skill in soccer: Implications for talent identification and development. *Journal of Sports Sciences, 18,* 727-736.

Original research

Donders, F. C. (1967). On the speed of mental processes, In W. G. Koster (Ed. & Trans.). *Attention and Performance II.* Amsterdam: North-Holland. (Original work published in 1868).

Hick, W. E. (1953). On the rate of gain of information. *Quarterly Journal of Experimental Psychology, 4,* 11-26.

Hyman, R. (1953). Stimulus information as a determinant of reaction time. *Journal of Experimental Psychology, 45,* 188-196.

Mann, D. T. Y., Williams, A. M., Ward, P. & Janelle, C. M. (2007). Perceptual-Cognitive Expertise in Sport: A Meta-Analysis. *Journal of Sport and Exercise Psychology, 29,* 457-478.

Memmert, D. & Furley, P. (2007). "I spy with my little eye!": breadth of attention, inattentional blindness, and tactical decision making in team sports. *Journal of Sport and Exercise Psychology, 29,* 365-381.

Merkel, J. (1885). Die zeitlichen Verhältnisse der Willensthätigkeit. *Philosophische Studien, 2,* 73-127. (Cited in Woodworth, R.S., 1938, Experimental Psychology. New York: Holt).

Poplu, G., Baratgin, J., Mavromatis, S. & Ripoll, H. (2003). What kind of processes underlie decision making in soccer simulation? An implicit-memory investigation. *International Journal of Sport and Exercise Psychology, 1,* 390-405.

Raab, M. (2007). Think SMART, not hard—a review of teaching decision making in sport from an ecological rationality perspective. *Physical Education and Sport Pedagogy, 12,* 1-22.

Vaeyens, R., Lenoir, M., Williams, A. M., Mazyn, L. & Philippaerts, R. M. (2007). The Effects of Task Constraints on Visual Search Behavior and Decision-Making Skill in Youth Soccer Players. *Journal of Sport and Exercise Psychology, 29,* 147-169.

Vaeyens, R., Lenoir, M., Williams, A. M. & Philippaerts, R. M. (2007). Mechanisms Underpinning Successful Decision Making in Skilled Youth Soccer Players: An Analysis of Visual Search Behaviors. *Journal of Motor Behavior, 39,* 395-408.

Williams, A. M., Ward, P., Bell-Walker, J. & Ford, P. R. (2012). Perceptual-cognitive expertise, practice history profiles and recall performance in soccer. *British Journal of Psychology, 103,* 393-411.

MOTOR SKILL ACQUISITION
AND THE LEARNING PROCESS (PART 3 AND 4)

Books

Magill, R. A. & Anderson, D. I. (2013). *Motor learning: Concepts and applications (10th ed.).* Singapore: McGraw-Hill International Editions.

Williams, A. M. & Hodges, N. J. (Eds.) (2004). *Skill Acquisition in Sport: Research, Theory and Practice.* London, UK: Routledge.

Schmidt, R. A. & Lee, T. D. (2011). *Motor Control and Learning: A Behavioral Emphasis (5th ed.).* Champaign, IL: Human Kinetics.

Schmidt, R. A. & Lee, T. D. (2015). *Motor Learning and Performance: From Principles to Application. (5th ed.).* Champaign, IL: Human Kinetics.

Reviews articles

Adams, J. A. (1987). Historical review and appraisal of research on the learning, retention and transfer of human motor skills. *Psychological Bulletin, 101,* 41-74

Annett, J. (1994). The learning of motor skills: Sports science and ergonomics perspectives. *Ergonomics, 37,* 5-16.

Janelle, C. M. & Hatfield, B. D. (2008). Visual attention and brain processes that underlie expert performance: Implications for sport and military psychology. *Military Psychology, 20,* 39-69.

Kalveram, K. T. (1999). A modified model of the Hebbian synapse and its role in motor learning. *Human Movement Science, 18,* 185-199.

Kantak, S. S. & Winstein, C. J. (2012). Learning-performance distinction and memory processes for motor skills: A focused review and perspective. *Behavioural Brain Research, 228,* 219-231.

Restle, F. (1970). Theory of serial pattern learning. *Psychological Review, 77,* 481-495.

Vereijken, B., van Emmerick, R. E. A., Whiting, H. T. A. & Newell, K. M. (1992). Freezing degrees of freedom in skill acquisition. *Journal of Motor Behavior, 24,* 133-142.

Original research

Bryan, W. L. & Harter, N. (1899). Studies on the telegraphic language: The acquisition of a hierarchy of habits. *Psychological Review, 6,* 345-375.

Fischman, M. G. (2015). On the continuing problem of inappropriate learning measures: Comment on Wulf et al. (2014) and Wulf et al. (2015). *Human Movement Science, 42,* 225-231.

Franks, I. M. & Wilberg, R. B., (1982). The generation of movement patterns during the acquisition of a pursuit tracking task. *Human Movement Science, 1,* 251-272.

Franks, I. M., Wilberg, R. B. & Fishburne, G. J. (1985). The planning organization and execution of serially ordered movement patterns: A coding perspective. In D. Goodman, R. B. Wilberg, and I. M. Franks (Eds.), *Differing Perspectives in Motor Learning, Memory and Control.* Amsterdam: North-Holland, pp. 175-191.

Heuer, H. & Luttgen, J. (2014) Motor Learning with fading and growing haptic guidance. *Experimental Brain Research, 232,* 2229-2242.

Land, W. M, Frank, C. & Schack, T. (2014). The influence of attentional focus on the development of skill representation in a complex action. *Psychology of Sport and Exercise, 15,* 30-38.

Lohse, K. R., Wadden, K., Boyd, L. A. & Hodges, N. J. (2015). Motor skill acquisition across short and long time scales: A meta-analysis of neuroimaging data. *Neuropsychologia, 59,* 130-141.

McNevin, N. H., Shea, C. H. & Wulf. G. (2003). Increasing the distance of an external focus of attention enhances learning. *Psychological Research, 67,* 22-29.

Pascua, L. A. M., Wulf, G. & Lewthwaite, R. (2015). Additive benefits of external focus and enhanced performance expectancy for motor learning. *Journal of Sports Sciences, 33,* 58-66.

Shmuelof, L., Krakauer, J. W. & Mazzoni, P. (2012). How is a motor skill learned? Change and invariance at the levels of task success and trajectory control. *Journal of Neurophysiology, 108,* 578-94.

Wolpert, D. M., Diedrichsen, J. & Flanagan, J. R. (2011). Principles of sensorimotor learning. *Nature Reviews Neuroscience, 12,* 739-751.

Wulf, G. (2013). Attentional focus and motor learning: A review of 15 years. *International Review of Sport and Exercise Psychology, 6,* 77-104.

Wulf, G., Chiviacowsky, S. & Drews, R. (2015). External focus and autonomy support: Two important factors in motor learning have additive benefits. *Human Movement Science, 40,* 176-184.

MOTOR SKILL ACQUISITION THROUGH DEMONSTRATION, MODELING AND OBSERVATION (PART 3 AND 4)

Books

Dowrick, P. W. & Biggs, S. J. (Eds.) (1983). *Using Video.* London: John Wiley and Sons.

Dowrick, P. W. (Ed.) (1991). *A Practical Guide to Using Video in the Behavioral Sciences.* New York: John Wiley and Sons.

Reviews articles

Dowrick, P. W. (1999). A review of self-modeling and related interventions. *Applied and Preventative Psychology, 8,* 23-29.

Franks, I. M. & Maile, L. J. (1991). The use of video in sport-skill acquisition. In P. W. Dowrick (Ed.) *A Practical Guide to Using Video in the Behavioral Sciences.* New York: John Wiley and Sons, pps. 231-243.

Hayes, S. J., Hodges, N. J., Scott, A. M., Horn, R. R. & Williams, A. M. (2007). The efficacy of demonstrations in teaching children an unfamiliar movement skill: the effects of object orientated actions and point-light demonstrations. *Journal of Sports Sciences, 25,* 559-579.

Hodges, N. J. & Franks, I. M. (2004). Instructions, demonstrations and the learning process: creating and constraining movement options. In A. M. Williams and N. J. Hodges (Eds.), 174.

Holmes, P. & Calmels, C. (2008). A neuroscientific review of imagery and observation use in sport. *Journal of Motor Behavior, 40,* 433-445.

Maslovat, D., Hayes, S., Horn, R. & Hodges, N (2010). Motor learning through observation. In D. Elliot and M. Khan, (Eds.). *Vision and Goal-Directed Movement: Neurobehavioral Perspectives.* Champaign, IL: Human Kinetics, pp. 315-339.

McCullagh, P. & Weiss, M. R. (2001). Modeling: Considerations for motor skill performance and psychological responses. In R. N. Singer, H. A. Hausenblas & C. M. Janelle (Eds.), *Handbook of sport psychology (2nd ed.).* London: Wiley Publishers, pp. 205-238.

Trower, P. & Keily, B. (1983). Video feedback: Help or hindrance? A review and analysis. In P. W. Dowrick and S. J. Biggs (Eds.), *Using Video.* London: John Wiley and Sons, pp.181-198.

Wulf, G. (2013). Attentional focus and motor learning: A review of 15 years. *International Review of Sport and Exercise Psychology, 6,* 77-104.

Wulf, G. & Prinz, W. (2001). Directing attention to movement effects enhances learning: A review. *Psychonomic Bulletin and Review, 8,* 648-660.

Original research

Calvo-Merino, B., Grezes, J., Glaser, D. E., Passingham, R. E. & Haggard, P. (2006). Seeing or doing? Influence of visual and motor familiarity in action observation. *Current Biology, 16,* 1905-1910.

Gould, D. & Roberts, G. (1982). Modeling and motor skill acquisition. *Quest, 33,* 214-230.

Gould, D. & Weiss, M. (1981). The effects of model similarity and model talk on self-efficacy and muscular endurance. *Journal of Sport Psychology, 3,* 17-29.

Hodges, N. J., Hayes, S. J., Eaves, D., Horn, R. & Williams, A. M. (2006). End-point trajectory matching as a method for teaching kicking skills. *International Journal of Sport Psychology, 37,* 230-247.

Martini, R., Rymal, A. M. & Ste-Marie, D. M. (2011). Investigating self-as-a-model techniques and underlying cognitive processes in adults learning the butterfly swim stroke. *International Journal of Sports Science and Engineering, 5,* 242-256.

McCullagh, P. & Caird, J. K. (1990). Correct and learning models and the use of model knowledge of results in the acquisition and retention of a motor skill. *Journal of Human Movement Studies, 18,* 107-116.

Ram, N. & McCullagh, P. (2003). Self-modeling: Influence on psychological responses and physical performance. *Sport Psychology, 17,* 220-241.

Ste-Marie, D. M., Rymal, A. M., Vertes, K. & Martini, R. (2011). Self-Modeling and competitive beam performance enhancement examined within a self-regulation perspective. *Journal of Applied Sport Psychology, 23,* 292-307.

Ste-Marie, D. M., Vertes, K., Law, B. & Rymal, A. M. (2013). Learner controlled self-observation is advantageous for motor skill acquisition. *Frontiers in Psychology, 3,* Article 556, 1-10.

Ste-Marie, D. M., Vertes, K., Rymal, A. M. & Martini, R. (2011) Feedforward self-modeling enhances skill acquisition in children learning trampoline skills. *Frontiers in Psychology, 2,* Article 155, 1-7.

MOTOR SKILL ACQUISITION AND THE EFFECTS
OF PRACTICE AND PLAY (PART 3 AND 4)

Books

Christina, R. W. & Corcos, D. M. (1988). *Coaches guide to teaching sport skills.* Champaign, IL: Human Kinetics.

Syed, M. (2010). *Bounce: Mozart, Federer, Picasso, Beckham and the Science of Success.* New York: HarperCollins Publishers.

Ericsson, K. A., Charness, N., Feltovich, P. J. & Hoffman R. R. (Eds.) (2006). *The Cambridge handbook of expertise and expert performance.* New York: Cambridge University Press.

Starkes, J. L. & Ericsson, K. A. (Eds.) (2003). *Expert Performance in Sports: Advances in Research on Sport Expertise.* Champaign, IL: Human Kinetics.

Thorndike, E. L. (1906). *The principles of teaching, based on psychology.* New York: Seiler.

Reviews articles

Côté, J. The influence of family in the development of talent in sport. *The Sport Psychologist, 13,* 395-417.

Côté, J. & Abernethy, B. (2012). A developmental approach to sport expertise. In S. Murphy (Ed.). *The Oxford handbook of sport and performance psychology.* New York, NY: Oxford University Press, pp. 435-447

Côté, J., Baker, J. & Abernethy, B. (2007) Practice and Play in the Development of Sport Expertise. In R. Eklund and G. Tenenbaum, (Eds.). *Handbook of Sport Psychology.* Hoboken, NJ: Wiley.

Ericsson, K. A. (2008). Deliberate Practice and Acquisition of Expert Performance: A General Overview. *Academic Emergency Medicine, 15,* 988–994.

Ford, P. R., Coughlan E. K., Hodges N. J. & Williams, A. M. (2015). Deliberate practice in sport. In D. Farrow and J. Baker (Eds.), *The Handbook of Sport Expertise.* London: Routledge/Taylor and Francis, pp. 347-362.

Ford, P. R. & Williams, A. M. (2013). The acquisition of skill and expertise: The role of practice and other activities. In Williams, A. M. (Ed.), *Science and soccer III.* London: Routledge, pp. 122-138.

Ford, P. R. & Williams, A. M. (2008) Expertise and expert performance in sport. *International Review of Sport and Exercise Psychology, 1,* 4-18.

Helsen, W. F., Hodges, N. J., Van Winckel, J. & Starkes, J. L. (2000). The roles of talent, physical precocity and practice in the development of soccer expertise. *Journal of Sports Sciences, 18,* 727-736.

Helsen, W. F., Starkes, J. L. & Hodges, N. J. (1998). Team sports and the theory of deliberate practice. *Journal of Sport and Exercise Psychology, 20,* 12-34.

Henry, F. M. (1968). Specificty vs. generality in learning motor skill. In R. C. Brown & G. S. Kenyon (Eds.), *Classic studies on physical activity.* Englewood Cliffs, NJ: Prentice Hall, pp. 331-340.

Holding, D. H. (1991). Transfer of training. In Morrison, J. E. (Ed), *Training for performance: Principles of applied human learning. Wiley series, human performance and cognition.* Oxford: John Wiley & Sons, pp. 93-125.

Macnamara, B. N., Hambrick, D. Z. & Oswald, F. L. (2014). Deliberate practice and performance in music, games, sports, education, and professions: A meta-analysis. *Psychological Science, 25,* 1608-1618.

Nyland, J. (2014). Coming to terms with early sports specialization and athletic injuries. *Journal of Orthopaedic and Sports Physical Therapy, 44,* 389-390.

Rhodri, L. et al. (2015). Long-Term Athletic Development- Part 1: A Pathway for All Youth. *Journal of Strength and Conditioning Research, 29,* 1439-1450.

Starkes, J. L., Deakin, J. M., Allard, F., Hodges, N. J. & Hayes, A. (1996). Deliberate practice in sports: What is it anyway? In Ericsson, K. A. (Ed.) *Road to excellence: The acquisition of expert performance in the arts and sciences, sports, and games.* Manawah, NJ: LEA Publishers, pp. 81-106.

Ward, P., Hodges, N. J., Starkes, J. L. & Williams, M. A. (2007). The road to excellence: deliberate practice and the development of expertise. *High Ability Studies, 18,* 119-153.

Williams, A. M. & Hodges, N. J. (2005). Practice, instruction and skill acquisition in soccer: Challenging tradition. *Journal of Sports Sciences, 23,* 637-650.

Original research

Hendry, D., Crocker, P. R. E. & Hodges, N. J. (2014). Practice and play as determinants of self-determined motivation in youth soccer players. *Journal of Sports Sciences, 32,* 1091-1099.

Hornig, M., Aust, F. & Güllich, A. (2014). Practice and play in the development of German top-level professional football players. *European Journal of Sport Science.* DOI: 10.1080/17461391.2014.982204.

Meinz, E. J. & Hambrick, D. Z. (2010). Deliberate practice is necessary but not sufficient to explain individual differences in piano sight-reading skill: the role of working memory capacity, *Psychological Science, 21,* 914–919.

Miriam A., Mosing, M. A., Madison, G., Pedersen, N. L., Kuja-Halkola, R. & Ullén, F. (2014). Practice does not make perfect: no causal effect of music practice on music ability. *Psychological Science, 25,* 1795-1803.

Vink, K., Raudsepp, L. & Kais, K. (2015). Intrinsic motivation and individual deliberate practice are reciprocally related: Evidence from a longitudinal study of adolescent team sport athletes, *Psychology of Sport and Exercise, 16,* 1-6.

MOTOR SKILL ACQUISITION AND FEEDBACK (PART 3, 4 AND 6)

Books

Bernstein, N. (1967). *The cordination and regulation of movements. (Ocherki po fiziologii dvizhenii i fiziologii aktivnosti).* Oxford: Pergamon Press.

Clegg, B. (2007). *The Man Who Stopped Time.* London: Joseph Henry Press

Marey, E. J. (1895). *Movement.* London.

Whiting, H. T. A. (Ed.) (1984). H*uman Motor Actions: Bernstein Reassessed.* Amsterdam: North Holland.

Reviews articles

Butler, D. L. & Winne, P. H. (1995). Feedback and self-regulated learning: A theoretical synthesis. *Review of Education Research, 65,* 245-281.

Franks, I. M. & Maile, L. J. (1991). The use of video in sport skill acquisition. In P. W. Dowrick (Ed.), *Practical guide to using video in the behavioral sciences.* New York: Wiley, pp. 231-243.

Franks, I. M. (1996). Use of feedback by coaches and players. In T. Reilly, J. Bangsbo and M. Hughes (Eds.), *Science and Football III.* London: E. and F. N. Spon. pp. 267-278.

Ginsburg, P., Anderson, C. E. & Dolby, J. (1957). Videotape recorder design. *ISMPTE, 66* (4).

Magill, R. A. (2001). Augmented feedback in motor skill acquisition. In R. N. Singer, H. A. Hausenblas & C. M. Janelle (Eds.), *Handbook of sport psychology (2nd ed.).* New York: Wiley, pp. 86-114.

Magill, R. A. & Anderson, D. I. (2012). The roles and uses of augmented feedback in motor skill. In N. J. Hodges & A. M. Williams (Eds.), *Skill Acquisition in Sport, (2nd ed.)*. New York, NY: Routledge, pp. 3-21.

McCallum, J. (1987). Videotape is on a roll. *Sports Illustrated, 66,* 14, 136-44.

Newell, K. M. (1981). Skill learning. In D. Holding (Ed.), *Human Skills.* New York: John Wiley and Sons.

Salmoni, A. W., Schmidt, R. A. & Walter, C. B. (1984). Knowledge of results and motor learning: A review and critical reappraisal. *Psychological Bulletin, 95,* 355-386.

Swinnen, S. P. (1996). Information feedback for motor skill learning: A review. In H. N. Zelaznik (Ed.), *Advances in motor learning and control.* Champaign, IL: Human Kinetics, pp. 37-66.

Wulf, G. & Shea, C. H. (2004). Understanding the role of augmented feedback: The good, the bad, and the ugly. In N. J. Hodges and A. M. Williams (Eds.), *Skill Acquisition in Sport.* New York, NY: Routledge, pp. 121-144.

Wulf, G., McConnel, N., Gärtner, M. & Schwarz, A. (2002). Feedback and attentional focus: Enhancing the learning of sport skills through external-focus feedback. *Journal of Motor Behavior, 34,* 171-182.

Original research

Badami, R. et al. (2011). Feedback after good versus poor trials affects intrinsic motivation. *Research Quarterly for Exercise and Sport, 82,* 360-364.

Badami, R. et al. (2012). Feedback about more accurate versus less accurate trials: Differential effects on self-confidence and activation. *Research Quarterly for Exercise and Sport, 83,* 196-203.

Chiviacowsky, S. & Wulf, G. (2002). Self-controlled feedback: Does it enhance learning because performers get feedback when they need it? *Research Quarterly for Exercise and Sport, 73,* 408-415.

Chiviacowsky, S. & Wulf, G. (2007). Feedback after good trials enhances learning. *Research Quarterly for Exercise and Sport, 78,* 40-47.

Janelle, C. M. et al. (1997). Maximizing performance feedback effectiveness through videotape replay and a self-controlled learning environment. *Research Quarterly for Exercise and Sport, 68,* 269-279.

Saemi, E. et al. (2012) Knowledge of results after relatively good trials enhances self-efficacy and motor learning. *Psychology of Sport and Exercise, 13,* 378-382.

Schmidt, R. A., Lange, C. & Young, D. E. (1990). Optimizing summary knowledge of results for skill learning. *Human Movement Science, 9,* 325-348.

Schmidt, R. A., Young, D. E., Swinnen, S. & Shapiro, D. E. (1989). Summary knowledge of results for skill acquisition: Support for the guidance hypothesis. *Journal of Experimental Psychology: Learning, Memory, and Cognition, 15,* 352-359.

Shea, C. H. & Wulf, G. (1999). Enhancing motor learning through external-focus instructions and feedback. *Human Movement Science, 18,* 553-571.

Winstein, C. J. & Schmidt, R. A. (1990). Reduced frequency of knowledge of results enhances motor skill learning. *Journal of Experimental Psychology: Learning, Memory and Cognition, 16,* 677-691.

Wulf, G. & Weigelt, C. (1997). Instructions about physical principles in learning a complex motor skill: To tell or not to tell. *Research Quarterly for Exercise and Sport, 68,* 362-367.

Yousif, N., Cole, J., Rothwell, J. & Diedrichsen, J. (2015). Proprioception in motor learning: lessons from a deafferented subject. *Experimental Brain Research, 233,* 2449-2459.

WARM-UP FOR TRAINING AND MATCH DAY (PART 5)

Website

FIFA 11+

f-marc.com/11plus/home/

(F-MARC refers to FIFA's Medical Assessment and Research Centre)

Original research

Bishop, D. (2003). Warm Up I: Potential mechanisms and the effects of passive warm up on exercise performance. *Sports Medicine. 33,* 439-454.

Bishop, D. (2003). Warm Up II: Performance changes following active warm up and how to structure warm up. *Sports Medicine, 33,* 483-498.

Bizzini, M., Junge, A. & Dvorak, J. (2013). Implementation of the FIFA 11+ football warm up program: How to convince the Football associations to invest in prevention. *British Journal of Sports Medicine, 47,* 803-806.

Junge, A., et al. (2011). Country-wide campaign to prevent football injuries in Swiss amateur players. *American Journal of Sports Medicine, 39,* 57-63.

Soligard, T., et al. (2008). Comprehensive warm-up programme to prevent injuries in young female footballers: cluster randomised controlled trial. *The BMJ, 337,* doi: http://dx.doi.org/10.1136/bmj.a2469a.

Steffen, K., Myklebust, G., Olsen, O. E., Holme, I. & Bahr, R. (2008). Preventing injuries in female youth football: A cluster-randomized controlled trial. *Scandinavian Journal of Medicine and Science in Sports, 18,* 605-614.

THE COACHING PROCESS (PART 6)

Books

Flanders, N. A. (1970). *Analyzing teaching behavior.* Oxford, England: Addison-Wesley.

Jones, R., Kingston, K. & Hughes, M. (Eds.) (2007). *An Introduction to Coaching.* London: Routledge.

Lyle, J. (2002). *Sports Coaching Concepts: A. Framework for Coaches' Behaviour.* London: Routledge.

Prinz, W. & Bridgeman, B. (Eds.) (1995). *Handbook of Perception and Action: Volume 1, Perception.* London: Academic Press.

Review articles

Fairs, J. R. (1987). The coaching process: the essence of coaching, *Sports Coach, 11,* 17-19.

Groom, R. & Cushion, C. J. (2004). Coaches perceptions of the use of video analysis: A case study. *Insight, 7,* 56-58.

Gilbert, W. D. & Trudel, P. (2004). Analysis of Coaching Science Research Published from 1970-2001. *Research Quarterly for Exercise and Sport, 75:4,* 388-399.

Hodges, N. J. & Franks, I. M. (2002). Modelling coaching practice: the role of instruction and coaching. *Journal of Sports Sciences, 21,* 793-811.

Horn, T. S. (2002). Coaching effectiveness in the sport domain. In T. S. Horn (Ed.). *Advances in sport psychology.* Champaign, IL: Human Kinetics, pp. 309-354.

Locke, L. F. (1984). Research on teaching teachers: Where are we now? *Journal of Teaching Physical Education. Monograph #2,* Summer.

Metzler, M. (1989). A Review of Research on Time in Sport Pedagogy. *Journal of Teaching in Physical Education, 8,* 87-103

More K. G. & Franks, I. M. (2004). Measuring coaching effectiveness. In M. Hughes & I. M. Franks (Eds.). *Notational Analysis in Sport (2nd ed).* Systems for Better Coaching and Performance, London: E. and F. N. Spon, pp.242-256.

O'Donoghue, P. G. & Mayes, A. (2013). Coach Behaviour. In T. McGarry, P. D. O'Donoghue & J. Sampaio (Eds). *Routledge Handbook of Sports Performance Analysis.* London: Routledge, pp. 127-139.

Olsen, E. & Larsen, O. (1997). Use of match analysis by coaches. In T. Reilly, J. Bangsbo, and M. Hughes (Eds.). *Science and Football III.* London: E. and F.N. Spon, pp. 209-220.

Original research

Brown, E. & O'Donoghue, P. G. (2008). A split screen system to analyse coach behaviour: a case report of coaching practice. *International Journal of Computer Science in Sport, 7,* 4-17.

Cushion, C., Harvey, S., Muir, B. & Nelson, L. (2012). Developing the Coach Analysis and Intervention System (CAIS): Establishing validity and reliability of a computerised systematic observation instrument. *Journal of Sports Sciences, 30,* 201-216.

Ford P. R., Yates, I. & Williams, A. M. (2010). An analysis of practice activities and instructional behaviours used by youth soccer coaches during practice: Exploring the link between science and application. *Journal of Sports Sciences, 28,* 483-495.

Franks, I. M., Hodges, N. J. & More, K. (2001). Analysis of coaching behaviour. *International Journal of Performance Analysis in Sport,1,* 27-36.

Franks, I. M. & Miller, G. (1986). Eyewitness testimony in sport. *Journal of Sport Behavior, 9,* 39-45.

Franks, I. M. & Miller, G. (1991). Training coaches to observe and remember. *Journal of Sports Sciences, 9,* 285-297.

Franks, I. M., Sinclair, G., Thomson, W. & Goodman, D. (1986). Analysis of the coaching process. *Science Periodical on Research and Technology in Sport, GY-1,* 12pp.

Laird, P. & Waters, L. (2008). Eyewitness recollection of sport coaches. *International Journal of Performance Analysis in Sport, 8,* 76-84.

More, K. G. & Franks, I. M. (1996). Analysis and modification of verbal coaching behaviour: The usefulness of a data driven intervention strategy. *Journal of Sports Sciences, 14,* 523-543

Newtson, D. & Engquist, G. (1976). The perceptual organization of ongoing behavior. *Journal of Experimental Social Psychology, 12,* 436-450.

Partington, M. & Cushion, C. (2013). An investigation of the practice activities and coaching behaviours of professional top-level youth soccer coaches. *Scandinavian Journal of Medicine and Science in Sports, 23,* 374-382.

Partridge, D. & Franks, I. M. (1996). Analyzing and modifying coaching behaviours by means of computer aided observation. *The Physical Educator, 53,* 8-23.

Potrac, P., Jones, R. & Cushion, C. (2006), Understanding power and the coach's role in professional English soccer: A Preliminary Investigation of Coach Behaviour. *Soccer and Society, 8,* 33-49.

Sinclair, G. D., Johnson, R. B. & Franks, I. M. (1990). Monitoring coaching-teaching feedback: a computer managed, real-time feedback analysis protocol. In M. Lirette, C. Pare, J. Dessureault and M. Pieron (Eds.) *Physical education and coaching: present state and outlook for the future.* Quebec, Canada: University of Quebec Press, pp. 55-62.

Smith, M. & Cushion, C. J. (2006). An investigation of the in-game behaviours of professional, top-level youth soccer coaches. *Journal of Sports Sciences, 24,* 355–366.

MODEL DEVELOPMENT AND PREDICTION (PART 6)

Books

Crilly, A. J. (1991). *Fractals and Chaos.* London: Springer-Verlaag.

Gleick, J. (1988). *Chaos : Making a New Science.* London: Penguin Books.

Ladany, S. P. & Machol, R. E. (Eds.). (1977). *Optimal Strategies in Sports.* Amsterdam: North Holland.

Lewis, M. (2003). *Moneyball: The art of winning an unfair game.* London: W.W. Norton and Company Ltd.

McGarry, T., O'Donoghue, P. & Sampaio, J. (2015). *Routledge Handbook of Sports Performance Analysis.* London: Routledge.

Morris, D. (1981). *The Soccer Tribe.* London: Jonathan Cape Ltd.

Anolli, L., Riva, G., Duncan Jr., S. & Magnusson, M. J. (Eds.). (2005). *The Hidden Structure of Interaction: From Neurons to Culture Patterns.* Amsterdam: IOS Press.

Review articles

Alexander, D., McClements, K. & Simmons, J. (1988). Calculating to win. *New Scientist. Dec,* 30-33.

Balague, N., Torrents, C., Hristovski, R., Davids, K. & Araújo,D. (2013). Overview of complex systems in sport. *Journal of Systems Science and Complexity, 26,* 4-13.

Bartlett, R. M. (2004). Artificial intelligence in performance analysis. In P. O'Donoghue and M. Hughes (Eds.). *Notational Analysis of Sport VI,* pp. 213-219.

Flanagan, J. C. (1954). The Critical Incident Technique. *Psychological Bulletin, 51,* 327-358

Franks, I. M. (2000).The structure of sport and the collection of relevant data. In A. Baca (Ed.). *Computer Science in Sport.* Vienna: Oebv & Hpt. pp. 226-240.

Franks, I. M. and Goodman, D. (1984). A Hierarchical Approach to Performance Analysis. *Science Periodical on Research and Technology in Sport, GY-1,* 4pp.

Hodges, N. J., McGarry, T. & Franks, I. M. (1998). A dynamical system's approach to the examination of sport behaviour: Implications for tactical observation and technical instruction. *Avante, 4,* 16-38.

Hughes, M. (2004). Notational analysis—a mathematical perspective. *International Journal of Performance Analysis in Sport, 4,* 97-139.

Leser, R., Hoch T., Moser, B. & Baca, A. (2015). Expert oriented analysis of football duels by means of position data. In Baca (Ed.). *Book of Abstracts, 8th World Congress on Science & Football.* Copenhagen, Denmark, p. 65.

McGarry, T. & Franks, I. M. (1996). Development, application and limitation of a Stochastic Markov Model in explaining championship squash performance. *Research Quarterly for Exercise and Sport, 67,* 406-415.

McGarry, T. & Franks, I. M. (1996). In search of invariant athletic behavior in competitive sport systems: An example from squash match-play. *Journal of Sports Sciences, 14,* 445-456.

McGarry, T. & Franks, I. M. (2003). The science of match analysis. In T. Reilly and A. M. Williams (Eds.). *Science and Soccer (2nd ed.).* London: Routledge. pp. 265-275.

McGarry, T. & Perl, J. (2004). Models of sports contests: Markov processes, dynamical systems and neural networks. In M. Hughes and I. M. Franks (Eds.). *Notational Analysis of Sport: Systems for Better Coaching and Performance in Sport.* London: Routledge, pp. 227-242.

McGarry, T., Anderson, D. I., Wallace, S. A., Hughes, M. & Franks, I. M. (2002). Sport competition as a dynamical self-organizing system. *Journal of Sports Sciences, 20,* 771-781.

Nelson, L. J. & Groom, R. (2012). The analysis of performance: some practical and philosophical considerations. *Sport, Education and Society, 17,* 687-701.

O'Hare, M. (1996). Chaos pitch. *New Scientist, June,* Issue 2033.

Perl, J. (2002). Adaptation, antagonism and system dynamics. In G. Ghent, D. Kluka and D. Jones (Eds.). *Perspectives. The multidisciplinary series of physical education and sport science.* pp. 105-125. Oxford, UK: Meyer & Meyer Sport.

Pollard, R., Benjamin, B. & Reep, C. (1977). Sport and the negative binomial distribution. In S. P. Ladany & R. E. Machol (Eds.). *Optimal Strategies in Sport.* pp. 185-195. Amsterdam: North-Holland.

Pollard, R. & Reep, C. (1997). Measuring the effectiveness of playing strategies at soccer. *Statistician, 46,* 541-550.

Reep, C. & Benjamin, B. (1968). Skill and chance in association football. *Journal of the Royal Statistical Society, Series A, 131,* 581-585.

Reep, C., Pollard, R. & Benjamin, B. (1971). Skill and chance in ball games. *Journal of the Royal Statistical Society, Series A, 134,* 623-629.

Serafini, A., Leser, R., Hoch, T., Moser, B. & Baca, A. (2015). Towards Data-Based Assessment of Individual Tactics Skills in Team Sports Based on Fuzzy Petri Nets. In F. Breitenecker, A. Kugi & I. Troch (Eds.). *Abstract Volume, Mathmod 2015, 8th Vienna Conference on Mathematic Modelling.* Vienna, Austria. p. 301.

Sussman, H. J. & Zahler, R. S. (1978). A Critique of Applied Catastrophe Theory in the Behavioural Sciences. *Behavioural Science, 23,* 28-39.

Stefani, R. (1998). Predicting Outcomes. In J. Bennett, (Ed.) *Statistics in Sport.* London: Arnold, pp. 249-275.

Original research

Bauer, H. U. & Schöllhorn, W. I. (1997). Self-organizing maps for the analysis of complex movement patterns. *Neural Processing Letters, 5,* 193-199.

Borrie, A., Jonsson, G. K. & Magnusson, M. (2002). Temporal pattern analysis and its applicability in sport: an explanation and exemplar data. *Journal of Sports Sciences, 20,* 845-852.

Grehaigne, J. F., Bouthier, D & David, B. (1997). Dynamic-system analysis of opponent relationships in collective actions in soccer. *Journal of Sports Sciences, 15,* 137-149.

Hughes, M. (2001) Perturbations and critical incidents in soccer. In M. Hughes and F. Tavares (Eds.). *Notational Analysis of Sport IV.* Porto: Faculty of Sports Sciences and Education, University of Porto, Portugal, pp. 23-33.

Lees, A., Barton, G. & Kershaw, L. (2003). The use of Kohonen neural network analysis to qualitatively characterize technique in soccer kicking. *Journal of Sports Sciences, 21,* 243-244.

McGarry, T. (2008). Probability analysis of notated events in sport contests: Skill and chance. In M. Hughes and I. M. Franks (Eds.). *The Essentials of Performance Analysis: An Introduction.* London: Routledge, pp. 206-225.

McGarry, T., Khan, M. A, & Franks, I. M. (1999). On the presence and absence of behavioural traits in sport: An example from championship squash match-play. *Journal of Sports Sciences, 17,* 297-311.

Mosteller, F. (1979). A resistant analysis of 1971 and 1972 Professional Football, In J. H. Goldstein (Ed.). *Sports, Games and Play.* New Jersey: Lawrence Erlbaum Associates, pp. 371-401.

Moura, F. A., Martins, L. E. B. & Cunha, S. A. (2014). Analysis of football game-related statistics using multivariate techniques, *Journal of Sports Sciences, 32,* 1881-1887.

Perl, J. (2002). Game analysis and control by means of continuously learning networks. *International Journal of Performance Analysis in Sport, 2,* 21-35.

Pollard, R. & Reep, C. (1997). Measuring effectiveness of playing strategies in soccer. *The Statistician, 46,* 541-550.

MISCELLANEOUS INFORMATION FOR COACHES AND STUDENTS

Commercial Match Analysis and Coaching Analysis Systems

www.prozonesports.com

www.matchanalysis.com

www.performanceinnovation.net

www.sportstec.com

www.nacsport.com

www.longomatch.com

www.optasports.com

www.statdna.com

www.apollo-mis.co.uk

Physics of Soccer

https://thescienceclassroom.wikispaces.com/Physics+of+Soccer

http://www.soccerballworld.com/Physics.htm

http://www.real-world-physics-problems.com/physics-of-soccer.html

http://newsoffice.mit.edu/2014/explained-how-does-soccer-ball-swerve-0617

http://www.bbc.co.uk/guides/zgxdwmn

Academic Societies and Conferences

http://iacss.org/index.php?id=29

www.ispas.org

http://www.sportsengineering.co.uk/

http://wcsf2015.ku.dk/

http://www.footballmedic.co.uk/

http://www.sloansportsconference.com/

PART 8
EPILOGUE

In this book we have used findings from research (see bibliography) in soccer analysis and skill acquisition to develop practices that would be the most beneficial for players of all ages. Throughout the book we have stressed certain imperatives that need to be taken into consideration by coaches. In this final section we have summarized some of the important key factors that lead to successful coaching and performance of soccer.

REALISM

We have stressed the importance of making each practice as realistic as possible within the limitations of the coaching practice objective. Realistic practices can be assured if the practice is developed as a consequence of match performance. Realistic practices will also ensure that transfer of training will be at a maximum.

PRACTICE

It is now clear that practicing a skill with adequate feedback and sufficient information about the skill will lead to improved performance of that skill. The more a player practices a skill with the correct feedback the better they will become at the skill.

PREPARATION

Coaches should prepare every practice carefully with a theme that will center on a specific skill or set of skills that have been identified as important from match analysis and coach observation.

DECISION MAKING

Players make decisions throughout the game. These decisions usually precede performance. If decisions can be made ahead of time then more time can be devoted to the performance of a technique. Decision making should be an integral part of each practice with the coach trying to cut down on the number of choices that a player has to deal with. The more choices that confront the player, the more indecisive they may become and the slower their reaction time will be.

ACTIVITY

The practice must be active and structured to keep the players moving and motivated. Practices that have players waiting and lining up will likely produce inattentive players.

ENJOYMENT

Along with activity comes enjoyment. Players should enjoy their soccer experience.

TIME ON THE BALL

Players will improve if they spend time playing soccer. Therefore coaches should try to ensure that there is an adequate supply of balls and their practices should encourage ball contact.

SUPPORT

In both attacking and defending aspects of play, the aim is to provide numerical superiority for your team in and around the ball. In order to achieve this, the whole team must understand the importance of giving support to either the player on the ball or the challenging defensive player who is pressuring the ball.

PENETRATION

Allen Wade (former coaching director of the English FA) emphasized the most important principle of attack, that being penetration (the ability to play the ball between and behind defenses with accurate passes). This book and the analysis upon which it has been based also places a strong emphasis on the principle of penetration.

DEFENDING

Defending as a team is as important as any attacking skill. The defensive principles of team play should be clearly understood by all players such that each team member is working towards the same objective (e.g. stop the opposition from scoring and regain possession).

OPPORTUNITIES

The game can be seen as a series of opportunities. Players should understand how to create and recognize opportunities and when to take these opportunities.

PROGRESSION

During a coaching session each practice should be progressive. Progression toward a game-like situation will make the practice more meaningful for players.

KNOWLEDGE OF PLAYERS

It is important that the coach realize there are individual differences within the team. Although the team must attack and defend with a common objective, individuals understand and learn at their own rate and in their own manner. Coaches should be aware of these differences and be able to accommodate for these during the practice.

COACHING POINTS

The coaching points made in this book should be thought of as coaching hints or tips the coach wishes to share with the players. For example, the coach should not spend too long explaining the biomechanical principles of techniques or making sure that every coaching point is delivered at every practice. Players want easy and quick tips on how to improve and then they need lots of practice. If the organization of the practice is correct, this will aid the player in reducing reliance on the guidance from the coach. There may be times when the coach will only intervene with a verbal comment one or two times during a skill practice. Better yet the coach will demonstrate or use a model and say very little. Remember, an ounce of information and a ton of practice and a picture is worth a thousand words.

INFORMATION

The term information is a paradox for soccer players. While it is important that players receive as much objective and accurate information about the performance as possible (see match analysis), it is also important that the coach attempts to reduce the mass of information they are faced with during the game (see decision making).

TEAMWORK

The team should examine each game with a collective responsibility. If they each understand the overall objective of each play, be it in attack or on defense, then they will readily accept responsibility as a unit for the performance. This allows the coach to progress toward the next level.

OBSERVATION

Coaches should observe performances and not spectate. Observing soccer performance is a skill and should be practiced. Alternate methods of objective observation have been detailed in this book and listed in the bibliography.

KNOWLEDGE OF SOCCER

Understanding the sequential nature of match play and the consequences of actions is important for coaches. Understand what led to the resulting performance and not just the results of the performance. Coaches should try to observe as many games as possible at all levels of performance.

ANALYSIS

The objective analysis of soccer games (and if possible coaching practices) should be undertaken before making decisions on team and individual performance. This can be done using a simple pencil and paper checklist or a sophisticated computer-video software program. The field of performance analysis in general has expanded and progressed greatly over the last 30 years. As with most things, technology and research have led the way in terms of development, particularly for notation analysis systems. Currently the most advanced systems may be desirable, but the cost is likely to be prohibitive to all but the wealthiest and, by logical extension, successful sports teams. The main development over the last 10 years has been the decreasing cost of computers and video cameras. This has led to the formation of a number of companies selling specialist software for different types of performance analysis (see bibliography). Currently most sports teams and individuals can afford the equipment necessary to record and analyze their performances. However, having the equipment and using it effectively is not necessarily the same thing. Over the next 10 years it is likely that the process of analyzing performances will become significantly easier. With the growing popularity of notational analysis in professional sport comes the need to adequately educate sports scientists in this area. Currently Cardiff Metropolitan University, Liverpool John Moores University, Loughborough University, Chester University, Nottingham Trent University, Middlesex University, University of Birmingham, Worcester University, University of Central Lancashire and Chichester University (UK only) have teaching and research programmes in place with others developing courses and the expertise to meet the demand. Many other universities around the world (e.g. University of Lisbon, University of British Columbia, University of Queensland, Universitat Magdeburg, University of Vienna, Carlow Institute of Technology, University of Victoria, University of Limerick, German Sport University) also offer courses and specific certificate programmes in the areas of coaching science and sport analysis, most at the graduate level. This demand will strengthen notational analysis as a discipline leading to better research by way of methodological advances, more appropriate statistical procedures and simpler output formats. These advances will in turn be fed back into sports organizations and companies to the benefit of all prospective analysts, coaches and players.

CREDITS

Cover design: Eva Feldmann

Layout: Sannah Inderelst

Illustrations: Ian Franks, Rachel Apted

Typesetting: www.satzstudio-hilger.de

Copyediting: Anne Rumery

COACHING SOCCER THE MODERN WAY

Timo Jankowski

COACHING SOCCER LIKE

GUARDIOLA AND MOURINHO

The Concept of Tactical Periodization

250 p., 16 1/2" x 9 1/4", in color

100 Halftone, 150 Illustrations

Paperback

ISBN 978-3-1-78255-072-3

$ 19,95 US/$ 29,95 AUS

£ 12,95 UK/€ 18,95

A soccer player is more than the sum of his parts: endurance, speed, shooting technique, passing technique, and many more. All of these factors need to be turned into one system to create good players. Traditional training theory doesn't achieve that because each skill is trained individually. This is why the concept of Tactical Periodization has become the preferred training theory for many of the current most successful soccer coaches: Pep Guardiola, José Mourinho, Diego Simeone, André Villas-Boas, and many others train according to these principles. By creating match-like situations in practice, players learn to link their technical, tactical, and athletic abilities to match intelligence. They will learn to transfer their skills to soccer matches and they can improve endurance, technique, and tactics all at the same time while enjoying the practice sessions more.

All information subject to change © Thinkstock/iStock

MEYER & MEYER Sport
Von-Coels-Str. 390
52080 Aachen
Germany

Phone   +49 02 41 - 9 58 10 - 13
Fax   +49 02 41 - 9 58 10 - 10
E-Mail   sales@m-m-sports.com
Website   www.m-m-sports.de

All books available as E-books.

MEYER
& MEYER
SPORT

THE HISTORY OF SOCCER

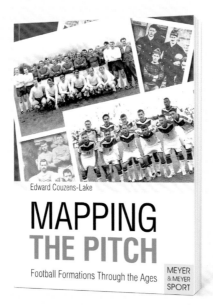

Edward Couzens-Lake

MAPPING THE PITCH

Football Formations Through the Ages

304 p., 5 3/4" x 8 1/4", b/w

31 Halftones, 13 Illustrations

Paperback

ISBN 978-1-78255-060-0

$ 14,95 US/$ 22,95 AUS

£ 9,95 UK/€ 14,95

This book takes an informal and entertaining look at some of the most influential football coaches and teams in the game's history as well as exploring some of the origins of football's more wellknown formations and the players who were an integral part of them.

THE OFFICIAL
NSCAA BOOK SERIES

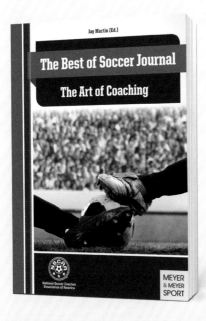

Jay Martin (Ed.)

THE BEST OF SOCCER JOURNAL:

THE ART OF COACHING

192 p., 6 1/2" x 9 1/4", in color

1 Halftone, 6 Illustrations

Paperback

ISBN 978-3-1-78255-049-5

$ 19,95 US/$ 32,95 AUS

£ 14,95 UK/€ 19,95

The NSCAA continues their successful book series "The Best of Soccer Journal" with this new highly anticipated entry in the instructional soccer book field. The book explores the Craft and Art of Coaching. The best coaches in the US describe how they get it done on the field. In addition, this book explores the 'Last Frontier' – the mental side of the game. Successful players and coaches must train the mind as well as the body to succeed and master the game!

MEYER & MEYER Sport

Von-Coels-Str. 390

52080 Aachen

Germany

Phone   +49 02 41 - 9 58 10 - 13

Fax   +49 02 41 - 9 58 10 - 10

E-Mail   sales@m-m-sports.com

Website   www.m-m-sports.de

All books available as E-books.

MEYER
& MEYER
SPORT